MODERN CHINA PHYSICAL

Scale 1:15,000,000

0   100   200   300   100   500   600 km

0   100   200   300   400 miles

ters
et)

5000
(16,400)

3000
(9840)

2000
(6560)

1000
(3280)

500
(1640)

200
(660)

0

Land below sea level

200
(660)

D1174677

YABLONOVYY KHREBET

Vitim R.

NERCHINSKIY KHREBET

Argun R.

Kerulen R.

Dalai Nor

TA-HSING-AN LING

HSIAO-HSING-AN LING

Heilung Chiang (Amur)

Amur R.

Sung-hua Chiang (Sungari R.)

Ussuri R.

Ch'i-ch'i-ha-erh

Ha-erh-pin

CHANG-KUANG-TSAI LING

Khanka
La...

Vladivostok

Chi-lin (Kirin)

Ch'ang-ch'un

Sungari Res.

Tumen Chiang

PAI-T'OU SHAN

ALIN KHREBET

SEA OF JAPAN

Hsi-liao Ho

Shen-yang (Mukden)

Liao Ho

Fu-shun

Ya-lu Chiang

P'yongyang

Soul (Seoul)

LIAO-TUNG WAN

Luan Ho

YIN SHAN

Pao-t'ou

DESERT

Great Wall

Pei-ching (Peking)

T'ien-ching (Tientsin)

PO HAI

KOREA BAY

Lü-ta (Dairen - Port Arthur)

Po-hai Strait

SHAN-TUNG PENINSULA

YELLOW SEA

Pusan

Seoul (Soul)

Kyushu

Korea Strait

Cheju

LU-LIANG SHAN

Tai-yüan

CHUNG-TIAO SHAN

T'AI-HANG SHAN

Hu-t'o Ho

Chi-nan
T'AI SHAN
T'ai Shan
1545

MENG SHAN

Ch'ing-tao (Tsingtao)

Hsi-an (Sian)

LING

Lo-yang

Huang Ho (Yellow River)

Wei-shan Hu

Yün Ho (Grand Canal)

Sha Ho

Hung-tse Hu

Huai Ho

Kao-yu Ho

EAST CHINA SEA

TA-PA SHAN

A-lan Chiang

TA-PIEH SHAN

Nan-ching (Nanking)

Ch'ao Hu

T'ai Hu

Shang-hai

Ch'ang Chiang (Yangtze R.)

Wu-han

SHAN

Tung-t'ing Hu

Yüan R.

Nan-ch'ang

P'o-yang Hu

Yung-chia

SEA

GAN SHAN

Ch'ang-sha

Hsiang Chiang

WU-KUNG SHAN

WU I SHAN

Min Chiang

Fu-chou (Foochow)

T'ai-pei

Ryūkyū Islands

KAO-TENG SHAN

NAN LING

Mei-ling Pass
397

Che-ling Pass
305

Formosa Strait

Hsin-kao Shan
3950

T'ai-wan (Formosa)

Kao-hsiung

Luzon

Batan Islands

Hsi Chiang

Kuang-chou (Canton)

Hong Kong

Macao

LEI-CHOU PENINSULA

Ch'iung-shan

SOUTH CHINA SEA

Babuyan Islands

Luzon Strait

ALF OF
ONKIN

Nan-ning

SHAN

Wu-chih Shan
1879

Hai-nan Tao

Luzon

An historical atlas of China

by

ALBERT HERRMANN

late Professor of Historical Geography, University of Berlin

NEW EDITION

General editor

NORTON GINSBURG

Professor of Geography, University of Chicago

Prefatory essay by

PAUL WHEATLEY

Professor of Geography, University of California

ALDINE PUBLISHING COMPANY CHICAGO

Based on *Historical and Commercial Atlas of China* by Albert Herrmann, published in 1935 by the Harvard-Yenching Institute (Monograph Series, Volume I).

New edition first published 1966 by
Aldine Publishing Company, Chicago
Djambatan n.v., Publishers & Cartographers, Amsterdam
Edinburgh University Press, Edinburgh

Printed in the Netherlands

Contents

Preface

Since 1935, when the Harvard-Yenching Institute first published Albert Herrmann's *Historical and Commercial Atlas of China*, the *Atlas* has been an indispensable companion of scholars and students of Chinese civilization and history. Indeed, it has had no rival in the Western-language literature and has been, in many ways, more convenient and reliable than rival modern publications in Chinese and Japanese. For these reasons, it was particularly unfortunate that the volume was out-of-print following the Second World War, when interest in China was reaching new heights and the scholarly communities, in both Europe and North America, concerned with China were expanding at an unprecedented rate.

Several solutions to the problem were considered. One possibility, of course, was to compile an entirely new atlas which would reflect the rapid advances in scholarly research on early China in particular, but it was rejected as requiring an extraordinary investment of time and the collective energies of a panoply of scholars, without the possibility of satisfying the existing demand for some years. Another possibility was to revise Herrmann's work, but to retain his organization and basic structure. This course, too, was rejected, since it would have required imputs almost as substantial as the first possibility, without substantial advantages other than those relating to the actual printing of the maps themselves.

Other possibilities also presented themselves, but the one chosen was designed to meet the need for an historical atlas of China as quickly as possible, and at the same time provide a cartographic introduction to modern and contemporary China. For the most part, Professor Herrmann's scholarship was not tampered with, except in a few instances where there were obvious misprints or syntactical inconsistencies. Thus, the first fifty-five pages of this *Atlas* consist of a redrafting of the historical maps in the original edition, with some reorganization and changes in sequence and with the use of completely new cartographic techniques, which make for greater clarity and legibility.

The modern maps in the original edition were dropped, however, and were replaced completely by a series of economic and cultural maps of modern and contemporary China, which, with due qualification on reliability-of-data grounds, is probably the most useful set of multi-colored, atlas-scale, systematic maps of China available in a European language. These include maps of population, ethnolinguistic groups, land use, major political-administrative units, minerals, industries, transportation facilities, and the Chinese in Southeast Asia, all of which are based on the most reliable information available. Although a general physical map of China is included in the group, no attempt has been made to reproduce maps of other physical elements, such as temperature, precipitation, and soils, which are readily available in other sources.

The editor and publishers are well aware of the inadequacies of even this portion of the atlas, however, since there remains a serious need for cartographic rendering of the fascinating kaleidoscope of political and social transformation that has characterized China within the past century and most conspicuously within the last half century; but they resort to the comfort of later editions-to-be, which might remedy this defect.

More important, they fully recognize that this new volume in its present state does not satisfy the need for a substantially original historical atlas of China, which would properly reflect the scholarly wisdom of contemporary Sinology. Fortunately, however, they, like other users of the *Atlas*, are the beneficiaries of Professor Wheatley's erudition and perspicacity, as displayed in his prefatory essay, a unique contribution in literary and scholarly criticism that physically precedes, rather than follows, the object of its concern. Every reader should profit from reading and re-reading this essay, which properly can be regarded as a guide to the *Atlas*, illuminating shadowy areas of obfuscation and raising caveats where caution is necessary, for scholar, student, and interested amateur alike.

NORTON GINSBURG

The assistance of Mr. Joseph R. Whitney and Mr. James Osborn in the preparation of this volume is gratefully acknowledged.

Longa nimis longo via dividit aequore Seras
Nec patiens tantae est mens generosa morę
HESSEL GERRITSZ, *Tabula Nautica*[1]

Refurbishing the nine cauldrons

Only a very bold or a very needy scholar would set out to compile an historical atlas of any description. Only one possessed of unusual audacity would select China as his field of endeavor, and only the most presumptuous would seek to include more or less the whole of Asia within the purview of his studies. Yet the price commanded by second-hand copies of the *Atlas of China* some thirty years after its publication testifies to the accomplished manner in which Albert Herrmann carried off just such an undertaking. The difficulties inherent in the enterprise were appalling, requiring an intimate acquaintance with scholarship relating to each of the great Asian cultural traditions, and committing the author to decisions on some of the most obscure and ambivalent questions in the history of that continent. Unlike the historian, the cartographer has no really effective means of registering doubt. He cannot easily qualify his opinions, but must either settle for a definite statement or omit the information altogether. He must, additionally, possess an intuitive appreciation of what is and what is not practicable and appropriate in matters of cartography. Professor Herrmann had intended to complement his atlas with a *Handbook of China*, which was to include an extended commentary on the maps, explain the rationale of his toponymic selections, and presumably justify his choice of names and localities in cases of controversy, as well as provide a detailed bibliography.[2] Since this clearly would have constituted a work of massive proportions, it is not surprising that he was unable to complete it before the outbreak of the Second World War, which he was unfortunately not to survive. He was killed while passing through Plzeň on 19 April, 1945.

Although Herrmann did not begin his quinquennium of labor on the atlas until 1930, he had already served a long apprenticeship in the study of the historical geography of Asia. After reading history and geography at Göttingen, he had spent two semesters studying Chinese at the University of Berlin. His doctoral thesis, written on the old trans-Asian Silk Route and presented at Göttingen in 1909, foreshadowed the main theme of his scholarly interests for the rest of his life, namely the relations between China and the West. It also brought him to the attention of Sven Hedin, to whose *Southern Tibet* he contributed a chapter on the treatment of Western countries in Chinese cartography. Subsequently he turned his attention to the sea route between the Middle East and China, and finally to the tradition of Chinese cartography. All this amounted to the sort of training that might ideally have been prescribed for the future author of an atlas of China.[3]

When the atlas finally appeared in 1935, it consisted of some sixty maps (not counting numerous insert maps), of which fifty or so were designed to convey historical information of one sort or another. The remainder either were vehicles for the representation of contemporary economic distributions or took the form of conventional atlas maps depicting

1. From Gerritsz's *Descriptio ac delineatio Geographica Detectionis Freti . . .* (Amsterdam, 1612), now in the James Ford Bell Collection, Walter Library, University of Minnesota.

2. This information was conveyed in two lines of very small print at the head of the bibliography on p. 85 of the first edition of the *Atlas of China*.

3. Some of the more important investigations into the historical geography of Asia undertaken by Albert Herrmann before the completion of his atlas include the following:
Die alten Seidenstrassen zwischen China und Syrien. Quellen und Forschungen zur alten Geschichte und Geographie, no. 21 (W. Sieglin, Berlin, 1910). Reproduced photographically in Tientsin in 1941.
"Die alten Verkehrswege zwischen Indien und Süd-China nach Ptolemäus," *Zeitschrift der Gesellschaft für Erdkunde* (Berlin, 1913), pp. 771–787.
"Ein alter Seeverkehr zwischen Abessinien und Süd-China bis zum Beginn unserer Zeitrechnung," *Zeitschrift der Gesellschaft für Erdkunde* (Berlin, 1913), pp. 553–561.
"Alte Geographie des unteren Oxusgebiets," *Abhandlungen der Königlichen Gesellschaft der Wissenschaften zu Göttingen, Philologisch-Historische Klasse* (Berlin, 1914), pp. 54–57.
"Marinus, Ptolemäus und ihre Karten," *Zeitschrift der Gesellschaft für Erdkunde* (Berlin, 1914), pp. 780–787.
"Die Seidenstrassen vom alten China nach dem Römischen Reich," *Mitteilungen der geographischen Gesellschaft in Wien*, vol. 58 (Wien, 1915), pp. 472–500.
"Die ältesten chinesischen Karten von Zentral- und West-Asien," *Ostasiatische Zeitschrift*, vol. 8 (Berlin, 1919), pp. 185–198.

mainly political units and current nomenclature. Although the volume constituted the first in the Harvard-Yenching Monograph Series and was published by Harvard University Press, the plates—designed, of course, by Professor Herrmann—were executed and printed by the German firm of Georg Westermann. As such they reflected not only the high standards of German cartography of the period but also its technical predilections, such as, for example, the representation of relief by means of shaded brown caterpillars, a carry-over into photolithography of the style of shading favored on the old black-and-white maps. As it so happens, this was not too inappropriate, for the caterpillar method of depicting relief is of a respectable antiquity in China, possibly dating back to the T'ang dynasty.[4] Both the letter-press and the transcription of names in the atlas were designed for the convenience of the English-speaking reader (cf. p. 66 of this edition), though occasional lapses in matters of capitalization, vocabulary, idiom, and spelling—some of which remain in the historical maps of the present edition—betrayed the foreign origin of the work. The production as a whole might be described as functional rather than extravagant.

Generally speaking, the atlas was well received by the community of Asian and specifically Chinese scholars. At one end of the spectrum of opinion Dr. Carl Bishop praised it as "excellent both in conception and execution,"[5] Cyrus H. Peake characterized it as "an indispensable aid,"[6] and Professor Georg Wegener, Herrmann's colleague at Berlin, referred to "der Neuheit und Grösse der Versuchs."[7] At the other extreme crusty old John Ferguson could not understand "how such an atlas could be published by the Harvard-Yenching Institute without any mark of Chinese scholarship,"[8] but such strictures were rare and comment was predominantly favorable. Eduard Erkes[9] and Gustav Fochler-Hauke,[10] knowledgeable in widely differing realms of East Asian scholarship, and anonymous authors in Forschungen und Fortschritte[11] and Ostasiatische Rundschau[12] wrote complimentary reviews, though voicing certain reservations about content and technique. Wolfram Eberhard,[13] then of Leipzig, and Julean Arnold[14] accorded the atlas qualified commendation while expressing disappointment at both the quantity and quality of the detail incorporated in the maps. Karl Haushofer[15] regretted the absence of a series of charts depicting climate, an omission with which I have some personal sympathy: such information is a prerequisite for understanding the crop distributions and ocean sailing routes that were included in the atlas and, at the level of generalization required for this work, the necessary data were easily obtainable even in 1935. The reviewer in the Scottish Geographical Magazine[16] would have liked to see the agricultural section expanded; Baron Osten-Sacken[17] wanted maps of Christian missions included; one good soul demanded a geological map, somebody else a map of population densities, and so on; but all acknowl-

Die Verkehrswege zwischen China, Indien und Rom um etwa 100 nach Chr. Geb. Veröffentlichungen des Forschungsinstituts für vergleichende Religionsgeschichte an der Universität Leipzig, no. 7 (Leipzig, 1922).

"Die Westländer in der chinesischen Kartographie," in Sven Hedin, Southern Tibet; discoveries in former times compared with my own researches in 1906–1908, vol. 8 (Swedish Army General Staff Lithographic Institute, Stockholm, 1922), pp. 89–406.

"Chinesische Umschreibungen von älteren geographischen Namen," in Sven Hedin, Southern Tibet, vol. 8 (1922), pp. 433–452.

[With Sven Hedin], "The Ts'ung-ling Mountains," in Sven Hedin, Southern Tibet, vol. 8 (1922), pp. 1–88.

[With A. von Le Coq], "Zwei Osttürkische Manuskriptkarten," in Sven Hedin, Southern Tibet, vol. 8 (1922), pp. 407–432.

"Die ältesten chinesischen Weltkarten," Ostasiatische Zeitschrift, vol. 11, pt. 2 (Berlin and Leipzig, 1924), pp. 97–118.

"Die Hephthaliten und ihre Beziehungen zu China," Asia Major, vol. 2, pts. 3/4 (Leipzig, 1925), pp. 564–580.

"Die Lage des Landes Ta Ts'in," Ostasiatische Zeitschrift, vol. 14, pt. 4 (1927), pp. 196–202.

"Die älteste Reichsgeographie Chinas und ihre kulturgeschichtliche Bedeutung," Sinica, vol. 5, pts. 5/6 (1930), pp. 232–237.

"Marinus von Tyrus," Petermanns Geographische Mitteilungen, Ergänzungsheft 209 (1930), pp. 45–54.

Lou-lan. China, Indien und Rom im Lichte der Ausgrabungen am Lobnor (Leipzig, 1931).

"Die Gobi im Zeitalter der Hunnenherrschaft," Hyllningsskrift tillägned Sven Hedin. Bihang till Geografiska Annaler (1935).

"Die älteste türkische Weltkarte (1076 n. Chr.)," Imago Mundi, vol. 1 (1935), pp. 21–28.

Subsequently, investigations carried out in connection with the atlas resulted in three further significant contributions to the historical geography of Asia:

"Das geographische Bild Chinas im Altertum," Sinica (Forke-Festschrift Sonderausgabe, 1937).

"Der Magnus Sinus und Cattigara nach Ptolemaeus," Comptes Rendus du Congrès International de Géographie, Amsterdam,

edged that the atlas constituted a remarkable achievement by one man. Even the great Paul Pelliot, who was at home in the literatures of almost all the Great Traditions of Asia and who was probably the scholar best qualified to comment on the historical features of the atlas, refrained from using the artillery that he undoubtedly commanded and contented himself with a volley of small-arms fire. On concluding an erudite evaluation of Herrmann's work,[18] he remarked that the undertaking, "dans l'état actuel de nos connaissances, en était peut-être un peu ambitieuse, et l'industrie d'un seul homme ne pouvait dominer l'ensemble d'un sujet si vaste dans l'espace et dans le temps." That, I think, is the point to be borne in mind in any evaluation of this atlas.

Albert Herrmann was the pioneer on the road to China who, in the words of Hessel Gerritsz quoted at the head of this essay, "was impatient of undue delay," and who was prepared to accept imperfection as the price of progress. By the nineteen-thirties the tradition of European sinology had attained its apogee, the dominance of a training in classical and medieval textual and epigraphic skills was still unchallenged and a symposium questioning the validity of sinology as an autonomous discipline[19] was still thirty years in the future. Most of the giants of this phase of Asian studies had already made their major contributions to scholarship. So far as China itself was concerned, a large portion of the classical corpus had been translated into one or another of the European languages, and medieval accounts of foreign countries had received considerable attention from scholars such as Stanislas Julien, W. P. Groeneveldt, Le Marquis d'Hervey de Saint-Denys, Edouard Chavannes, Takakusu Junjirō, Gustave Schlegel, Henri Maspero, Berthold Laufer, Friedrich Hirth and W. W. Rockhill.

For the other cultural realms of Asia there were also substantial corpora of relevant translation and exegesis. The material relating to the Muslim world of the Middle East was particularly plentiful, for a good many of the first texts to be edited and translated into European languages by such early Arabists as J. T. Reinaud, the Abbé Renaudot, P. A. Jaubert, Kurt von Schlözer, A. Sprenger, F. Wüstenfeld, T. G. J. Juynboll, C. Barbier de Meynard, Stanislas Guyard, and MacGuckin de Slane had been geographical in nature. M. J. de Goeje's great corpus of Arabic texts with Latin prefaces, *Bibliotheca geographorum Arabicorum*, had appeared at Leiden between 1870 and 1894, and had been supplemented by Gabriel Ferrand's compendium of translations of Arabo-Persian sources relating to East Asia in 1913/4. For South and Southeast Asia Sanskritists had already accumulated a vast body of material relevant to ancient toponymy, while the kaleidoscopic ethnography of Central Asia had for decades exercised a fascination for scholars in all the major cultural traditions of Asia, as well as for the grand masters in this field such as Barthold, Grum-Grzhimailo and Grünwedel.

1938, vol. 2 (1938), pp. 123–128. *Das Land der Seide und Tibet im Lichte der Antike.* Quellen und Forschungen zur Geschichte der Geographie und Völkerkunde, vol. 1 (K. F. Koehler Verlag, Leipzig, 1939).

4. Ogawa Takuji, "Kinsei Seiyō Kōtsū Izen no Shina Chizu ni tsuite," *Chigaku Zasshi*, vol. 22 (1910), p. 413. Reprinted in Ogawa's *Shina Rekishi Chiri Kenkyū*, 2 vols. (Kyoto, 1928); Joseph Needham, *Science and civilisation in China*, vol. 3 (Cambridge, at the University Press, 1959), p. 546.

5. Carl Whiting Bishop, *The Geographical Review*, vol. 27, no. 3 (1937), p. 517.

6. *The Social Studies.* Journal of the National Council for the Social Studies, vol. 24, no. 6 (1936), p. 422.

7. Georg Wegener, *Zeitschrift der Gesellschaft für Erdkunde*, parts 3/4 (Berlin, 1937), p. 135.

8. John C. Ferguson, *T'ien Hsia Monthly*, vol. 3, no. 3 (1936), p. 301.

9. *Artibus Asiae*, vol. 7, pts. 1–4 (1937), pp. 247–249.

10. *Mitteilungen der Geographischen Gesellschaft in München*, vol. 28, pt. 1 (1935), pp. 195–196.

11. Vol. 11, no. 30 (1935), pp. 385–387.

12. Vol. 16, no. 18 (1935), pp. 485–487.

13. *Monumenta Serica*, vol. 2 (1936–7), pp. 248–250.

14. Julean H. Arnold, *Journal of the North China Branch of the Royal Asiatic Society* vol. 67 (1936), pp. 188–189.

15. *Zeitschrift für Geopolitik*, vol. 13, no. 7 (1936), p. 491.

16. Vol. 53, no. 1 (1937), p. 80.

17. Baron O. B. Osten-Sacken in letters of 26 February and 8 May, 1937, quoted in *Monumenta Serica*, vol. 2 (1936–7), p. 486

18. Paul Pelliot, *T'oung Pao*, vol. 32, pt. 5 (1936), pp. 363–372. Another detailed review of the atlas was provided by Gustav Haloun in *Orientalistische Literaturzeitung*, vol. 42 (Leipzig, 1939), pp. 46–51.

19. *The Journal of Asian Studies*, vol. 23, no. (1964).

The time appeared to be ripe for an attempt to crystallize the spatial
ad chronological relationships of this material in just such an atlas as
errmann set out to produce. But the world-bestriding stature of a
andful of scholars should not blind us to the fact that the nineteen-
irties still belonged to the formative period of Asian studies. Awestruck
ith admiration as we must be when we contemplate the erudition of a
havannes or a Pelliot, a de Goeje, a Barthold or a Finot, let us not
rget that a well trained graduate student of today can often ascribe
gnificance and meaning to a text that defeated one of the great masters
the earlier decades of this century. To this extent Herrmann was, as
elliot said, "un peu ambitieuse."

Yet, paradoxically, this may have been the one period when the
holarly community would have countenanced such an ambitious
adertaking by one man. The 'thirties' may well have seen the last of the
olyhistors, the men who could claim to have mastered a significant
oportion of the major textual traditions of Asia. Of course, some of the
ants lived on beyond the 'thirties'—Pelliot himself until 1945, and a very
w, such as George Coedès, are with us yet—but by the end of the
cond World War the intellectual climate had changed. During that
ar the social scientists had discovered Asia and opened up innumerable
citing new approaches to the investigation of the non-Western world.
t the same time history and philology, the twin pillars of traditional
sian studies, were in the process of dissolving their long established
artnership. Formerly the highly philological character of Asian historio-
aphy had imparted a universality to its principles and practice, and had
duced an illusory unity in its intellectual universe that was reflected in
e use of such rubrics as 'Oriental Studies' or 'Asian History.' However,
is apparent unity was a measure of the disciplinary structure of the
ne rather than a quality inherent in reality, and in this respect the
amanistic studies of the period were often as devoid of cultural relativity
were the social sciences that arose on their ruins. But after 1945 the
d universality, valid enough in its way, had dissolved and the spurious
aity of Asian studies had been shattered. Henceforward no one man
uld hope to produce an acceptable atlas of China—let alone of Asia.
s Pelliot remarked at the conclusion of his review, "le travail de pionnier
t fait, et il appartiendra à chacun de nous, dans son domaine propre,
e le reprendre et de le compléter." In the future the compilation of such
atlas would of necessity have to be a collaborative venture. Even then
would be no easy task.

Let us turn now to the atlas itself. In this edition the plates relating to
ntemporary China have been completely redrawn to incorporate
-to-date information, so that it is necessary to concern myself only
ith the historical maps. These will be discussed under two headings,
ose relating to China Proper, the old Eighteen Provinces, the "Land

within the Great Wall," and those depicting the rest of Asia, including the Chinese dependencies. It will be my purpose not to point to lacunae in the composition of these maps, even less to suggest additional plates, but rather to draw attention to instances in which the passage of time has rendered some of the information that does appear erroneous or misleading.

MAPS OF CHINA PROPER

The maps of China Proper present a conspectus of Chinese development from prehistoric times up to the beginning of the twentieth century, often with considerable detail in the matter of territorial adjustments (cf., e.g., Plates 21, 25 and 33). Herrmann himself pointed out that he intended them to serve the purposes not only of sinologists but also of "other orientalists, historians of art, theologians, geographers and politicians,"[20] to whom we at the present day may add the flood (of a magnitude that Herrmann could never have envisaged) of students of social science, law, natural science, and technology (not to mention the omnipresent military), who are now bending their efforts to the study of things Chinese. This atlas is still virtually their only cartographic guide to the political, ecological, economic, and toponymic patterns of historic China.

Having said this, I must straightway enter certain caveats, the most pressing of which concerns the principles underlying the selection of information to be portrayed. Despite a superficial appearance of comprehensiveness, this information often seems to have been selected somewhat arbitrarily. By way of illustration, let us glance at the map of *The T'ang Dynasty: A.D. 618–906*, on Plate 29. This shows the boundaries and capitals of the ten great *tao* or provinces into which the empire was divided at the time of the Emperor T'ai Tsung, as well as some, but by no means all, of their constituent *chou* or prefectures. The difficulty arises when we try to discern the method by which Herrmann selected the *chou* that do appear on the map. Of the more than seventy (the exact number varied slightly from year to year) that were constituted in the southernmost *tao* of Ling-nan (B/C 3), for example, only twenty-eight appear on the map, and these do not readily betray the rationale of their choice. Some, such as Kuang, Hsün, and Shao, were reasonably populous centers of Chinese settlement with important economic and communication functions; others, such as Huan, I, and T'ien, were remote outposts in aboriginal territory. Of the seven Regular Prefectures *(Cheng Chou)* that were located in the Tong-king delta and on the coastal plains as far south as Hoành-sơn, only five appear on the map. Moreover, the seat of the Protectorate-General of *Kau (Mand.=Chiao; Sino-Việt.=Giao), later reconstituted as the Protectorate-General of the Pacified South, was known in T'ang times as *Suong-b'iwong (Mand.=Sung-p'ing; Sino-Việt.=Tông-bình) rather than as "Chiao" (B 3). In any case, this

21. The caption "An-nan 681–757" on Pl. 29, B3 is actually misleading for, although the name of the Protectorate-General was changed to *$\widehat{T}\breve{\imath}\underset{\wedge}{e}n$-nậm (Mand. = Tien-nan) in 757, it subsequently reverted to *·Ân-nâm (Mand. = An-nan) in 768 [*Chiu T'ang-shu*, chüan 41, f. 33 verso; *Yüan-ho chün-hsien t'u-chih*, chüan 38, f. 9 verso; *Hsin T'ang-shu*, chüan 43A, f. 8 recto].

administrative apparatus functioned only on the plains; in the neighbouring uplands Chinese control was often only nominal. From time to time attempts were made to bring these territories within the prefectural hierarchy, but more often than not the more remote tracts, at least, were constituted as Prefectures (or Subprefectures)-under-Restraint *(Chi-mi Chou* [*Hsien*]*)*, where local headmen acted on behalf of Chinese authority—what analogy might lead us to call Scheduled Territories today. None of these, of which there were sizable clusters along the southwestern frontier of the T'ang empire, appears on Plate 29. Neither is the significance of the Protectorate-General, an instrument of government developed by the T'ang to cope with the exigencies of border administration, adequately brought out. Although there were seven of these territories spaced in an arc round the land frontiers of the Empire, apart from the attachment to certain place-names of dates whose implications are apparent only to those already knowledgeable in the intricacies of T'ang administrative history, they receive no recognition on Plates 29 and 30/31.[21]

At an earlier epoch we find that on the map of the Ch'un-Ch'iu period (Pl. 6/7) only the larger feudal states are indicated, together with a very small proportion of the total number of ethnonyms and toponyms mentioned in the classical texts. Once again I have been unable to discover any consistency in their selection. The same uncertainty arises in connection with the map of the Han dynasty (Pl. 14/15), which depicts only the seats of princely fiefs, those ruled by governors, and a scattering of additional names which cannot be correlated with any easily discernible criteria of importance. The other maps of China Proper from Chou to Ch'ing, on close inspection exhibit comparable inconsistencies, or at least apparent anomalies which cannot be resolved on the basis of the evidence inserted on the map. Perhaps Professor Herrmann himself would have provided a rationale for his choice of information had he lived to complete his handbook. As it is, students of, say, T'ang or Sung China would do well to remember that the administrative hierarchies are depicted only imperfectly.

Whether or not the anomalies just described resulted specifically from Herrmann's choice of sources I have not been able to decide, but both the bibliography and the internal evidence of the maps indicate that he relied to a high degree on commentary and exegesis in European languages. Moreover, his evaluation of Chinese sources was not always judicious or overly critical. For example, much of the information relating to Yünnan in earlier times is clearly derived from the *Nan-Ch'ao Yeh-shih*, a work belonging to a genre of "unconventional histories" which, although of value in other respects, are of dubious reliability. The publications of twentieth-century Chinese geographers are represented only sketchily in the bibliography, and virtually not at all in the construction of the maps.

22. On the other hand, sundry sites from the historic period, notably the excavation in 1930, under Japanese auspices, of the Ch'un-ch'iu and Chan-kuo city of **G'å-to* (Mand. = Hsia-tu) are missing from the map. *Vide* Fu Chen-lun, "Yen Hsia-tu fa-chüeh pao-kao," *Kuo-Hsüeh Chi-k'an*, vol. 3 (Peking University, 1932), pp. 175–182.

23. *Yün-nan Chin-ning Shih-chai-shan kù mu ch'ün fa-chüeh pao-kao* (Wen-wu Press, Peiping, 1959).

24. An Chin-huai, "Cheng-Chou ti-ch'ü-ti ku-t'ai i-ts'un chiai-shao," *Wen-wu Ts'an-k'ao Tzŭ-liao*, no. 8 (Peking, 1957), pp. 16–20; Tsou Heng, "Shih-lun Cheng-Chou hsin-fa-hsien-ti Yin-Shang wen-hua i-chih," *K'ao-ku Hsüeh-pao*, no. 3 (Peking, 1956), pp. 77–103; An Chih-min, "I-chiu-wu-erh nien ch'iu-chi Cheng-Chou Erh-li-kang fa-chüeh chi," *K'ao-ku Hsüeh-pao*, no. 8 (1954), pp. 65–108, and "Cheng-Chou-shih Jen-Min-Kung-Yüan fu-chin-ti Yin-t'ai i-ts'un," *Wen-wu Ts'an-k'ao Tzŭ-liao*, no. 6 (1954), pp. 32-37; Chao Ch'üan-ku *et al.*, "Cheng-Chou Shang-t'ai i-chih-ti fa-chüeh," *K'ao-ku Hsüeh-pao*, no. 1 (1957), pp. 53–73; "Cheng-Chou Lo-ta-miao Shang-t'ai i-chih shih-chüeh tan-pao," *Wen-wu*, no. 10 (1957), pp. 48–51; Chao Ch'ing-yün, "1957-nien Cheng-Chou hsi-chiao fa-chüeh chi-yao," *K'ao-ku T'ung-hsün*, no. 9 (1958), pp. 54–56; Chao Ch'ing-yün *et al.*, "Cheng-Chou Ko-ta-wang-ts'un i-chih fa-chüeh pao-k'ao," *K'ao-ku Hsüeh-pao*, no. 3 (1958), pp. 41–62.

Perhaps this was because the work of these geographers was not highly regarded by the group of scholars with whom Herrmann was associated at Berlin, but this excuse cannot be advanced in explanation of his neglect of the writings of the Japanese school of historical geographers. In any case, in my opinion Herrmann would have profited considerably from some acquaintance with the *Li-t'ai yü-ti yen-k'o Hsien-yao t'u* of Yang Shou-ching and Jao Tun-chih and with the maps prepared by T'ung Shih-heng, Su Chia-jung and Ou-yang Ying, as well as from the writings of contemporary Chinese historical geographers such as Ku Chieh-kang and Fu Tseng-hsiang. It is noticeable, too, that Herrmann resorted to English-language secondary sources only very sparingly, a reflection of the prevailingly low esteem in which British scholarship was held on the continent of Europe at that time. By contrast, his coverage of French and German literature—judging from the maps rather than the bibliography, which is clearly only skeletal in character—was extremely thorough. In fact, it is scarcely an exaggeration to characterize the atlas as a monument to the achievements of continental European scholars, to the virtual exclusion of Chinese and Japanese contributions.

Without doubt the map that has worn the least well of all the historical plates is the one concerned with prehistory (Pl. 1). Although it depicts more than a hundred individual sites, and numerous others under collective rubrics, it was not quite complete even in 1935 (largely owing to the author's neglect of English-language sources mentioned above). Moreover, a number of the sites, including some of the more significant, are not strictly speaking prehistoric: I am thinking of the Han tombs, for example, or of the Ordos bronzes, or of the tomb of Ch'in Shih-huang.[22] Perhaps "archeological" would be a more apposite term than "prehistoric" in the caption to this plate. The non-specialist in matters Chinese who makes use of this map should also be warned that the arrows denoting immigrations from the northwest, northeast and southeast do not imply synchronous movements, nor are they directly associated with the sites that occur along their routes. But much more important than anything on the map is that which is missing, for this plate necessarily omits all mention of the extremely important excavations carried out by Chinese archeologists during the last fifteen years or so, which in fact far outnumber the aggregate of all previous discoveries. In fact, it would be my guess that this map records less than a tenth, possibly very much less, of the total investigations undertaken to date. At least nine new Paleolithic and about a score of Mesolithic sites have been opened up since Herrmann plotted his single site at Chou-k'ou-tien, and Neolithic finds have also become proportionately more numerous. Today at least eighty prehistoric sites are known in Ssŭ-ch'uan alone, where Herrmann was able to plot only two, and at least thirty in An-hui where he had none. In the middle Yang-tzŭ valley an abundance of finds has thrown new

ght on the origins and expansion of the kingdom of **Ts'io (Mand. =
h'u), and excavations at Shih-chai Shan, in the vicinity of Tien Lake,
ave revolutionized our conception not only of conditions in southwest
hina from the later Chan-kuo period onward but also of the character
f Dong-son culture in general.[23] Finally, it should be remarked that the
reat Shang ceremonial centers at Cheng Chou,[24] Lo-yang[25] and Hui
sien,[26] together with their constellations of associated sites, have all
ome to light since this map was compiled. What I have been saying
mounts to a pretty direct warning that anyone seeking the spatial
attern of modern Chinese archeological research should supplement the
formation on Pl. 1 with a perusal of recent issues of *K'ao-ku*, *K'ao-ku*
süeh-pao, *Wen-wu* and *Ta-lu Tsa-chih*.[27]

Other maps which should be viewed with scepticism by the non-
ecialist in early Chinese history—such an admonition would, of course,
e otiose for the specialist—are those dealing with the Hsia and Shang
ynasties (Pl. 2/3 and 4). In the first place the historicity of the Hsia has
 far received no confirmation from archeological investigation, and it
still a moot point whether the origins of the archetyped tradition of that
ynasty should be sought, along with the three Sovereigns and Five
mperors, in the pre-Shang Lung-shan stage, in the earlier phases of the
hang, or possibly even as a projection backward from later times. Under
ese circumstances, to attempt to distinguish the Hsia culture hearth
om later accretions to the alleged polity, and to ascribe a date to this
ynasty (Pl. 2) betrays a wholly unwarranted devotion to the texts of the
hu Ching, Shih Chi, and Chu-shu Chi-nien. Much the same criticism can
e directed against the maps of the Shang state (or perhaps states?),
here Herrmann again seems to have accepted the Chinese textual
adition at its face value. Once more he has attempted to discriminate
etween, and assign dates to, an original nuclear hearth and subsequent
rritorial acquisitions. Even if it could be demonstrated that the Shang
ate of the texts exercised sole political authority within the Shang
lture area—which, in my opinion, is by no means certain—the Shang
etropolitan territory as depicted on the map would still be considerably
ore extensive than that attested by archeology. It is true that a late
loss on a passage in the *Chu-shu Chi-nien* delimits the state under
u-ting, twenty-second of the Shang monarchs, as stretching far into west
nd south China, but this is certainly an exaggeration born of the an-
istoricity of Han, or later, perceptions of the past. The ceremonial
enters which were the distinguishing marks of metropolitan Shang terri-
ory appear so far to have been restricted to an arcuate zone in northern
o-nan running from the neighborhood of Lo-yang in the west, through
heng Chou, to An-yang in the north. Important settlements exhibiting
lly evolved Shang cultural characteristics formed a halo around this
ore area, extending from Shan Hsien in the southwest to Ch'ü-yang in

25. Kuo Pao-chün and Lin Shou-chin,
"I-chiu-wu-erh-nien ch'iu-chi Lo-yang
tung-chiao fa-chüeh pao-k'ao," *K'ao-ku
Hsüeh-pao*, no. 9 (1955), pp. 91–116;
Kuo Pao-chün *et al.*, "Lo-yang Chien-pin
ku-wen-hua i-chih chi Han-mu," *ibid.*,
no. 1 (1956), pp. 11–28; An Chih-min
and Lin Shou-chin, "I-chiu-wu-ssŭ-nien
ch'iu-chi Lo-yang hsi-chiao fa-chüeh-
chien-pao," *K'ao-ku T'ung-hsün*, no. 5
(1955), p. 26.

26. Kuo Pao-chün, Hsia Nai *et al.*, *Hui-Hsien
fa-chüeh pao-kao* (Science Press, Peking,
1956).

27. Three of China's four archeological
journals have undergone changes of title
since their inception: (i) From 1955 to
1958 *K'ao-ku* was known as *K'ao-ku
T'ung-hsün*; (ii) The first issue in 1936
of the journal now known as *K'ao-ku
Hsüeh-pao* appeared under the title
T'ien-yeh K'ao-ku Hsüeh-pao, while for
numbers 2–5 this was changed to
Chung-kuo K'ao-ku Hsüeh-pao; (iii)
From 1950–1958 *Wen-wu* was known as
Wen-wu Ts'an-k'ao Tzŭ-liao.
There are fairly recent compendious
surveys of Chinese archeology and
prehistory in English in William Watson,
Archaeology in China (Max Parrish,
London, 1960), and *Ancient peoples and
places. China before the Han dynasty*
(Frederick A. Praeger, New York, 1961);
Kwang-chih Chang, *The archaeology of
ancient China* (Yale University Press,
New Haven, 1963); and in a series of
continuing volumes by Cheng Te-k'un,
Archaeology in China (W. Heffer & Sons
Ltd., Cambridge, 1959–). Volumes on
Prehistoric China (1959), *Shang China*
(1960), and *Chou China* (1963) have
appeared to date. See also the same
author's *Archaeological studies in
Szechwan* (Cambridge, at the University
Press, 1957).

28. The German geographer Alfred Hettner had taken a more liberal view of the scope of historical geography at least as early as 1898: "Die Entwicklung der Geographie im 19. Jahrhundert," *Geographische Zeitschrift*, vol. 4 (1898), pp. 305–320. Cp. his much later summa statement on the character of this disciplin in *Die Geographie, ihre Geschichte, ihr Wesen und ihre Methoden* (Ferdinand Hirt, Breslau, 1927), pp. 150–151.

the north and Chi-nan in the east. Beyond that lay a much wider zone, extending into northern Ho-pei, central Shan-hsi, Shen-hsi, Hu-pei, northern An-hui, and eastern Shan-tung, in which certain Shang culture traits had diffused among pre-urban societies. This archeologically attested cultural zonation is, in fact, not incompatible with the ternary world view of the Shang themselves, in which the district governed directly from the capital was surrounded by feudal fiefs, and those in turn by tribal territories, the home of non-Shang peoples.

It is evident both from the atlas and from the corpus of Professor Herrmann's published work that he interpreted historical geography to mean primarily the reconstruction of the political and toponymic patterns of the past rather than the study of former modes of ecological adaptation.[28]

Attempts to depict information in this latter category are sporadic and usually not very successful. There is, for example, no attempt to plot the spread of wet-rice cultivation after the introduction of early-ripening varieties in the eleventh century A.D., or the diffusion of American food crops throughout China in post-Columbian times. A great deal of material of this nature is fairly readily available in the profusion of local topographies that constitute such a distinctive strand in the tradition of Chinese geographical writing, and it is significant that Herrmann made no use of this resource. Perhaps this was because such topographies were not well represented in the Berlin sinological collections, but I think it at least as likely that it reflected the overwhelming concern of the sinologists of the time with classical texts.

One map which does include such information from ancient times is that on Pl. 4, depicting the products which the *Yü Kung (Tribute of Yü)* assigned to the Nine Provinces of ancient China. It is curious that Herrmann, who himself offered a course at Berlin entitled "Historische Geographie Chinas (mit *Übungen)*," should have been one of the last scholars to persist in ascribing a Shang date to this text. In fact, it had already become evident before 1935 that the *Yü Kung* could not have been pre-Confucian, and was probably to be dated to the fifth century B.C., at which time it constituted a projection into the past of Chou-style conceptions. Plate 4 should be regarded, therefore, as a representation of possibly ancient economic information forced into a Late-Chou mould.

Two plates, based on information from the *Chou Li* and *Shih Chi* respectively, attempt to depict the contrasting economic condition of China during the Ch'un-ch'iu (Pl. 6/7, inset) and Former-Han periods (Pl. 12). Leaving aside the fact that the *Chou Li* was also a Former-Han compilation which possibly incorporated a certain amount of Late-Chou material, and that the insert on Pl. 7 should consequently be transferred to Pl. 8 at the earliest, it is difficult to see why Herrmann should have believed that, during the second half of the first millenium B.C., the

29. Ting I, "Chiang Han p'ing-yüan hsin-shih-ch'i-shih-t'ai hung-shao-t'u chung ti tao-ku k'ao-ch'a," *K'ao-ku Hsüeh-pao*, no. 4 (1959), pp. 31–33; Hu Yüeh-chien, *ibid.*, no. 1 (1957), p. 27; Hsieh Chun-chu, *Wen-wu Ts'an-k'ao Tzŭ-liao*, no. 8 (1955), pp. 50–51.

30. Hu Yüeh-chien, *K'ao-ku Hsüeh-pao*, no. 1 (1957), pp. 26.

31. *Nukhbat al-dhar fi' ajāïb al-barr wa al-baḥr*, p. 227 of A. F. Mehren's edition of the text in *Cosmographie de Chems-ed-Din Abou Abdallah Mohammed ed-Dimichqi* (Saint Petersburg, 1866). It is true, of course, that Dimashqī's information about East Asia was anything but reliable, and that he was simply repeating material from an earlier age.

northern and western limits of rice cultivation—presumably implying wet-rice cultivation—had retreated to the southeast. The truth, of course, is that these texts are inadequate sources for this kind of reconstruction. Their positive affirmations can be accepted with a degree of caution commensurate with the state and pedigree of the particular text, but arguments *ex silentio* are entirely untrustworthy. As rice had been domesticated in Southeast Asia, the frontiers of its cultivation were more likely to have moved in the opposite direction from that suggested in the atlas. The fact that they had done so long previously is attested by recent archeological reports, which imply that rice cultivation had formed part of the cultural repertoire of Lung-Shan farmers, though whether they planted wet or dry varieties is uncertain pending further analyses.[29] The introduction of wheat into the Huai region in about 1100 B.C. (Pl. 7, inset) is also based on a questionable evaluation of the sources which, since 1935, have been further discredited by the discovery of grains of that cereal from Lung-shan levels at Tiao-yü-t'ai in northern An-hui.[30] A last point in this general area of concern: paper, which appears on the map of economic development in about 100 B.C. (Pl. 12, B 2), was not invented for another two centuries.

Finally, I must enter a word of warning concerning some of the capitals that appear on Professor Herrmann's maps, more particularly as they represent the sort of information for which an atlas such as this is frequently consulted. First, as to their names. On Pl. 19 *Saraga* (a Sanscritized form of the *Sarag* of the Nestorian Inscription) is given as a name for Lo-yang. In actual fact this term is not encountered until T'ang times, and should therefore be transferred to Pl. 31, F3, where it is at present omitted. Moreover, on this latter map *Khamdan* is a poor reading for the Arabic *Khumdān*, deriving from **G'em-dịang (Mand.=Hsien-yang), the name of the Ch'in capital, which persisted in Arab geographical writings as the name of the Chinese metropolis at least as late as the fourteenth century, when Muhammad ibn Ibrāhīm al-Anṣārī al-Dimashqī was still making mention of it.[31] *Khubdan* on Pl. 27, F3 is merely a deviant reading of *Khumdān*, not an alternative appellation. On Pl. 40, G3, entitled *Beginnings of the Mongol Empire*, the name *Ta-t'ung* should be replaced by the old Ch'in name of *Hsi Ching* (Western Capital), which was retained in the early days of the Mongol hegemony. At the same time K'ai-feng or Pien-ching was known only as *Nan-ching* (= Southern Capital: Polo's *Namghin*). On the same map, which relates to A.D. 1234, Shang-tu (G2) is an anachronism, for this name did not replace that of K'ai-p'ing-fu until June 16, 1263. Indeed, K'ai-p'ing-fu itself had not been founded as a summer residence for Qubilai, then Heir-Apparent, until 1256. Meanwhile the official capital remained at Qara-qorum until Qubilai's accession to the throne in 1260, when it was transferred to Ta-hsing, that is Peking. Professor Herrmann was also mistaken in

32. *Vide* Paul Pelliot, *Notes on Marco Polo*, vol. 1 (Librairie Adrien-Maisonneuve, Paris, 1959), *sub Cambaluc* and *Ciandu;* vol. 2 (1963), *sub Namghin* and *Taidu*.

33. "T'ang-t'ai Ch'ang-an Ch'eng k'ao-ku chi-lüeh," *K'ao-ku*, no. 11 (1963), plates opposite pp. 596 and 610. See also "T'ang Ch'ang-an Ch'eng ti-chi ch'u-pu t'an-ts'e," *K'ao-ku Hsüeh-pao*, no. 3 (1958), pp. 79–94.

locating "Taidu" (G3) on this map and in relying on Bretschneider's date of 1271 for Qubilai's taking up of winter residence there. In actual fact the name of Chung-tu (which had been adopted in 1264) was changed to Ta-tu (Polo's *Taidu)* on March 4, 1272, but the palace was not completed until the end of 1273. Qubilai entered the great hall to receive the congratulations of the Court on New Year's Day (February 9) 1274.[32]

As for the plans of the Chinese capitals on Plates 13, 42/43, 45 and 49, they display clearly enough the material expression of a canon of city planning that was permeated with cosmic symbolism, but investigations subsequent to 1935 have modified some of the detail. In particular, the systematic excavations at Ch'ang-an undertaken by the Institute of Archeology of the Academia Sinica since 1957 have added several new features, including the layout of the Great Luminous Palace containing more than twenty halls, details of the Hsüan-wu Gate and the location of the P'eng-lai Pool. The best reconstruction of ancient Ch'ang-an to date is that in *K'ao-ku* for 1963,[33] and there is a series of plans of the chief capitals, published some twenty years after Herrmann completed his atlas, in *Chung-kuo li-shih ti-t'u chi*, compiled by Ch'eng Kuang-yü and Hsü Sheng-mu, and issued in Hong-Kong in 1956.

MAPS OF CHINA'S DEPENDENCIES AND OF THE REST OF ASIA

Even the primarily Chinese maps usually include information relating to neighboring territories, but what gives this atlas such a distinctive character is the way in which these maps are integrated into their Asian context. It was, of course, entirely logical and necessary to include the Central Asian territories over which the stronger Chinese dynasties claimed control, but there are in addition a series of maps showing, as it were, China-in-Asia, and there can be little doubt that these plates have contributed as much to the popularity of the atlas as have those relating specifically to the Eighteen Provinces. Yet, from a purely intellectual point of view, it may be queried whether such maps are justified by the largely autochthonous character of Chinese historical development. I think that the real reason for the inclusion of these maps of Asia is to be sought in the milieu in which Herrmann worked. When the treasures collected by Albert von Le Coq and Albert Grünwedel on their Turfan expeditions were brought back to Berlin in the early years of this century, that city almost at once became one of the premier European foci of Central Asian studies. In succeeding decades there gravitated toward the twin foci of the Anthropological Museum and the Prussian Academy a group of scholars who brought a mutually complementary array of skills to the study of Central Asia. Among those working there in Herrmann's time, in addition to von Le Coq and Grünwedel, were F. W. K. Müller, H. Schaeder, Ferdinand Lessing, O. Kümmel, Otto Franke, and, of a younger generation, Walter Henning, W. Gelpke, E. Waldschmidt, A. von

34. It is true that, prior to R. A. Stein's magistral study of *Liə̯m-·i̯ə̯p toponymy ["Le Lin-yi," *Han-Hiue*, vol. 2, pts. 1–3 (Peking, 1947)], the relationships of these tribal groups to each other and to Chinese authority were but ill understood, but their names and general locations were familiar enough to students of South Chinese ethnology.

35. With reference to Pl. 31, G2, it should be noted that the capital of Japan did not remain at Nara until A.D. 794, but was transferred to Nagaoka in the province of Yamashiro in 784. 794 was the year when the still uncompleted Nagaoka was abandoned for geomantic reasons in favor of Heian-kyō.

Gabein, and Wolfram Eberhard, all of whom exhibited a sustained interest in Central Asian scholarship.

It was not surprising that in this stimulating intellectual environment Albert Herrmann should also have been attracted to the study of Central Asia, specifically in his case to Sino-European relations in early times. In a sense his atlas is a true reflection of the way in which he himself viewed China—primarily as the country at the end of a long Central Asian corridor filled with shifting and elusive peoples whose history had to be unravelled before one could come to grips with the historical geography of China Proper, and secondarily as the country at the end of the long southern sea-route, a topic which had provided him with his other main scholarly interest. And always, in accordance with this order of priorities, the Central Asian sectors of the maps receive fuller treatment than do the South and Southeast Asian maps. This is equally true of the maps relating to China Proper: the ethnic groups of the northwestern frontiers are more fully represented than those of the southwest.

Compare, for example, these frontier zones on the map of T'ang China in Pl. 29. In the north and west we discover most of the names that one would expect to find on an atlas map: Uighurs, Bayirku, Pu-ku, T'u-chüeh, Huns, Avars, Tatabi, and Kitan, but where are the Eastern *Ts'uân or Black *Mwan in the hills to the south of the Tien Lake? Similarly one will look in vain for any mention of the turbulent tribal groups such as the *Luo-i̯wo, *Kuo-lâng, *Si̯ək-b'uk *Puâ-lieu, *Ki̯ə̯u-puə̯t-dẓ'i, *Mi̯uə̯n-i̯ng and *Zi̯wo-lâng who surged round the Chinese colonial foundations in *Ńźi̯ĕt-nậm Commandery in earlier centuries.[34] Not even the *Lâk (Sino-Việt.=Lặc) tribes, the main ethnic group in the Tong-king lowlands in Han times, are represented. And, farther afield, while the ruins of Lou-lan and Qara-qorum rate inset reproductions, those of Yaśodhara-pura (Aṅkor), Amarāvatī [Mĭ-sơn] and Arimaddanapura [Pagan] do not.

To some extent this northern and western bias, which reflected Herrmann's own predilections, was reinforced by a parallel tendency in the progress of Chinese studies. Prior to 1935 very few sinologists had devoted much attention to the southern parts of the Chinese culture realm. Even the band of scholars working at the Ecole Française d'Extrême-Orient in Hanoi had been concerned less with the south of China than with Chinese accounts of the *Nan Hai*. As for the countries lying to the east of China, it must be admitted that, compared with the attention that he bestowed on Central Asia, Herrmann treated both Korea and Japan in somewhat cavalier fashion. His competence and interest lay in directions remote from these two countries, with whose languages and literatures he was unfamiliar.[35]

It was in the compilation of the maps relating to Asia as a whole that Professor Herrmann once or twice allowed himself to indulge a favorite but nonetheless unlikely theory of his own invention. Generally speaking, the atlas is unusually free of such personal idiosyncrasies, and Herrmann customarily stayed fairly close to the Berlin consensus. However, two different identifications of the same toponym proposed by him have never achieved acceptance, namely the equation of Ta Ch'in *(*d'ai-dz'iĕn)* with Arabia Felix on Pl. 18, C3, and with Baghdād on Pl. 30, C2. Long before 1935 it had become clear that this name referred to the Roman Orient, particularly Syria. Similarly, few scholars have accepted the identity of Issedon[es] and Ch'i-t'un *(*ts'iĕt-d'uən*: implied by Pl. 20, inset, and 32, F/G3; cf. also *Corrigenda* on p. 112 of the 1935 edition of the *Atlas)*.

MAPS OF CENTRAL ASIA

As has been pointed out above, Central Asia is well represented in the atlas, and, in view of the amount of scholarly work that has been publish-ed since 1935, it is remarkable how well these maps have stood the test of time. Nevertheless, the non-specialist should take heed of a few points in which the recorded information is misleading. I shall ignore those matters which learned doctors are still debating, and mention only a few names which a layman might have occasion to look up in the atlas and which at the same time have been identified with reasonable certainty.

Some of the anomalies are anachronistic in character. The **T'uət-Kiuət* (Mand.=T'u-chüeh) for example, are not attested before the middle of the sixth century A.D. and should, therefore, be deleted from Pl. 24, E2.[36] Others have arisen through errors in transcription. On Pls. 16, E2, and 20 (inset), for instance, the Chinese transcription of Kuča should read Ch'iu-tz'ŭ (in Mandarin) rather than "Kuei-tzu". Still other anomalies involve the misplacement of names. The Kingdom of Fu *(*B'iu)*, which crops up in Sui and later texts and which Herrmann took for a transcription of *dBu* (for *dBus*, the vicinity of Lhasa), should be disassociated from this latter name and located farther eastward, occupy-ing territory lying approximately between Ta-chien-lu and Jyekundo (or Gyal-kun-mdo).[37] While it is true that T'u-jen *(*t'uo-ńźiĕn)*, or indigenes, assumed the overtones of an ethnic name in Chinese colloquial speech, it has not, as Herrmann implies in his index *(sub* Turen), been satisfactorily related to T'u-yü-hun *(*t'uo-k'iak-ɣuən)*.[38] In some instances a name is displaced from its proper situation, as when the "Men with black carri-ages" *(* Xək-kiwo-tsi)*, who occur in contexts which show them to have been Mongols, are located on the Orkhon and Selenga rivers instead of some distance farther to the east (Pl. 36, B/C 1).

The migrations of the nomadic groups of Central Asia in historic time are extremely obscure, but had the Chien-kun *(*kien-kuən)*, who are usually equated with the Qyrghyz, been on the "Hunger Steppe" between Lake Balkash and the Sary Su in the first century A.D. in the manner indicated on Pls. 11, C1, 16, B/C, 1 and 18, D2, then—as Otto Maenchen-Helfen once remarked—they would surely have starved to death.[39] On

36. See Edouard Chavannes, *Documents sur les Tou-Kiue (Turcs) occidentaux, recueillis et commentés par . . .* (Imp. Acad. Sci., St. Petersburg, 1903); Paul Pelliot, "L'origine de T'ou-kiue, nom chinois des Turcs," *T'oung Pao*, series 2, vol. 16 (1915), pp. 687–689; Peter A. Boodberg, "Three notes on the T'u-chüeh Turks," in Walter J. Fischel [ed.], *Semitic and Oriental Studies presented to William Popper*. University of California Publications in Semitic Philology, vol. 11 (University of California Press, 1951), pp. 1–11; Liu Mau-tsai, *Die chinesischen Nachrichten zur Geschichte der Ost-Türken (T'u-küe)*. Göttinger Asiatische Forschungen, vols. 10 and 11 (Wiesbaden, 1958); E. G. Pulleyblank, "The Chinese name for the Turks," *Journal of the American Oriental Society*, vol. 85, no. 2 (1965), pp. 121–12.

37. E.g., *Sui Shu*, chüan 83, f. 8 recto; *Pei Shih*, chüan 96, f. 10 recto. The reason-ing behind Herrmann's location of this toponym is set out in Sven Hedin's *Southern Tibet*, vol. 8, p. 235. For remarks on the Kingdom of Fu see R. A Stein, *Les tribus anciennes des marches sino-tibétaines, légendes, classification et histoire*. Bibliothèque de l'Institut des Hautes Etudes Chinoises, vol. 15 (Presses Universitaires de France, Paris, 1961), pp. 80–81, and Paul Pelliot, *Notes on Marco Polo*, vol. 2 (Librairie Adrien-Maisonneuve, Paris, 1963), pp. 693–694.

38. For references to the *T'u-yü-hun* see the bibliography on pp. 41–47 of Thomas D. Carroll, S.J., *Account of the T'ù-yü-hu in the History of the Chìn Dynasty*. Chinese Dynastic Histories Translations No 4 (University of California Press, 1953)

39. Otto [J.] Maenchen-Helfen, "Manichaean in Siberia," in Walter J. Fischel [ed.], *Semitic and Oriental Studies presented to William Popper*. University of California Publications in Semitic Philology, vol. 11 (University of California Press, 1951), p. 317, note 19.

l. 31 the "Toghuzghuz" (=Toquz Oghuz), who are equated with the Uighurs of Outer Mongolia (E/F2), are the same people as "the 9 Oguz" who are located around the headwaters of the Kerulen river (F2), the element *toquz* being simply a Turkish numerical designation frequently applied to tribal federations in the eastern and northern territories of the Orkhon Turkish empire (cp. the Chinese term *chiu hsing* applied to the Uighurs).[40] It also is a fact, which Professor Herrmann did not take into account, that Muslim writers retained the name Toquz Oghuz to denote the Uighur kingdom that was subsequently reconstituted in the vicinity of Turfan. Finally, anyone who is thinking of accepting uncritically the several locations of the ethnikon *Hun* in the pages of this atlas would do well to read Professor Maenchen-Helfen's papers on this topic.[41]

MAPS OF SOUTH AND SOUTHEAST ASIA

When Professor Herrmann came to compile those sectors of his maps relating to South and Southeast Asia, he was confronted with even greater difficulties than he had encountered in dealing with Central Asia. The nuclear corpus of Chinese, Arabic, Persian, Greek, and medieval European texts with which he had been familiar for a quarter of a century were still relevant to his work, but the Turkish, Mongolian, and Tibetan materials were now replaced by Sanskrit and Dravidian literary-annalistic and archeological-epigraphic sources, supplemented by documents from nearly a dozen ancient civilizations in Southeast Asia *sensu stricto*. The fragmentation and ambivalence of the primary source materials certainly posed no less formidable problems than in Central Asia, but the available corpus of translation and exegesis was considerably smaller, and very probably of poorer quality. It is true that Paul Pelliot's magnificent excursus, "Deux itinéraires de Chine en Inde à la fin du VIIIe siècle,"[42] by integrating hitherto obscure and splintered scraps of information into a coherent whole, had provided a framework for the historical geography of early Southeast Asia. At the same time a succession of French scholars at the Ecole Française d'Extrême-Orient had made available to a wider public the historical resources of Indochina. Pelliot had collated the texts relating to **B'iu-nậm* (Mand.=Fu-nan) in 1903,[43] Georges Maspéro those relating to *Campā* in 1910,[44] and in 1909 George Coedès had published a compendium of translations of Greek and Latin texts bearing on the geography of ancient Southeast Asia.[45] In the then Netherlands East Indies the labors of members of the Archeological Commission (from 1913 the Archeological Service) had been synthesized by N. J. Krom in his *Hindoe-Javaansche Geschiedenis*,[46] and Coedès, by delineating the form of an hitherto unknown thalassocracy as an integrating principle permeating apparently unrelated texts, had revealed the existence of the kingdom of Srī Vijaya.[47] Moreover, between 1924 and 1929 Coedès had published, transcribed, translated, and annotated a substantial corpus of

40. Boodberg, "Three notes," pp. 3–5. Note particularly the reference on p. 3, note 18 to Grum-Grzhimailo in *Zapadnaiia Mongoliia*, pp. 285–289; L. Bazin, "Notes sur les mots 'Oġuz' et 'Türk', "*Oriens*, vol. 6 (1953), pp. 315–322; E. G. Pulleyblank, "Some remarks on the Toquzoghuz problem," *Ural-Altäische Jahrbücher*, vol. 28 (1956), pp. 35–42.

41. Otto J. Maenchen-Helfen, "Huns and Hsiung-nu," *Byzantion*, vol. 17 (1945), pp. 222–243; "The ethnic name Hun," in Søren Egerod and Else Glahn [eds.], *Studia Serica Bernhard Karlgren Dedicata* (Copenhagen, 1959), pp. 223–238.

42. *Bulletin de l'Ecole française d'Extrême-Orient*, vol. 4 (1904), pp. 131–413.

43. "Le Fou-nan," *Bulletin de l'Ecole française d'Extrême-Orient*, vol. 3 (1903), pp. 248–303.

44. "Le royaume de Champa," *T'oung Pao*, series 2, vol. 11 (1910), pp. 125–136, 165–220, 319–350, 489–526, 547–566; vol. 12 (1911), pp. 53–87, 236–258, 291–315, 451–482, 589–626; vol. 14 (1913), pp. 153–201. Reprinted in book form by Les Editions G. van Œst, Paris, 1928.

45. *Textes d'auteurs grecs et latins relatifs à l'Extrême-Orient, depuis le IVe siècle av. J.C. jusqu'au XIVe siècle* (Paris, 1910).

46. The Hague, 1926.

47. "Le royaume de Çrīvijaya," *Bulletin de l'Ecole française d'Extrême-Orient*, vol. 18, no. 6 (1918), pp. 1–36.

Thai texts,[48] but his six volumes of *Inscriptions du Cambodge*[49] and his summary statement on the Indianized realms of Southeast Asia[50] were still in the future, as indeed was the work of Louis Malleret on Oc-èo,[51] of Pierre Dupont on Mōn archeology,[52] of L. C. Damais on Sino-Indonesian toponymy,[53] and of C. C. Berg[54] and J. G. de Casparis[55] on Indonesian epigraphy, as well as Rolf Stein's study of *Liəm-jəp* toponymy.[56]

Much else besides which today constitutes the communal store of received knowledge for workers in the field of Southeast Asian historical geography was unavailable to Herrmann in 1935. Under these circumstances his maps of South and Southeast Asia in former times, particularly in the earlier historical periods, represented an achievement of which he could well be proud. It will not be my purpose in the following notes —any more than it was in those concerning Central Asia—to undertake a modernization of these maps, which have actually survived the revisions of three decades uncommonly well. That would be a task to occupy a team of scholars over years. Rather I shall try to illustrate a few of the problems which confronted Professor Herrmann in this phase of his work, to demonstrate some of the uncertainties and ambivalencies which attend the identification of certain toponyms, and in general to sound a note of warning to the scholar from another discipline who may have occasion to use these maps.

A proportion of the necessary revisions, as was the case in Central Asia, are concerned with anachronisms. On Pl. 27 neither Haripuñjaya nor Pagan had come into existence by the beginning of the seventh century A.D. The former of these two kingdoms was, according to the *Jīnakālamālinī* of Ratanapañña, not founded until the eighth century.[57] The latter, according to none-too-reliable Burmese chronicles, developed through a process of synoecism that was completed in A.D. 849 when nineteen hitherto discrete settlements were enclosed within a wall.[58] However, there is no epigraphic reference to the city earlier than a Cham inscription of A.D. 1000-1050.[59] In any case the legend "KINGD. OF PAGAN" should be deleted from Pl. 27, E3, which relates to c. A.D. 610. So, too, should the toponym "Pyū," though for different reasons. It is true that the people known to the Chinese in early times as *P'iău*,[60] and to the Burmese in later centuries as *Pyu* and *Pru*,[61] appear to have been the dominant ethnic group in the middle Irawadi valley during the period to which the map refers, but there is no evidence that their capital was ever called "Pyū." In fact they styled themselves *Tirčul* or something similar,[62] and their capital seems to have been known by the honorific *Śrī Kṣetra*. There is scope for disagreement as to its precise location, but there is no evidence whatever to suggest that it was on the site later to be occupied by Pagan. Meager archeological and epigraphic evidence, Burmese chronicles of less than desirable authenticity, and a few incidental remarks by two Chinese Buddhist travellers have led several

48. *Recueil des inscriptions du Siam*, 2 vols. (Bangkok, B.E. 2467–2472: A.D. 1924–1929).

49. *Ecole française d'Extrême-Orient: Collection de textes et documents sur l'Indochine, III. Inscriptions du Cambodg* 6 vols. (Hanoi/Paris, 1937–54).

50. *Histoire ancienne des états hindouisés d'Extrême-Orient* (Hanoi, 1944). Second edition under the title *Les états hindouisé d'Indochine et d'Indonésie* (Editions E. de Boccard, Paris, 1948; third edition, 1964

51. *L'archéologie du delta du Mékong.* Publications de l'Ecole française d'Extrême-Orient, no. 43 (Paris, 1959–63 vol. 1, *L'exploration archéologique et les fouilles d'Oc-èo;* vol. 2, *La civilisation matérielle d'Oc-èo;* vol. 3, *La culture du Fou-nan;* vol. 4, *Le Cisbassac.*

52. *L'archéologie mône du Dvāravatī.* Publications de l'Ecole françaised 'Extrên Orient, no. 41, 2 vols. (Paris, 1959).

53. Louis-Charles Damais, "Etudes d'épigraphie indonésienne," *Bulletin de l'Ecole française d'Extrême-Orient*, vol. 45, pt. 1 (1951), and "Etudes sino-indonésiennes," *ibid.*, vol. 52, pt. 1 (1964), pp. 93–114.

54. This author's interpretations of Indonesian history, which are scattered through numerous and not always easily accessible journals, are summarized in C. C. Berg, "Javanese historiography—a synopsis of its evolution," in D. G. E. Hall, *Historians of South-East Asia* (Oxford University Press, 1961), pp. 13–23. See also his "The Javanese picture of the past," in Soedjatmoko, Mohammad Ali, G. J. Resink and G. McT. Kahin [eds.], *An introduction to Indonesian Historiography* (Cornell University Press, Ithaca, N.Y., 1965), pp. 86–117.

55. J. G. de Casparis, *Inscripties uit de Çailendra-Tijd (= Praśasti Indonesia, diterbitkan oleh Djawatan Purbakala Republik Indonesia I)*, Masa Baru, Bandung, 1950, and *Praśasti Indonesia diterbitkan oleh Dinas Purbakala Republi Indonesia* (1956).

56. Cf. note 34 above.

57. George Coedès, "Documents sur l'histoi politique et religieuse du Laos occidental, *Bulletin de l'Ecole française d'Extrême-Orient*, vol. 25 (1925), p. 19.

58. Pe Maung Tin and G. H. Luce, *The Glass Palace Chronicle of the Kings of Burma* (Oxford University Press, 1923), pp. 28–29 (reprinted with identical

holars to identify Srī Ksetra, at least during the seventh century, with
e ruins at Hmawza, about five miles to the southeast of Prome.[63]
deed, the city is so located on Pl. 27 of this atlas. However, ninth-
ntury Chinese descriptions of the capital *may* be held to imply that the
pital was transferred at a later date to Upper Burma.[64] Even so there is
 reason to seek a site at Pagan; in fact it is the ruins at Halingyi which
st come to mind, though nothing has so far been found to link these
mains specifically with a Pyu capital.[65]

On the same map the form "Ramaniyadesa" (presumably for *Ramañ-*
desa) attached to the Mōn territories of Lower Burma (E4) is actually
t attested prior to the Kalyānī inscriptions from the end of the fifteenth
ntury. It was in fact a clerkly Pāli term coined by Buddhist monks,
en though it was apparently solidly based on a Middle Mōn form
man < Rmañ which did occur in Khmer epigraphy of the seventh
ntury.[66] Nevertheless, it was still a little too late to be included on this
ap. Moreover, in connection with Plate 31, F3 relating to c. A.D. 750
yādhapura (= City of the Hunter[s?]; cp. Chinese **D'ək-mĭuk,* a tran-
ription of Old Khmer *dmâk* with the same connotation)[67] had been
nounced as capital of **B'ĭu-nậm* in favor of *Naravaranāgara* late in the
xth century A.D. By the first half of the eighth century the capital of
aritime **Tśĭen-lâp* (Mand.=Chen-la) had probably been constituted
 Bālādityapura, and that of Continental **Tsien-lâp* at *Sambhupura,*
ither of which appear on this map.

If Mlle. Jacqueline Pirenne succeeds in sustaining her recent contention
at the *Periplus Maris Erythraei* should be ascribed to the early decades
 the third century rather than to the close of the first century A.D.,[68]
ates 19 and 27 will incorporate a special suite of anachronisms for
hich Herrmann can hardly be held responsible. The ensuing revisions
ould entail a series of readjustments hingeing on the substitution of
tolemaic toponyms for those of the *Periplus.* The city of *Minnagara*
l. 19, D3) in the Indus delta, for example, would be replaced by *Patala.*
f course, some of these changes would be made on the assumption that
e Ptolemaic evidence was applicable to the end of the first century A.D.,
en though the text has traditionally been dated to the middle of the
cond century.[69] If strict contemporaneity were insisted on, however,
en the *Minaei* (C4) should be omitted from what is presently the nor-
ern Yemen and *Salike* from Ceylon (E4). In any case *Carna* (C4)
ould be sited somewhat farther north, more or less on the latitude of
akoraba. In Ceylon the name "Palaesimundus" (= *Palaisimoundou;*
), monstrous though long cherished child of mislection, should read
moundou.[70] Moreover, it follows from Mlle. Pirenne's investigations
at the Kusāna king Kaniska was not reigning until about the second
cade of the third century A.D.,[71] which would imply that the Kusāna
ngdom had not yet extended its control over Northwestern India (D3).

pagination, Rangoon, 1960); *Mahā Yazawin Gyi,* I, 163 (Burma Research Society Publication, series no. 5, 1926). See also J. S. F. [John Sydenham Furnivall], "The foundation of Pagan," *Journal of the Burma Research Society,* vol. 1, pt. 2 (1911), pp. 6–9; Maung Htin Aung, "The Lord of the Great Mountain," *ibid.,* vol. 38, pt. 1 (1955), pp. 75–82; Maung Maung, "A history of Lower Burma," *ibid.,* vol. 11, pt. 2 (1921), p. 83.

59. Etienne Aymonier, "Première étude sur les inscriptions tchames," *Journal Asiatique,* 8th series, vol. 17 (1891), p. 29; Louis Finot, "Notes d'épigraphie," *Bulletin de l'Ecole française d'Extrême-Orient,* vol. 3 (1903), p. 633.

60. *Hou-Han Shu,* chüan 116, f. 18 verso; *Fa-yüan Chu-lin* by Tao Shih (A.D. 668), chüan 49, f. 16 verso; *Kuang Chih* by Kuo I-kung [4th century. *Apud Yü-han Shan-fang Chi-i-shu* (1853), chüan 74]; *T'ai-p'ing Yü-lan,* chüan 353, f. 2 verso, chüan 359, f. 3 recto, chüan 956, f. 4 verso, chüan 981, f. 7 recto, and chüan 982, f. 3 verso; *Hua-yang-kuo Chih* by Ch'ang Ch'ü (A.D. 347), chüan 4, f. 16 recto; *T'ang Hui-yao,* chüan 100, ff. 17 verso-18 recto; *T'ai-p'ing Huan-yü Chi,* chüan 179, ff. 16 recto-17 recto, quoting *Hsi-nan I-fang Chih* and *Nan-chung Pa-chün Chih,* both of uncertain date; *Chiu T'ang-Shu,* chüan 197, ff. 16 verso-17 verso; *Hsin T'ang-Shu,* chüan 222C, f. 9 *et seq.;* *Man Shu,* chüan 10, pp. 45–46; and later works.

61. *Vide* G. H. Luce, "Names of the Pyu," *The Journal of the Burma Research Society,* vol. 22, pt. 2 (Rangoon, 1932), p. 89.

62. Cf. *Hsin-T'ang Shu: *T'uət-lâ-tśĭu;* Kyanzittha's palace inscription of c. 1011/2: *Tircul;* Marvazi's *Tabā'i 'al-hayawān* (c. 1120): *T.rshul;* *Hudūd al-'Ālam: Tusūl.*

63. For a bibliography relating to the archeological remains at Hmawza see G. H. Luce and Pe Maung Tin, "Burma down to the fall of Pagan" [Part I only published], *The Journal of the Burma Research Society,* vol. 29, pt. 3 (Rangoon, 1939), pp. 264–282 (reprinted in the *Burma Research Society Fiftieth Anniversary Publication No. 2* [Rangoon, 1960], pp. 385–403). The two Chinese travellers were (i) Hsüan-Tsang, *Ta-t'ang Hsi-yü Chi,* chap. 10, f. 51 recto (see also

A sprinkling of names in South and Southeast Asia are inaccurately transcribed or are derived from deviant recensions. On Pl. 27, E4, for instance, *Kānśipura* should read *Kāncipura*.[72] On Pl. 39, F5, "Chaban" was not precisely the same place as the "New Town," Herrmann's translation of the name *Hsin Chou*, by which the Chinese designated Quinhon. On Pl. 19, E4, by inscribing "Telingāna" across Lower Burma, Herrmann made it clear that he subscribed to the popular belief that the ethnikon *Talaiṅ*, by which the Burmese referred to the Mōn, was in some way related to the name customarily applied to the Madras district. In fact *Talaiṅ* derives from an older **Tanluiṅ*[73] which, though not attested epigraphically until A.D. 1204,[74] was surely the basis of the *Tanlwing* mentioned in the *'Akhbār aṣ-Ṣīn wa'l-Hind* as early as 851,[75] and which may have been constructed from a stem **tluiṅ* and the ancient infix *-in-* or *-an-*. Neither **tluiṅ* nor **Tanluiṅ* can be derived from Telingā[na].[76] On Pl. 31, F4, "Sribuza," long considered the form by which the Arabs rendered *Srī Vijaya*, should now be rejected. Jean Sauvaget has shown that in the early Arab system of transcription, in which a foreign *v* was denoted by *b*, and *j* by *z*, *Srbza* was a phonetically perfect transcription of *Srī Vija[ya]*.[77] The apocope of the last syllable may have been accidental or, possibly, the result of mistaking it for the Arabic termination *-ya*. In any case "Zabag" *(= Zābaj)* could not have been a transcription, as Herrmann believed, of "Sribuza" (had that been the correct reading), *Srī Vijaya* or **Śi-lji-b'iuət-źi̯äi* (Mand.=Shih-li-fo-shih): it was, in fact, a transcription of the widespread ethnikon *Jāvaka*.

Incidentally, it should be remarked that so far as Southeast Asia is concerned, Herrmann does not follow his stated intention (p. 88 of the first edition) of rendering "non-Chinese names which have been handed down in the Cinese language" in the Chinese pronunciation current at the time. There are many examples of this but one must suffice for all. Let us take "Strait of Chih" on Pl. 31, F3. In Chia Tan's itinerary this is categorized as "a strait *(hsia)* which the foreigners call **tśi̯ĕt*.[78] As it was located unequivocally somewhere between the Malay Peninsula and Sumatra (Herrmann's position may not be too accurate), Pelliot was probably correct in regarding **tśi̯ĕt* as a transcription of Malay *sĕlat*,[79] but Herrmann's retention of the Mandarin pronunciation *chih* effectively obscures the possibility of this identification.

The name "Kakola" on Plate 31, E3, deserves special consideration. It is an imprecise transcription[80] of the *Qāqulla* which early Arab authors located rather vaguely in the Orient, and which the Chinese seem to have denoted by the graphs **Kâ-kuk-lâ* or **Kât-kuo-lâ*.[81] Because of an apparent interchangeability of *t-* and *k-* in Sanskrit and Pāli texts,[82] some authors have equated *Qaqulla/*Kâ-kuk-lâ* with *Takola Emporion* of the Ptolemaic corpus. None of this is very satisfactory, and I should prefer to treat the two names as distinct. Yet so far the locating of *Qāqulla* as a

Ta-T'ang Ta-tzŭ-en-ssŭ San-ts'ang Fa-shi *Chuan* by Hui-Li, which includes a parallel passage, chap. 2053, f. 240), and (ii) I-Ching, *Nan-hai Chi-kuei Nei-fa Chuan*, chap. 1, f. 3 verso.

64. From one point of view, information provided by Pyu embassies to the Chinese court in A.D. 802 and 807 and subsequently incorporated in both T'ang histories [*Chiu T'ang-Shu*, chüan 197, ff. 16 verso 17 recto and *Hsin T'ang-Shu*, chüan 222 ff. 9 recto - 12 recto], as well as in sundry other annals and encyclopedias, does not agree with the picture of *Srī Ksetra* derived from archeology and Burmese chronicles. From another point of view, one of Chia Tan's itineraries [*Hsin T'ang-shu*, chüan 43B, f. 29 recto] and Fan Ch'o's *Man Shu* [chüan 10, p. 45] both imply that the capital *may* have been situated in Upper Burma.

65. *Archaeological Survey of Burma (1905)*, pp. 7–10; *(1906)*, p. 7; Charles Duroiselle, "Excavations at Halin," *Archaeological Survey of India (1929–1930)*, pp. 151–155. A legendary account of Halin is summarized in the *Shwebo District Gazetteer* (Rangoon) and Charles Duroiselle, *Archaeological Survey of India, 1914–15*, pp. 44–45. At various times the city seems to have been known under the following honorifics: *Hamsava* (nothing to do with Pegu which shared the same honorific), *Hamsanagara*, *Pachchimanagara* and *Kāmavatī*. According to a local legend, the city was founded by a King Karabho, son of the famous Mahāsammata. Subsequently, 798 kings reigned at Halin, followed by a monarch styled Pyu-bhandhava [Duroiselle, *Arch. Survey India*, 1929–30, p. 152].

66. Pierre Dupont, *L'archéologie mône de Dvāravatī*, pp. 2–4.

67. George Coedès, "Etudes cambodgiennes quelques précisions sur la fin du Founan," *Bulletin de l'Ecole française d'Extrême-Orient*, vol. 43 (1943–6), p. 4, and *Inscriptions du Cambodge*, vol. 2 (1942), p. 110, note 5.

68. Jacqueline Pirenne, "Un problème-clef pour la chronologie de l'Orient: la date du 'Périple de la Mer Erythrée'," *Journal Asiatique*, vol. 249, pt. 4 (1961), pp. 441–459.

69. These remarks raise the problem of the precise mode of transmission and date of the Ptolemaic text, on which see pp. xxv below. Here I am assuming that the

oponym independent of *Takola* has proved an insoluble problem. The only thing that can be said with a reasonable degree of certainty is that it seems to have been on the northern shores of the Bay of Bengal. My own preference would be to look for it in the neighborhood of Chicacole, the old *Uttarakākula*, but this is no more than a guess after a fairly intensive investigation of alternative possibilities in Southeast Asia has proved unrewarding.

The mere fact of putting a name on a map implies a certitude which is sometimes at variance with the ambiguities and perplexities of the texts from which its location is deduced. *Kalāh* is just such a name (Pl. 31, F3). There can be no doubt that it was the same name which the Chinese rendered as **Kâ-lâ*, but beyond that there is little agreement. *Quot homines . . .* in this instance is no exaggeration, but perhaps the more sober theories as to its location may be grouped into three categories: those which would place it in the vicinity of Kĕlang at the narrowest part of Mĕlaka Strait, those which seek it in Kĕdah, and those which prefer a more northerly site on or near the Kra isthmus. Sayyid Qadratullah Fatimi is the exponent of the first thesis;[83] Groeneveldt, Schlegel, Ferand, and Wheatley have espoused the third; and most other investigators of this problem, including Quatremère, Walckenaer, Van der Lith, de Goeje, Tomaschek, Le Strange, Nilakanta Sastri, Jean Sauvaget, and Herrmann, have preferred the second.[84] The reader who consults this atlas may take his choice, and Herrmann is certainly aligned with the majority opinion. What is unsatisfactory about his representation is that he depicts *Kalāh* as the point of departure for I-Ching's voyage across the Indian Ocean. Now I-Ching did not mention *Kalāh*. His last port of call in Southeast Asia was **γât-tṣ'ăt* (Mand.=Chieh-ch'a) = *Kaṭāha* ⟩ Kĕdah. Some of us may think it odd that *Kaṭāha* should also have been known as *Kalāh* at this time, for the names cannot possibly have been etymologically related; but even if they were, **γât-tṣ'ăt/Kaṭāha* should still appear on the map as the name of I-Ching's port of call. In any case this name exemplifies only too well the problems which beset the cartographer who would attempt to reconstruct the toponymy of ancient Southeast Asia.

One more example. The legend "City of red soil" on Pl. 27, E/F4, illustrates Herrmann's occasional fondness for translation as opposed to transcription. In this instance the phrase represents the author's translation of **Tṣ'iăk-t'uo* (Mand.=Ch'ih-t'u), meaning Red Earth, a name which was brought back from the *Nan Hai* by imperial envoys in 607–8.[85] Strictly speaking, it denoted a kingdom *(kuo)* rather than a city, probably the same country which featured as *Raktamṛttikā* on a Buddhist votive inscription from Kĕdah.[86] The capital of this kingdom was *Siṁhapura* (= Lion City), known to the Chinese in both transliterated *(*Səng-g'jiĕ źiäng)* and translated *(*Ṣi-tsi źiäng)* forms. It should be noted in passing

Southwest Asian material does indeed date from the middle of the second century A.D.

70. Pirenne, "Un problème-clef," p. 453.

71. *Loc. cit.*, p. 457.

72. As, indeed, should "Kanchipura" on Pl. 22, C/D 4.

73. C. O. Blagden, "Notes and reviews: etymological notes, I: Talaing," *Journal of the Burma Research Society*, vol. 4, pt. 1 (1914), p. 57.

74. G. H. Luce, "Notes on the peoples of Burma in the XIIth–XIIIth. cent. A.D.," *Burma Census Report* (Rangoon, 1931), Appendix F. Reprinted, with slight changes in the references, in *Journal of the Burma Research Society*, vol. 42, pt. 1 (1959), pp. 52–112.

75. Jean Sauvaget, 'Akhbār aṣ-Ṣīn wa'l-Hind. Relation de la Chine et de l'Inde (Paris, 1948), p. 54.

76. Louis-Charles Damais, "Etudes sino-indonésiennes. III. La transcription chinoise Ho-ling comme désignation de Java," *Bulletin de l'Ecole française d'Extrême-Orient*, vol. 52, pt. 1 (1964), pp. 97–100.

77. Jean Sauvaget, in George Coedès, *Les états hindouisés d'Indochine et d'Indonésie* (Third edition, Paris, 1964), p. 242, note 2.

78. *Hsin-T'ang Shu*, chüan 43B, f. 30 recto and chüan 222C, f. 8 verso.

79. Pelliot, "Deux itinéraires," p. 232.

80. In transliterating Arabic names Herrmann does not distinguish between the letters *qāf* and *kāf* so that, for example, on Pl. 31 we find both *Qāqulla* (E3) and *Kalāh* (F3) transcribed with *k*.

81. The relevant Arabic texts have been translated and collated by G. R. Tibbetts ["The Malay Peninsula as known to the Arab geographers," *The Malayan Journal of Tropical Geography*, vol. 9 (1956), pp. 33–38], the Chinese texts by Wheatley [*The Golden Khersonese* (University of Malaya Press, 1961), pp. 56–58 and 270–271.]

82. Sylvain Lévi, "Ptolémée, le Niddesa et la Bṛhatkathā," *Etudes Asiatiques*, vol. 2 (Paris, 1925), pp. 1–55 and 431–432.

83. S. Q. Fatimi, "In quest of Kalah," *Journal [of] Southeast Asian History*, vol. 1, no. 2 (1960), pp. 62–101.

84. References in Wheatley, *Khersonese*, p. 222.

85. *Ch'ih-t'u Kuo Chi apud Sui Shu*, chüan 82, ff. 3 recto - 5 verso; *Pei Shih*, chüan 95, ff. 11 verso - 14 recto; *T'ai-p'ing Yü-lan*,

that this penchant for translation sometimes obscures the cultural origins of a toponym. For example, there is nothing to show that the "Great Gulf" on Pl. 19, F4, was a Greek term rather than a Chinese, Mōn, Khmer, Indian, or Malaysian name.[87]

ROUTES TO AND FROM CHINA

The determination of routes is one of the main points on which an atlas such as this is likely to be consulted, and Herrmann has accordingly traced out the journeys of the most celebrated travellers in ancient and medieval times. The least acceptable of these routes is that ascribed to Chang Ch'ien (Pl. 10/11, II), which leaves out of account that envoy's decennary detention at the court of the Shan-yü of the Huns, at that time situated in Mongolia.[88] On the same plate the date of the campaign of Li Kuang-li to Ferghana that appears on the map contradicts that in the key. However, I think that 104–102 B.C. is more probable than either of the dates proposed by Herrmann.

On Pl. 22/23 Fa Hsien's return voyage is depicted as calling at "Yava-dvipa (in Sumatra)." It is true that Fa Hsien did spend five months in a country which he called *Ḭa-bʻuâ-dʻiei, a phonetically perfect transcription of the name of the Ptolemaic island 'Ιαβαδιου, itself a transcription of a Prākrit Yāvadiu ⟨ Sanskrit Yāvadvīpa. There is no doubt that this name is the Sanskritized form of an island of Java, but Java was a fairly widespread ethnonym in early Southeast Asia, and it has been suggested that this particular Java was situated somewhere north of the equator.[89] The argument in favor of this point of view takes note of the fact that Fa Hsien's vessel allegedly set a course northeastwards from "Java" in May, in other words at the onset of the southwest monsoon. If this information is to be taken literally, then such a course could have been set only from a position north of the equator. However, it is possible, even probable, that the course should be understood in the more general sense of a voyage in a predominantly northeasterly direction. In any case, there has been virtually no support among scholars for the location of *Ḭa-bʻuâ-dʻiei in Sumatra.

On Pl. 30/31 the itinerary of another Buddhist monk, Hsüan Tsang, should be continued farther northeastwards into Kāmarūpa in the Brahmaputra valley. The voyage of I-Ching outward bound from Canton to India (Pl. 30/31) also requires some adjustments. Although Herrmann was correct in restricting sailing in the China sea virtually to cabotage at the end of the first century A.D. (Pl. 19), direct sailing before the northeast monsoon was regular practice by the seventh century. I-Ching's account of his voyage in the closing months of 671, a voyage (as he puts it) "over the illimitable deep where the sea was intersected by mountainous waves and where enormous swells, slanting across the mighty ocean, reached cloud-like to the sky,"[90] implies an ocean crossing, and the time that it

chüan 787, ff. 1 verso - 3 recto; ff Wen-hsien T'ung-k'ao, chüan 331, ff. 2602–3.

86. James Low, "An account of several inscriptions found in Province Wellesley on the Peninsula of Malacca," *Journal of the Asiatic Society of Bengal*, vol. 17 (1848), pp. 62–66 (reprinted in E. Rost [ed.], *Miscellaneous papers relating to Indo-China*, vol. 1 (London, 1887), pp. 223–226). See also J. W. Laidlay, *Journal of the Asiatic Society of Bengal*, vol. 17 (1848), pp. 66–72; R. L. Mitra, *loc. cit.*, vol. 17, p. 71; Hendrik Kern, *Verspreide Geschriften onder zijn Toesich Verzameld*, vol. 3 (The Hague, 1915), pp. 255–262; and B. Ch. Chhabra, *Journal of the Asiatic Society of Bengal (Letters)*, vol. 1 (Calcutta, 1935), pp. 14–20.

87. It is not clear why Herrmann, who accepted as an article of faith the second century dating of the whole of the Ptolemaic corpus, should have also inserted this name on Pl. 27, F4, which relates to c. A.D. 610. Could it be that h equated the Great Gulf with the *T̬iang Xai of the Chinese and the Ṣankhay of later Arab writers?

88. Herrmann followed the majority opinion in ascribing Chang Ch'ien's embassy to the years 138–126 B.C., but it is worth noting that Gustav Haloun believed that it did not begin until 133 ["Zur Üe-Tsï-Frage," *Zeitschrift der deutschen morgenländischen Gesellschaft*, vol. 91 (1937), p. 243].

89. A. Grimes, "The journey of Fa-Hsien from Ceylon to Canton," *Journal of the Malayan Branch of the Royal Asiatic Society*, vol. 19, pt. 1 (1941), pp. 76–92.

90. *Ta-T'ang Hsi-yü Ch'iu-fa Kao-seng Chuar* f. 98 recto.

ook, less than twenty days from Canton to Śrī Vijaya, confirms this
mpression. Neither is there the slightest reason to suppose that his vessel
assed through Singapore Main Strait ("Strait of Chih") as Pl. 31, F3,
ould indicate.

When dealing with Marco Polo's itineraries (Pl. 42/43) Herrmann was
t a disadvantage compared with modern cartographers in that Moule
nd Pelliot had not then completed their scrupulously exact collation of
he variant traditions which resulted in the establishment of a definitive
ext and English translation.[91] Neither had Herrmann the benefit of
elliot's annotations, published posthumously but the outcome mainly
f his courses at the Collège de France from 1918 to 1930 and from 1936
o 1939.[92] These "annotations" are nothing less than a series of treatises,
nany of monographic proportions, which serve as vehicles for that
cholar's prodigious erudition in virtually all aspects of Chinese history
nd culture. These and other developments have had less effect on the
recise tracks of Polo's journeys than on the readings of his place-names
nd similar matters. Professor Herrmann's views on the former reflect
ssentially the consensus of modern scholars with one or two exceptions,
otably the depiction of a sea passage from Basra to Ormuz. There can
e little doubt that on both his outward and return journeys Polo avoided
uch a passage and followed the old caravan route along the eastern
oothills of the Zagros. I am also presumptuous enough to agree with
elliot—though in the teeth of Leonardo Olschki[93]—that Polo did not
imself visit the kingdom of Pagan but reported on the campaigns there
rom hearsay. Neither do I think that he called at any point on the east
oast of the Malay Peninsula on his homeward voyage, but this inter-
retation depends on the identification of *Lochac*, which in turn depends
ot only on philological arguments but also on one's view as to the
tructure of Polo's narrative at this point. If it is accepted that his notice
n *Lochac* (like those on Java and *Malaiur*) is a digression, then Pelliot
ay be correct in equating that toponym with *La-γuk* (Mand.=*Lo-hu*) <
Lavo[k?], the ancient Thai name of Lopburī. However, not even
elliot's ingenuity could explain away Polo's clearly worded direction,
500 miles by the sirocco" [i.e., southeast] from Pulau Kundur: "it is a
nistake," he says, "whatever solution one may adopt for 'Lochac'."[94]

There is, however, one way in which this difficulty might be circum-
ented. If we accept Polo's direction and distance as being reasonably
ccurate, then they would have implied a landfall in western Kalimantan,
here Francisco Rodrigues two centuries later was to place the kingdom
f *Llouçam*,[95] and where subsequent cartographers were to locate *Laue,
auwe, Lave* or *Lao*.[96] Jan Broek has demonstrated that this name was
ssociated with the Kapuas delta.[97] The *-m* in *Llouçam* is simply a
ortuguese nasalized termination, so that the original name from which
he above transcriptions derived was probably not too dissimilar from the

91. A. C. Moule and Paul Pelliot, *Marco Polo. The Description of the World*, 2 vols. (George Routledge & Sons Ltd., London, 1938).

92. Paul Pelliot, *Notes on Marco Polo* (Imprimerie Nationale, Librairie Adrien-Maisonneuve, Paris: vol. 1, 1959; vol. 2, 1963; vol. 3 [analytical index], in press).

93. *Marco Polo's Asia, an introduction to his* Description of the World *called il Milione* (University of California Press, 1960), pp. 328–335 and map at end. This work is a translation by John A. Scott of the same author's *L'Asia di Marco Polo* (G. C. Sansoni, Florence, 1957).

94. Pelliot, *Notes*, vol. 2, pp. 766–770.

95. Armando Cortesão, *The Suma Oriental of Tomé Pires ... and the Book of Francisco Rodrigues ...* vol. 2: The Hakluyt Society, second series, no. LXXXIX (London, 1944), Pl. XXVI.

96. For a discussion of the maps, charts and MSS. in which this name occurs see Jan O. M. Broek, "Place Names in 16th and 17th Century Borneo," *Imago Mundi*, vol. 16 (Amsterdam, 1962), pp. 135–137. Cp. also the territory of *Lawai* which figures among the Bornean dependencies of Mapapahit in the *Nāgara-Kertāgama* (A.D. 1365). *Vide* Theodore G. Th. Pigeaud, *Java in the fourteenth century. A study in cultural history*, vol. 1 (Martinus Nijhoff, The Hague, 1962), p. 11; vol. 3 (1960), p. 16; vol. 4 (1962), p. 31.

97. Broek, *loc. cit.*

98. Pelliot, *Notes*, vol. 2, pp. 766 and 768.
99. For *kuo* represented by -*gu* in Polo's toponymy cp. *Çipingu*=Jih-pen Kuo.
100. Pelliot, *Notes*, vol. 2, pp. 646–647.
101. Pelliot, *Notes*, vol. 1, pp. 150–153.
102. Cp. *Sājū* in the *Hudūd al-'Ālam*, *Sājū* in Gardīzī, *Sa-cu* in Tibetian sources and *Sacu* in Khotanese documents [Pelliot, *Notes*, vol. 2, p. 822]. For -*chou* rendered by -*ciou* (instead of -*giu*), cp. *Campciou* above.
103. *Carachoço* in Z.
104. Kuwabara Jitsuzo, "On P'u Shou-keng, a man of the western regions who was the Superintendent of the Trading-Ships' Office in Ch'üan-chou towards the end of the Sung dynasty," *Memoirs of the Research Department of the Tōyō Bunkō*, no. 2 (Tōkyō, 1928), pp. 30-33.

Lavo or *Lvo* with which Pelliot was concerned. In the same article he had advanced reasons for believing that in Polo's dictation the name sounded something like *Logac,[98] which, in view of the easy phonetic interchange between -*g*- and -*v*- (-*w*-), could well have represented *Lauwe*, *Lave*, etc. The final -*k* (which may also occur in the Arabic phrase "*Lawāqī* aloes-wood": *int. al.* Ya'qūbī, *Kitāb al-Buldān*, c. A.D. 891, de Goeje's edition, vol. 7, p. 795) is a difficulty, and in both interpretations must be held to imply an early *Lawāk/Lawek*. In either case it is to be assumed that Polo resumed his narrative from Pulau Kundur with an account of a voyage of 500 miles *per meridionem* (= southward) to *Pentan* = Bintan. This is not the place to argue the respective merits of these interpretations; suffice it to say that there is little reason to locate *Lochac* on the Malay Peninsula.

So much for the journeys depicted on Pl. 40. Polo's placenames are quite another matter. The publication of the Zelada codex [Z] in 1938, which could then be compared with the previously available Franco-Italian (F) and French texts and with Ramusio's Italian translation (R), has necessitated a revision of numerous Polan toponyms. Herrmann's "Cangigu" (F3), for example, a mislection which he apparently took over from Benedetto and Penzer, should read *Caugigu*, a form which Quatre-mère and d'Ohsson long ago derived correctly from *Chiao-chih Kuo*,[99] the old Chinese name for Tong-king. It is true that Polo heard of this country while he was in Yün-nan and was thereby led to append to the name a description of the district around the headwaters of the Red River, but the term should properly be located in the delta. Similarly *Aniu*, which Herrmann locates in present-day northeastern Burma, is nothing other than a corrupt version of Annam. Turning to Central Asia, "Erguiul" (Pl. 40, F3) and "Erginul" (Pl. 43, F3) both should read *Ergiuul* ⟨ *Ärǰü'ül* ⟨ *Äriǰä'ü*, a form which appears in the Mongol text of the *Secret History*, § 265, possibly for *Ärǰi'ü*. The final element -*ül*, although attested by all the Mss., has not been satisfactorily explained. *Ärǰi'ü* itself must have been a Hsi-Hsia toponym.[100] Somewhat farther westward (Pl. 40, E3) the form "Canpicou" does not occur in any manuscript. The Z reading is *Campçio*, which probably comes closest to an original orthography of *Campciou* (cp. the Catalan Map of 1375: *Cansio*) ⟨ *Kam Chou*, the pronunciation of Kan Chou in the Mongol period.[101] On the same map, "Saciu" E2/3, should read *Saciou* (=Sha-chou = Tun-huang),[102] and "Karakhocho" (E2) is an unorthodox transcription of *Qarā-qoǰo* or *Qarā-ḥōǰo*,[103] an ancient Uighur capital. In China Proper, *Kaitam* (Pl. 43, G3) is not an alternative designation of, but merely an aberrant reading for, *Caitun* ⟨ *Çaitun* = *Zaitun*, the name by which Ch'üan-chou was popularly known after *tz'ŭ-t'ung* trees were planted round the city wall in about the middle of the Five Dynasties.[104] There are other textually inferior readings of Polan toponymy on Pl. 40, but exigencies of space require that the examples above stand both as

105. *Geographia* or *Cosmographia* was the name under which later centuries knew the   or *Guide to map making* of Klaudios Ptolemaios of Alexandria.

106. Louis Renou, *Géographie de Ptolémée, l'Inde (VII, 1–4)* (Librairie de la Société de Linguistique de Paris, 1925).

107. W. Kubitschek, "Die sogenannte B-Redaktion der ptolemäischen Geographie," *Klio*, vol. 28 (Göttingen, 1935), pp. 108–32, and "Studien zur Geographie des Ptolemäus: I, Die Ländergrenzen," *Akademie der Wissenschaften in Wien, philosophisch-historische Klasse:* Sitzungsberichte, vol. 215, pt. 5 (1935); P. Schnabel, "Die Entstehungsgeschichte des kartographischen Erdbildes des Klaudios Ptolemaios," *Sitzungsberichte der Preussischen Akademie der Wissenschaften, philosophisch-historische Klasse*, vol. 14 (1930), and *Text und Karten des Ptolemäus* (Leipzig, 1938); H. von Mžik, "Neue Gesichtspunkte zur Würdigung der 'Geographie' des Klaudios Ptolemaios für die Orientalistik mit den einleitenden Abschnitten der 'Weltschau' des (Pseudo-)Moses Xorenaçi in deutscher Übersetzung," *Litterae Orientales*, no. 54 (Leipzig, 1933), pp. 1–16. For Bagrow's contributions see note 108.

108. Leo Bagrow, review of Joseph Fischer's *De Cl. Ptolemaei vita operibus Geographia praesentim eiusque fatis* in *Imago Mundi*, vol. 1 (Stockholm, 1935), pp. 76–77; "Entstehung der 'Geographie' des C. Ptolemaeus," *Comptes Rendus du Congrès International de Géographie, Amsterdam, 1938*, vol. 1 (1938), pp. 380–387; and "The origin of Ptolemy's Geographia," *Geografiska Annaler*, vol. 27, pts. 3/4 (1945), pp. 318–387. The most recent statement of this point of view is to be found in the same author's *History of Cartography* (a translation of Bagrow's *Geschichte der Kartographie*, Safari-Verlag, Berlin, 1944 by D. L. Paisey, revised and augmented by R. A. Skelton, C. A. Watts & Co. Ltd., 1964), pp. 34–37.

presentative of the rest and as invitations to the users of this atlas to supplement its information by reference to the text, translation, and annotations of Moule and Pelliot.

THE PTOLEMAIC PROBLEM

The *Geography*[105] of Claudius Ptolemy is of such central importance in any reconstruction of the ancient geography of Asia that it requires a few comments in connection with Pl. 18/19. Professor Herrmann himself had devoted much of his life to the study of Ptolemaica, and there was already a massive quantity of exegetical material to hand. For the difficult problems of place-name identification inherent in Book VII *(Cis- & Trans-Gangetic India)* he could draw on the text established by Louis Renou in 1925,[106] but Herrmann was a little unfortunate in that he was engaged in the compilation of his atlas at the very time when Kubitschek, Schnabel, von Mžik, Bagrow, and others were elucidating the relations between the Ptolemaic textual and cartographic traditions.[107] Out of these investigations came the suggestion, first adumbrated by Bagrow in 1935 but formalized only in 1945,[108] that the information transmitted by the surviving manuscripts, all from the closing centuries of the Byzantine Empire, might not be all from the hand of Ptolemy. Problems raised by textual inconsistencies and contradictions, the inclusion of material which could not have been known to Ptolemy, and discrepancies between text and maps were, according to Bagrow, to be resolved by attributing the work as we now have it to a later cartographer, a Byzantine author of the tenth or eleventh century, who incorporated some original Ptolemaic data with a great deal of later material, the whole of which he endowed with authority in the form of a spurious Ptolemaic imprimatur. Although not all scholars working in this field have applied Bagrow's interpretation to their studies of early Asian history, no sustained refutation of this drastic revision of the nature of the Ptolemaic tradition has so far appeared. If it is sustained successfully, then it will mean that the *Geography* provides a composite rather than a synoptic framework for the early geography of Asia. By widening the scope of the inquiry this goes some way towards simplifying some of the problems of toponymic identification, but in other ways it evokes a multiplicity of new difficulties. Because of a relative scarcity of other sources relating to Western, South, and Central Asia in the second century A.D., a vast superstructure of toponymy has of necessity been erected on the hitherto apparently secure foundation of a synoptic Ptolemaic map. If Bagrow is right, this will have to be revised on the basis of the independent dating of individual names.

Pivotal in any interpretation of the Ptolemaic geography of East Asia is the position to be ascribed to the Golden Khersonese. On this decision depends the identification of the *Sinae*, the Great Gulf, *Kattigara*, the

109. This point of view is implicit in Pelliot's discussion of *Caugigu*, *Notes*, *sub verbo*. It is also the present author's conclusion in *The Golden Khersonese*, chap. X.

110. George Coedès, review of Wheatley, *The Golden Khersonese* in *T'oung Pao*, vol. 49, pts. 4/5 (1962), pp. 433–439.

111. Unlike the bulk of the information relating to the *Sinai* which is in Book VII, these remarks occur in Book I, chap. 11, § 4 of the *Geography*.

112. Pelliot, *Notes*, vol. 1, *sub Caugigu*.

113. *Das Land der Seide und Tibet im Lichte der Antike*. Quellen und Forschungen der Geographie und Völkerkunde, vol. 1 (K. F. Koehler Verlag, Leipzig, 1939), p. 80; "Der Magnus Sinus und Cattigara nach Ptolemaeus," *Comptes Rendus du Congrès International de Géographie, Amsterdam, 1938*, vol. 2 (1938), p. 123. Cf. the review of *Das Land der Seide* by R. A. Stein in *Bulletin de l'Ecole française d'Extrême-Orient*, vol. 40 (1940), p. 459.

Theriodic Gulf, the Islands of the Satyrs, and so on. It has long been realized that the Ptolemaic coordinates are unreliable guides to the identification of place-names, particularly toward the eastern limits of the known world, that they represent not a framework for the construction of the map but rather partake of the nature of an index to it. Leaving aside the conclusions of several early workers in this field who, in the process of devising correction factors with which to convert Ptolemaic to true coordinates, were led to the conclusion that the Golden Khersonese was in Lower Burma, there are seemingly only two acceptable alternatives. In the first of these the Golden Khersonese is identified with the Malay Peninsula. Supporters of this interpretation point to what they regard as an essential correspondence in the essential land patterns of the Ptolemaic and modern maps, the probable testimony of Chinese, Indian, and Arab sources that some of the place-names of the Golden Khersonese were located on the Malay Peninsula, the fact that the designation "golden" agrees well with what is known of the early history of the peninsula, and the custom of European cartographers of the fifteenth and sixteenth centuries of adopting this identification, perhaps—it is suggested—in the light of evidence since lost. This was the interpretation espoused by Professor Herrmann and, apparently, favored by Pelliot in his *Notes on Marco Polo*.[109]

Recently, however, Professor George Coedès has proposed an alternative solution, in which he has suggested that the Golden Khersonese may have constituted only the southern tracts of the Malay Peninsula, approximately present-day Malaya in other words.[110] In support of this argument he equates the unexplored reed-covered swamps which Ptolemy located to the eastward of the *Sinai* with the marshes of the Mekong delta, particularly the Plaine des Joncs,[111] and likens the relative positions of the capital of the *Sinai* and the port of *Kattigara* to those of the capital of *B'iu-nâm and the port excavated by Louis Malleret at Oc-èo. Neither of these two interpretations is at present capable of proof, and their implications cannot be debated here. Let these few remarks serve notice that the data on Pl. 18/19 should be consulted with the present state of Ptolemaic scholarship in mind.

The port of *Kattigara* must needs play an important role in either of the reconstructions discussed above. On Pl. 19, F3, Professor Herrmann placed it in Tongking, an identification with which Pelliot, who saw the name as an Hellenized version of *Kau-tśi (Mand.=Chiao-chih; Sino-Việt.=Giao-chỉ), was in agreement.[112] Subsequently, however, Herrmann changed his mind and located the port in the neighborhood of present-day Saigon.[113] We do not have to accept his concomitant derivation of the name from the Indian *Kottiara* (present-day Cochin), of which he believed *Kattigara* to be a colony, in order to agree that a case can be made for such an identification. It is, in fact, in close accord with the reconstruction subsequently proposed by Professor Coedès. A decade or

114. R. A. Stein, "Le Lin-yi, sa localisation, sa contribution à la formation du Champa et ses liens avec la Chine," *Han-Hiue*, vol. 2, pts. 1–3 (Pekin, 1948), pp. 122 *et seq.* Stein refers to Levy's study on p. 1 but, as far as I have been able to ascertain, it was never published.

115. *Chin Shu ti-tao chi, apud Shui-Ching Chu*, chüan 36, f. 23 recto. But cf. J. J. L. Duyvendak's review of "Le Lin-yi" in *T'oung Pao*, vol. 40 (1951), pp. 336–351.

116. For the irregular declension of accusative θῖνα, genitive θινός, which occurs in the *Periplus Maris Erythraei*, § 64 (as opposed to θῖναι in Ptolemy, VII, 3, 6 and Martianus of Heraclia, I, 16), see H. Frisk, "Le périple de la Mer Erythrée," *Högskolas Årsskrift*, vol. 33 (1927), p. 126, and Pelliot, *Notes*, vol. 1, pp. 266–267. Pelliot, however, categorically rejects Frisk's hypothesis of a nominative * θίς. "Either," he says, "the name was θῖνα in the nominative (with a final - α, which was not necessarily etymological) and the declension is irregular and due to analogy [of θίς = sand-heap, acc. θῖνα , gen. θινός]; or the nominative was * θῖν, with a regular declension due perhaps to the attraction of that of θίς." The formal distinction between *Seres* and *Sinae* is peculiar to the Ptolemaic corpus and its adherents.

117. *Han Wu-ti nei-chuan* (probably 4th century A.D.). Ts'ung-shu Chi-ch'eng edition, Shanghai, 1937, p. 10.

after Herrmann had advanced this thesis, Paul Lévy and Rolf Stein had also come to the same conclusion by wholly independent arguments.[114] Stein further equated *Kattigara* with *K'iwət-tuo-kuən/kân, a settlement founded by migrants from the Chinese subprefecture of *Tśįu-nguo (Mand.=Chu-wu; Sino-Viêt.=Châu-ngô) in the commandery of *Ńźįĕt-âm.[115] This, in his opinion, was the reason why the Ptolemaic text referred to *Kattigara* as ὅρμος Σιγων, "the roadstead (or anchorage) of the Sinai." In any case, acceptance of the general thesis, whether in the form proposed by Herrmann, Lévy, Stein, or Coedès, does require that the identification of the *Sinai* (or *Thinai*)[116] with the Chinese *sensu stricto* be abandoned, and that the name *Thinae* on Pl. 19, F3, be deleted, along with *Saraga* discussed above, from the neighborhood of Lo-yang. Even if the older interpretation be retained, it is still more than doubtful that *Thinai* should be located at Lo-yang.

ENVOI

This then, is the *Atlas of China* after thirty years. It is still, as far as the Western world is concerned, the only atlas to present a conspectus of Chinese toponymy in the amplitude of its historical development; it is still the only atlas of China which attempts historical reconstruction in any degree of detail; it is still the only atlas to set China in its historical Asian context; and, rarest of all, it is the only atlas to record Chinese renderings of foreign toponyms through the ages side by side with the indigenous names that they transcribed and translated.

It cannot be claimed that Albert Herrmann was uniformly successful in carrying out this enterprise, but he probably achieved all that lay within the power of one man. The atlas reflects the preoccupations of an age no less than the predilections of the author and, occasionally, the fallibility of human judgment as well. Yet, although Herrmann's reach exceeded his grasp, he did manage to forge a tool which even today, chipped though it is after three decades of constant use, gives no indication that it is likely to be superseded in the near future. The long and arduous task of depicting the face of China that allegedly began when Yü the Great cast cauldrons bearing symbolic representations of the Nine Provinces is by no means complete, but the definitive historical atlas of China which lies somewhere in the future will certainly be the work, not of one man, but of a team of sinologues coming together in collaboration to produce a likeness worthy of a great civilization. Albert Herrmann, by contrast, belongs in the company of scholars such as P'ei Hsiu (A.D. 224–271), Chia Tan (730–805), the incomparable Chu Ssŭ-pen (1273–1337), Li Tse-min (fl. c. 1330), and Ch'ing Chün (1328–1392), who labored alone and with inadequate resources to furbish up the cauldrons as best they could. Like Emperor Wu of Han, who also made great sacrifices in order to acquire a map, Herrmann "manifested the spirit of the true scholar and never lost sight of the Tao."[117]

Selected bibliography

LIST OF ABBREVIATED TITLES

AM = Asia Major, Leipzig.
BEFEO = Bulletin de l'École française d'Extrême-Orient, Hanoi.
GR = Geographical Review, New York.
JA = Journal asiatique, Paris.
JRAS = Journal of the Royal Asiatic Society of Great Britain and Ireland, London.
MSOS = Mitteilungen des Seminars für Orientalische Sprachen, I. Abt., Berlin.
OZ = Ostasiatische Zeitschrift, Berlin.
PELO = Publication de l'École des Langues orientales vivantes, Paris.
PM = Petermanns Geographische Mitteilungen, Gotha.
TP = T'oung pao, Archives concernant l'histoire, les langues, la géographie, l'ethnographie et les arts de l'Asie orientale, Leide.
VS = Variétés sinologiques, Shang-hai.
YJ = Yenching Journal of Chinese Studies, Pei-ching.
ZGE = Zeitschrift der Gesellschaft für Erdkunde, Berlin.

I. GENERAL BIBLIOGRAPHY

Books and Collections: CH'ÊNG-CHÜN, FÊNG, Hsi-yü-ti-ming (Dictionary of geographical Names of Western Regions), 1930 — S. COUVREUR, Géographie ancienne et moderne de la Chine, 1917. — G. B. CRESSEY, China's Geographic Foundations, 1934; Land of the 500 Million, New York: McGraw-Hill, 1955. — Great Britain, Admiralty, Naval Intelligence Division. China Proper. London, 1944, 3 volumes. — O. FRANKE, Geschichte des chinesischen Reiches, I, 1930. — R. GROUS-SET, Histoire de l'Extrême-Orient, I, II, 1929. — A. HERRMANN, Die Westländer in der chinesischen Kartographie; in S. HEDIN, Southern Tibet, VIII, 1922, pp. 89–406. — HSING-LANG, CHANG, Chung-hsi-chiao-t'ung-shih-liao-hui-p'ien (Materials to the History of the Chinese Relations to West), 6 Vols; Collections of Catholic Univ. at Peking, 1, 1926–30. — A. KOLB, Ostasien, Heidelberg: Quelle and Meyer, 1963. — LI, CHI, The formation of the Chinese people, 1929. — Nien-ssŭ-shih (24 Imperial Annals, B.C. 220-A.D. 1644, with important geographical chapters). — H. SCHMITTHENNER, China im Profil, 1934. — SHOU-CH'ANG, HSIEH, Chung-kuo ku-chin ti-ming ta-tzŭ-tien (Great Dictionary of ancient and present Place Names of China), 1931. — J. SION, Asie des Moussons; Géographie Universelle, IX, 1928, pp. 66–188. — T. R. TREGEAR, A Geography of China, Chicago: Aldine Publishing Co., 1966. — U.S. Board on Geographical Names, Mainland China: Administrative Divisions and Their Seats, Gazetteer No. 70, Washington: 1963. — WIEGER, Textes historiques, 2 Vols, 2nd Edit., 1922–23. — H. G. W. WOODHEAD, and others, The China Yearbook, 1930–33.

Maps: L. M. ABRAMOVIČA, Karta Manczurii, ca. 1924. — ANDREES ALLGEMEINER HANDATLAS, 8th Edit., 1930, sheets 146/7, 164/7. — JOHN BARTHOLOMEW, ed. The Times Atlas of the World, Mid-Century Edition, London: 1958–59, 5. Vols., Plates 16, 20, 21, 22, 23, 25. — C. Y. CHANG, Atlas of the Republic of China, T'ai-pei: National War-College, 1960–63, Five Vols. — CHUNG-HUA-YU-CHÊNG YÜ-T'U (China Postal Atlas), Edit. 1933. — CHUNG-KUOLI-TAI CHIANG-YÜ CHANG-CHÊNG HO-T'U (Historical Atlas of China, adjacent Countries and the Wars), 1931. — E. J. DINGLE, The New Atlas and Commercial Gazetteer of China, 1918. — Ergebnisse der Expedition Dr. Handel-Mazzetti's nach China 1914 bis 1918; Denkschr. Akad. Wiss. Wien, math.-natur-wiss. Kl., 97, 100, 101. — A. HOSIE, Philips' Commercial Map of China, Edit. 1928; cf. LADY HOSIE, A Map of China in the Making, JNChina Br. RAS, 1926, p. 19. — G. KÖHLER, Hwang-ho-Einzugsgebiet; orograph.-hydrograph. Karte; PM, Ergänz.-H. 203, 1929. — F. v. RICHT-

HOFEN, Atlas von China, I, II (by M. Groll). — E. STANFORD, Comple Atlas of China, 2nd Edit., 1917. — STIELERS HANDATLAS, 10th Edi sheets 69, 74–76. — P. C. STREIT, Atlas Hierarchicus, 2nd Edit., 192 p. 47, sheets 22, 23. — TA-CHUNG-HUA MIN-KUO FÊN-SHÊNG T'U (Atl of the Provinces of Great Chinese Republic), 1932. — V. K. TIN W. H. WANG, and S. Y. TSEN, New Atlas of China (Chung-hua-min-k Hsin-ti-t'u), Shang-hai: Shen-pao, 1934. — Touring Club Italian Atlante Internazionale, Milan, 1956, pp. 97–100. — WATARU YAN Tôyô tokushi chizu (Tung-yang tu-shih-ti-t'u = Historical Atlas the Relations to the foreign Countries), 1926. — G. WEGENER, Dur die Provinz Kiangsi. Mit aufnahmen am Fukiang und Kankian ZGE 1926, pp. 124 sqq., 155 sqq.

II. SPECIAL BIBLIOGRAPHY

To page 1: J. G. ANDERSSON, Prähistorische Kulturbeziehungen zwische Nordchina und dem näheren Orient; OZ 1929, pp. 49 sqq. — D. BUXTO The Light thrown on ancient Chinese History by recent archaeologic Discoveries; JN China Branch RAS 1930, pp. 2 sqq. —W. EBERHAR Bericht über die Ausgrabungen bei An-yang Honan); OZ 1932, pp. sqq.; 1933, pp. 208 sqq. — D. C. GRAHAM, The ancient Caves Szechwan Province; Proc. U.S. National Museum 80, Art. 16, 1932. Guide to the Exhibitions of the Museum of Far Eastern Antiquitie Stockholm 1933. — Y. HARADA, Mu-yang-ch'êng. Han and pre-Ha sites at the foot of M. Lao-t'ieh in S. Manchuria, 1932. S. HEDI Rätsel der Gobi, 1931, pp. 264 sqq. (according to F. Bergman). R. HEINE-GELDERN, Urheimat und früheste Wanderung der Austron sier; Anthropos 1932, pp. 543 sqq. — HEINE-GELDERN, Bedeutung u Herkunft der Metalltrommeln; AM, 1932, pp. 519 sqq. — LI, CH Manchuria in History; Chinese Social and Political Science Review 1932, pp. 226 sqq. — P'ITZU WO, Prehistoric Sites by the River Pi-liu-h South Manchuria, 1929. —. H. SCHMIDT, Prähistorisches aus Ostasie Zeitschr. f. Ethnologie, 1924, pp. 133 sqq. — TE-K'UN, CHÊNG, Son Sketches of a Trip of archaeological Investigation in the Provinces Hopei, Honan and Shantung; YJ, Suppl. No. 1, pp. 79 sqq. — R. TOR Études archéologiques et ethnologiques. Populations primitives de Mongolie Orientale; J College of Science, Univ. of Tôkyô 36, 1914. YJ, Nr. 7.9, 1931, 1932; cf. TP 1932, pp. 268 sq.

To pages 2–4: E. CHAVANNES, Les Mémoires historiques de Se-m Ts'ien, I, 1895. — G. HALOUN, Contributions to the History of Cla Settlement in Ancient China; AM I, 1924, pp. 76 sqq., 587 sqq. HALOUN, Die Rekonstruktion der chinesischen Urgeschichte; Japan deutsche Zeitschr. f. Wiss., 1925, pp. 243 sqq.—A. HERRMANN, D ältesten chinesischen Weltkarten; OZ, 1924, pp. 97 sqq. — J. LEGG The Chinese Classics, III, 1, 1865, Proleg. 117 sqq., (Bamboo Annals pp. 92 sqq. (Yü-kung); cf. CHAVANNES, op. cit., V, pp. 446 sqq HERRMANN, Westländer etc., pp. 107 sqq., 152 sqq.—LI, CHI, Archaeol gical Survey of the Fên River Valley S. Shansi. Smithonian Miscella Collect. 78, 7, pp. 123 sqq. — MU, CH'IEN, The geography of China the beginning of the Chou Dynasty; YJ 10, 1931, pp. 1955 sqq., Supp 1, p. 73. — A. TSCHEPE, Die drei Kiang des Chou-King; MSOS, VII 1905, pp. 139 sqq. — TSCHEPE, Sur les Tartares et autres peuplades etc VS 31, 1910, pp. 157 sqq. — A. WEDEMEYER, and G. HALOUN, Kar zur Geschichte der Kaiser Yao, Shun und Yü; AM, Hirth Anniv. Vo 1922. — P. YETTS, The Shang-Yin Dynasty and the An-yang Find JRAS, 1933, pp. 657 sqq.

To pages 5–8: Chou-li, ch. 33; cf. E. BIOT, Le Tcheou-li, II, 1851, p 263 sqq. — G. HALOUN, Der Lehensstraat de Tschou-Dynastie unte König Süan (827–782 v. Chr.); Der Grosse Brockhaus IV, p. 32. HALOUN, Orientierungskarte zur Geschichte des vorchristlichen China E. A. VORETZSCH, Altchinesische Bronzen, 1924. — HALOUN, D Altchinesischen Groszstaaten um 350 v. Chr.; Der Grosse Brockhau IV, p. 33. — A. HERRMANN, Westländer, etc., pp. 131 sqq., 167 sqq. H. MASPERO, La Chine antique; Cavaignac, Histoire du Monde, 192 — G. SAINSON, Nan Tchao Ye-che; PELO, 1904; cf. P. PELLIO BEFEO, 1904, pp. 1094 sqq.

To pages 9–13: L. AUROUSSEAU, La première conquête chinoise des pay annamites; BEFEO, 1924, pp. 243 sqq.; cf. H. MASPERO, TP 1924, p 372 sqq. — Ch'ang-an-t'u-chih, edit. by Pi Yüan, 1784. — E. CHAVA NES, Se-ma Ts'ien (see above). — A. FORKE, Ch'ang-an im Altertume MSOS 1898, pp. 104 sqq.; Lo-yang im Altertume; ibid. pp. 120 sqq. J. J. M. DE GROOT, Die Hunnen der vorchristlichen Zeit, 1921. A. HERRMANN, Die Gobi im Zeitalter der Hunnenherrschaft; Hyllning skrift tillägned Sven Hedin; Bihang till Geografiska Annaler, 1935. F. HIRTH, Über Wolga-Hunnen und Hiung-nu; Sitzber. Akad. Wis

inchen, 1900. — Hirth, The Story of Chang K'ién; JAmer, Oriental
c., 1917. — Mei-ts'un, Wang, Shui-ching-chu-t'u, 1840, p. 76a. —
F. v. Möllendorff, Die Grosze Mauer von China; Zeitschr. D.
orgenländ. Gesellsch., 1881, pp. 75 sqq. — F. W. K. Müller, Toχrï
d Kuisan (Küsän); Sitzb. Akad. Wiss. Berlin, 1918. — O. Sirén,
urney to Sianfu; Revue des Arts asiatiques, IV, 1927, pp. 40 sqq. —
de Takács, L'art des grandes migrations en Hongrie et en Extrême-
ient; Revue des Arts asiatiques, VII, 1932, pp. 24, 57. — Tê-k'un,
êng, see above to p. 1.

pages 14–19: E. Chavannes, Se-ma Ts'ien etc., II, pp. 534 sqq. —
avannes, Les pays d'Occident d'après le Heou Han chou; TP, 107,
. 149 sqq. — Chavannes, Les pays d'Occident d'après le Wei lu; TP,
05, pp. 521 sqq. — J. J. M. de Groot, Die Westlande Chinas in der
rchristlichen Zeit, 1926. — Y. Harada, Lo-lang, 1930. — S. Hedin,
d A. Herrmann, The Ts'ung-ling Mountains; S. Tibet, VIII, 1922. —
errmann, Die alten Seidenstraszen zwischen China und Syrien, I,
11. — Herrmann, Die alten Verkehrswege zwischen Indien und Süd-
ina etc.; ZGE, 1913, pp. 771 sqq. — Herrmann, Die Seidenstrasse
n China nach dem Römischen Reich; Mitt. Geogr. Ges. Wien, 1915,
. 472 sqq. — Herrmann, Westländer etc., pp. 195 sqq. — Hermann,
er die Lage des Landes Ta Tsin; OZ, 1924, pp. 196 sqq. — Herr-
nn, Lou-lan, 1931. — Herrmann, Articles on Kattigara, Sakai,
res, Sinai, Tamaros, Taprobane, Thaguroi, Thina, Thogara, Throana
.; Paulys Realenzycl. d. klass. Altertums, 2nd Edit. — F. Hirth,
ina and the Roman Orient, 1885. — Ch. Joppen, Historical Atlas of
dia, 3rd Edit., 1923. — H. Maspero, Le Royaume de Champa, 1927.
Nundolal Dey, The early Course of the Ganges; Indian Antiquary,
21, pp. 8 sqq. — P. Pelliot, Le Fou-nan; BEFEO, 1903, pp. 248 sqq.
Pelliot, Note sur un ancien itinéraire chinois dans l'orient romain,
, 1921, I, pp. 139 sqq. — A. Stein, Ancient Khotan, 1907. — Stein,
rindia, 1921. — Stein, Maps of Chinese Turkistan, etc., 1923. —
ein, Innermost Asia, 1928. — A. Tschepe, Der Nan-kiang; MSOS,
06, pp. 134 sqq. — P. Vidal de la Blache, Les voies de commerce
ns la Géogr. de Ptolémée; Note sur l'origine du commerce de la soie
r mer; C. R. Acad. Inscr., 1896, 1897. — E. H. Warmington, The
mmerce between the Roman Empire and India, 1928. — R. B.
hitehead, The River Courses of the Panjab and Sind; Indian Anti-
ary, 1932, pp. 163 sqq.

pages 20–25: E. Chavannes, Voyages de Song Yun etc.; BEFEO,
03, pp. 379 sqq. — Chavannes, Documents sur les Tou-kiue occiden-
ux, 1903. — Chavannes, Gunavarman; TP, 1904, pp. 193 sqq.
Des Michel, Chih Louh Kouoh Kiang Yuh Tchi, Histoire géogra-
ique des Seize Royaumes; PELO, 1891. —. W. Fuchs, Das Turfan-
biet; OZ, 1926, pp. 124 sqq. — S. Hedin, A. Herrmann, see to pp.
—19. — Herrmann, Die Hepththaliten und ihre Beziehungen zu China;
M, 1925, pp. 564 sqq. —. J. Legge, A Record of Buddhistic Kingdoms,
86. — J. Markwart, Über das Volkstum der Komanen; Abh. Ges.
iss. Göttingen, 1914, pp. 25 sqq. — P. Pelliot, À propos des Comans;
, 1920, I, pp. 129 sqq. — F. W. Thomas, Some notes on the Kharosthî
ocuments from Chinese Turkistan; Acta Orient, 1934. pp. 37 sqq. —
Wedemeyer, Japanische Frühgeschichte, 1930, pp. 88 sqq., with
ap III of Korea.

pages 26–32: St. Balász, Beiträge zur Wirtschaftsgesch. der T'ang-
it; MSOS, 1931, pp. 1 sqq., 1932, pp. 93 sqq., 1933, pp. 1 sqq. —
W. Bushell, The Early History of Tibet; JRAS, 1880, pp. 538 sqq. —
Chavannes, Documents etc. (see above). — Chavannes, Mémoires
r les réligieux éminents etc., 1894. — G. L. M. Clauson, The Geo-
aphical Names in the Staël-Holstein Scroll; JRAS, 1931, pp. 297 sqq.
R. des Rotours, Les grands fonctionnaires des provinces en Chine
us les dynasties des T'ang; TP, 1928, pp. 219 sqq. — G. Ferrand,
oyage du marchand arabe Sulaymân etc.; TP, 1922, pp. 399 sqq. —
Ferrand et N. J. Krom, L'Empire Sumatranais de Crivijaya, 1922.
Ferrand, Wakwâk; Enzykl. d. Islam, IV, p. 1199. — A. H. Francke,
ntiquities of Indian Tibet, II, 1926, pp. 82 sqq. — A. v. Gabain, Ein
itrag zur Fu-lin-Frage; Sinica, 1933, pp. 195 sq. — Gander, Le
anal Impérial, 1894. — H. A. R. Gibb, The Arab Conquests in Central
sia, 1923. — S. Hedin and A. Herrmann, see to pp. 14–19. — Herr-
ann, Westländer etc., pp. 232 sqq., 424 sqq. — Herrmann, Alte
eographie des unteren Oxusgebiets; Abh. Ges. Wiss. Göttingen, 1914,
. 54 sqq. (Zemarchos). — H. B. Hulbert, The History of Corea, I,
05, pp. 85 sqq. — Ff. Jäger, Leben und Werk des P'ei Kü; OZ,
21/22, pp. 81 sqq., 216 sqq. — P. Kahle, Islamische Quellen zum
inesischen Porzellan; Zeitschrift D. Morgenländ. Ges., 1934, pp.
sqq. — Kosmas Indikopleustes, edited by Winstedt, 1909. — J.

Kuwabara, On P'u Shou-Kêng; Mém. Res. Dep. Tôkyô Bunko, II,
1928. — G. Le Strange, The Lands of the Eastern Caliphate, 1905. —
S. Lévi and E. Chavannes, L'itinéraire d'Ou-kong; JA, 1895, II, pp.
341 sqq. —. H Lüders, Zur Geschichte und Geographie Osturkestans;
Weitere Beiträge etc.; Sitzber. Akad. Wiss. Berlin, 1922, 1930. —
J. Markwart, Osteuropäische und ostasiatische Streifzüge, 1903. —
H. Maspero, Champa (see above). — Maspero, Le protectorat d'Annam
sous les T'ang; BEFEO, 1910, pp. 550 sqq. — Z. N. Matveef, The
State Bohai; Public. de l'Univ. d'Etat de l'Extrême-Orient, 6/7, 1929. —
J. Moravisik, Zur Geschichte der Onoguren; Ungar, Jbb., 1930, pp.
52 sqq. — P. Pelliot, Comans etc. (see above). — Pelliot, Le "Cha
techeou tou tou fou t'ou king" et la colonie sogdienne de la région du
Lob Nor; JA, 1916, I, pp. 111 sqq. — Pelliot, Note sur les T'ou-yü-hun
etc.; TP, 1920, pp. 323 sqq. — Pelliot, Tokharien et koutchéen; JA,
1934, I, pp. 23 sqq. — H. H. Schaeder, Iranica; Abh. Ges. Wiss.
Göttingen, 1934, pp. 24 sqq. (Fu-lin). — A. Stein, see to pp. 14–19. —
V. A. Smith, in Watters, On Yuan Chwang's travels in India, II, 1905,
pp. 329 sqq. — V. Thomsen, Alttürkische Inschriften aus der Mongolei;
Zeitschr. D. Morgenländ. Ges., 1924, pp. 121 sqq. —. C. E. Wilson,
The Wall of Alexander against Gog and Magog and the expedition sent
out to find it by Khalif Wâthiq in 842 A.D.; AM, Hirth Anniv. Vol.,
1922, pp. 575 sqq.

To pages 33–36: C. Brockelmann, Mitteltürk. Wortschatz, pp. 240
sqq. (Geography of Mahmûd al-Kâshgharî). — E. Chavannes, Le
royaume de Wou et de Yue; TP, 1916, pp. 129 sqq. —. Chavannes,
Voyageurs chinois chez les Khitan et les Joutchen; JA, 1897, I, pp. 377
sqq. — Hsi-Hsia-chi-shih-pên-mo, Edit. 1884 (with Map of Kingdom of
Hsi-Hsia). — Liao-shih (Annals of Liao Dyn.), 1343/45, ch. 36–41. —
J. Mullie, Les anciennes villes de l'empire des Grands Leao etc.; TP,
1922, pp. 105 sqq. —. G. Sainson, see above to 5–8. — Sung-shih
(Annals of Sung Dyn.), 1343/45, ch. 85–90. — A. Tschepe, Die Ebene
von Schanghai. MSOS, 1906, pp. 131 sqq. — Tschepe, Woher kommt
der Name des Stromes Jangtsekiang? MSOS, 1906, pp. 127 sqq.

To page 37: W. Barthold – R. Stübe, Zur Geschichte des Christen-
tums in Mittelasien bis zur mongolischen Eroberung. — E. Boerschmann, Chinesische Pagoden, I, 1931, — Ch. E. Bonin, Note sur les
anciennes chrétientés nestoriennes de L'Asie Centrale, JA, 1900, I, pp.
584 sqq. — E. Chavannes, Documents etc. (Manichaeism, Mazdeism).
— Chavannes, Mission archéologique dans la Chine septentrionale, II,
1915. — H. Cordier, Le Christianisme en Chine et en Asie Centrale
sous les Mongols; TP, 1917, pp. 49 sqq. — Encyclopaedia Judaica,
China, V, pp. 475 sqq. — H. A. Francke, see above. — O. Franke,
Zur Frage der Einführung des Buddhismus in China; MSOS, 1910. —
A. Foucher, L'Art Gréco-Bouddhique de Gandhara, I. II, 1905/22. —
A. Grünwedel, Alt-Buddhistische Kultstätten in Chinesisch-Turkistan,
1912. — S. Hedin, Scientific Results of a Journey in Central Asia, II,
1905. — A. Herrmann, Lou-lan, 1931. — A. v. Le Coq, Die Buddhisti-
sche Spätantike Mittelasiens, VII Vols., 1932/33. — A. C. Moule, The
Nestorians in China; JRAS, 1933, pp. 116 sqq. — P. Pelliot, Trois ans
en Asie Centrale; Bull. Comité de l'Asie Française, 1910. — Pelliot,
Chrétiens d'Asie Centrale, etc.; TP, 1914, pp. 623 sqq. — Pelliot, Les
traditions manichéennes au Fou-kien, TP, 1923, pp. 193 sqq. — Pelliot,
Sceaux-amulettes de bronze avec croix etc:; Revue des Arts asiat., 1931,
pp. 1 sqq. — Pelliot, Les Nestoriens en Chine après 845; JRAS, 1933,
pp. 115 sqq. — A. Stein, see above to pp. 14–19. — Tadashi Sekino,
Cave temple of Mount T'ien-lung; Kokka, 375, 1921. — Tê-k'un,
Chêng, see above to p. 1. — E. Waldschmdit, Gandhara, Kutscha,
Turfan, 1925.

To pages 38–39: W. Barthold, Turkestan down to the Mongol Inva-
sions, 2nd Edit., 1928. — Barthold, Karâ khitâi, and other articles in
Encycl. d. Islam. — E. Bretschneider, Mediaeval Researches from
Eastern Asiatic Sources, I., 1888. — A. H. Francke, Indian Tibet, II,
pp. 92 sqq. — De Harlez, Constitution de l'Empire Kin; JA, 1886, I,
pp. 469 sqq. — F. Hirth, and W. W. Rockhill, Chau Ju-kua, 1911. —
Ho-nan-shêng-ch'êng-ti-yü-t'u (Map of K'ai-fêng), 1097. — Kuo-Wei,
Wang, The Boundary Trenches under the Chin Dynasty; YJ, 1, 1931,
pp. 1 sqq., Suppl. 1, pp. 1 sq. — A. C. Moule, and L. Giles, Christians
at Chên-chiang-fu, TP, 1915, pp. 627 sqq. (with Map of Lin-an). —
A. Stein, Note on a map of the Turfan Basin; Geogr. J., 1933, II, pp. 236
sqq. — V. I. Tolmatcheff, Historic Manchurian Relics; Manch. Res.
Soc., 1925.

To pages 40–43: L. F. Benedetto, Marco Polo, il Milione, 1928. —
E. Bretschneider, Mediaeval Researches, I. II, 1888. — A. Herrmann,

Westländer etc., pp. 277 sqq., 455. — A. C. MOULE, Hang-chou to Shang-tu; TP, 1915, pp. 394 sqq. — L. IMPEY, Shangtu; GR, 1925, pp. 592 sq. — W. LENTZ, War Marco Polo auf dem Pamir? Zeitschr. D. Morgenl. Ges., 1932, pp. 1 sqq. — W. RADLOFF, Atlas des Altertümer der Mongolei, 1892, Pl. XXXVI. — P. PELLIOT, A propos des Comans, JA, I, 1920, pp. 129 sqq. — F. RISCH, Johann de Plano Carpini, 1930. — RISCH, Wilhelm von Rubruk, 1934. — SSANANG SETSEN, Gesch. der Ostmongolen, edit. by I. J. Schmidt, 1829. — A. STEIN, Marco Polo's Account of a Mongol Inroad into Kashmir; Geogr. J., 1919, II, pp. 92 sqq. — A. WALEY, Ch'ang-ch'un, 1931. — N. YAMADA, Ghenko, the Mongol invasion of Japan, 1916. — H. YULE, Cathai and the way thither, 2nd Edit. by H. Cordier, 4 Vols., 1913-16.

To pages 44-47: W. BARTHOLD, Articles on Caghatâi-khân, Bishbalik, Dûghlât, Shârukh Mîrzâ; Encycl. d. Islam. — M. BITTNER, and W. TOMASCHEK, Die topogr. Kapitel des indischen Seespiegels Mohît, 1897. — G. BOUILLARD, Note succincte sur l'historique du territoire de Peking etc.; Bull. Mus. Far Eastern Antiquities, 1, 1929. — E. BRETSCHNEIDER, see above.—BRETSCHNEIDER, Recherches archéolog. et histor. sur Pékin etc.; PELO, 1879. — CHIANG-NING FU-CHIH, edit. by Li Yen-chao, 1811. — J. J. L. DUYVENDAK, Ma Huan re-examined; Verh. Akad. Wet. Amsterdam, 1933; cf. P. PELLIOT, TP, 1933, pp. 237 sqq. — W. FILCHNER, Kumbum Dschamba Ling, 1933. — P. E. HAUER, Huang-Ts'ing-k'ai-kuo-fang-lüeh, Die Gründung des Mandschurischen Kaiserreiches, 1926. — O. F. v. MÖLLENDORFF, see to pp. 9-13. — H. B. MORSE, Lampaçao; JNChinaBr. RAS, 1933, p. 137. — NANKING, Ordnance Survey Office, 1927, 1:25 000. — W. W. ROCKHILL, Notes on the Relations and Trade of China with the Eastern Archipelago; TP, 1914/15. — H. YULE, see above.

To pages 48-52: M. COURANT, L'Asie Centrale aux XVIIe et XVIIIe siècles, 1912. — W. FILCHNER, and G. SCHOLTZ, Karte der chinesischen Provinz Kan-su; Wissenschaftl. Ergebnisse der Expedition Filchner, etc., III, 1910. — O. FRANKE, Beschreibung des Jehol-Gebietes, 1902, p. 103. — E. HAENISCH, Bruchstücke aus der Geschichte Chinas etc.; TP, 1911, pp. 197 sqq. 375 sqq. — HAENISCH, Eine chinesische Beschreibung von Tibet, and Das Goldstromland im chinesisch-tibetischen Grenzgebiete. — S. HEDIN, Southern Tibet, IX, 4, 1922. — HEDIN, Southern Tibet, I. II., 1917 — HEDIN, Jehol, 1932. — A. HERRMANN, Westländer etc., pp. 287-406. — ST. JULIEN, Sur les pays et peuples étrangers; JA, 1846, II, pp. 236 sqq. — A. TAFEL, Meine Tibetreise, I.II, 1914.

To page 53: G. BOUILLARD, Carte des environs de Pékin, 1923, 1:25 000. — H. DUGOUT, Carte de la province du Kiang-Sou, 1:200 000. — Guide to China, issued by the Japanese Gov. Railways, 2nd Edit., 1924. — F. ROUX, Carte du Setch'ouan occidental; VS, 1915. — E. OBERHUMMER, Schanghai; Mitt. Geogr. Ges. Wien, 1932, pp. 5 sqq. — Shanghai, Plan of, 1928, 1:16 000.

To page 55: K. BUCHANAN, The Changing Landscape of Rural China, Pacific Viewpoint, March, 1960, pp. 11-38. — J. L. BUCK, Land Utilization in China, Chicago: University of Chicago Press, 1937, (3 Vols.) — CENTRAL INTELLIGENCE AGENCY, The Program for Water Conservancy in Communist China, 1949-61, Washington, 1962. — China's Agriculture, FOCUS (American Geographical Society), April, 1960, pp. 1-6. — M. N. JEN, Agricultural Landscape of Southwestern China, Economic Geography, July, 1948, pp. 157-69. — T. H. SHEN, Agricultural Resources of China, Ithaca: Cornell University Press, 1951.

To pages 56-57: J. S. AIRD, The Size, Composition, and Growth of the Population of Mainland China, Int. Population Statistics Reports, Series P-90, No. 15. Washington: Bureau of the Census, 1961. — BRUK AND APENCHENKO, op. cit. — J. W. ALEXANDER, The Pre-war Population of China: Distribution and Density, Annals, Assn. of American Geographers, March, 1948, pp. 1-5. — LEO ORLEANS, China's Population Statistics: An Illusion? China Quarterly, January-March, 1965, pp. 168-78. — ORLEANS, The Recent Growth of China's Urban Population, Geographical Review, January, 1959, pp. 43-57. — T, SHABAD, The Population of China's Cities, Geographical Review. January, 1959, pp. 32-42. — G. T. TREWARTHA, New Maps of China's Population, Geographical Review, April, 1957, pp. 234-9. — M. B. ULLMAN, Cities of Mainland China, 1953-8, Int. Population Reports, Series P-95, No. 59, Washington: Bureau of the Census, 1961. — W. WYNNE, Jr., The Population of Manchuria, International Population Statistics Reports, Series P-90, No. 7, Washington: Bureau of the Census, 1958.

To pages 58-59: S. I. BRUK and U. S. APENCHENKO, Atlas Naroc Mira, Moscow: Gugk i Institut Etnografii AN SSSR, 1964, pp. 42 — Y. R. CHAO, Languages and Dialects in China, Geographical Journ July-December, 1943, pp. 63-7.

To page 60: Central Intelligence Agency, Lead in the Sino-Soviet Bl Washington, 1961. — Tin in the Sino-Soviet Bloc, Washington, 1961. Aluminum in the Sino-Soviet Bloc, 1950-65, Washington, 1962. D. J. DWYER, The Coal Industry in Mainland China since 1949, G graphical Journal, Sept., 1963, pp. 329-38. — V. C. JUAN, Mine Resources of China, Econom. Geology, June-July, 1946 (Supp pp. 399-474. — J. E. SPENCER, Salt in China, Geographical Revi July, 1935, pp. 353-66. — K. P. WANG, Mineral Resources of Chi Geogr. Review, Oct., 1944, pp. 621-35.

To page 61: M. ERSELCUK, The Iron and Steel Industry in China, Ec Geography, Oct., 1956, pp. 347-71. — T. HERMAN, Cultural Factors the Location of the Swatow Lace and Needlework Industry, Ann Assn. of American Geographers, March, 1956, pp. 122-7. — S. NIKOLAYEV and L. I. MOLODSOVA, The Present State of the Chir Iron and Steel Industry, Soviet Geography, Oct., 1960, pp. 55-70. I. K. OVDIYENKO, The New Geography of Industry of China, So Geography, April, 1960, pp. 63-77. — T. T. READ, Economic-Geograp Aspects of China's Iron Industry, Geogr. Review, Jan. 1943, pp. 42- — T. SHABAD, China's Resources for Heavy Industry, Focus (A Geogr. Society, Nov., 1958, pp. 1-6. — Y. L. WU, Principal Industr Cities on the Mainland: Regional Distribution and Ranking, in E. Kirby, ed., Contemporary China, V, 1961-62. — WU, Econom Development and the Use of Energy Resources in Communist Chi New York: Praeger, 1963. — WU, The Steel Industry in Commu China, New York: Praeger, 1965.

To pages 62-63: K. S. CHANG, The Changing Railroad Pattern Mainland China, Geogr. Review, Oct., 1961, pp. 534-48. — N. GINSBURG, China's Railroad Network, Geogr. Review, July, 19 pp. 470-74. — GINSBURG Manchurian Railway Development, Eastern Quarterly, Aug., 1949, pp. 398-411. — H. HUNTER, Transp in Soviet and Chinese Development, Econ. Development and Cultu Change, Oct., 1965, pp. 71-84. — R. MURPHEY, China's Transp Problem and Communist Planning, Econom. Geography, Jan., 19 pp. 17-28. — V. P. PETROV, New Railway Links between China and Soviet Union, Geogr. Journal, Dec., 1956, pp. 471-7. — J. E. SPENC Trade and Transshipment in the Yangtze Valley, Geogr. Review, Ja 1938, pp. 112-23. — F. H. A. STABLES, Present Conditions of Ro Travel in China, J. of the Royal Central Asian Society, April, 19 pp. 144-50.

To page 64: C. A. FISHER, South-East Asia: A Social, Economic, a Political Geography, London: Methuen, 1963. — N. GINSBURG a C. F. ROBERTS Jr., Malaya, Seattle: Univ. of Washington Press, 1958. V. PURCELL, The Chinese in Southeast Asia, Oxford: Univ. Press, 19 Revised Edition. — G. W. SKINNER, Chinese Society in Thaila Ithaca: Cornell Univ. Press, 1957. — L. UNGER, The Chinese in Sou east Asia, Geogr. Review, April, 1944, pp. 196-217.

To pages III-IV: (Rear End Paper) Central Intelligence Agency, Chir Provisional Atlas of Cummunist Administrative Units, Washingtc U.S. Dept. of Commerce, 1959. — N. S. GINSBURG, China's Changi Political Geography, Geogr. Review, Jan. 1952, pp. 102-17. — HERMAN, Group Values Toward the National Space: The Case China, Geogr. Review, April, 1959, pp. 164-82. — W. KIRK, The Sin Indian Frontier Dispute, Scottisch Geogr. Magazine, April, 1960, p 3-13. — Y. F. LAAI, F. MICHAEL, and J. C. SHERMAN, The Use of Ma in Social Research, Geogr. Review, Jan., 1962, pp. 92-111. — R. McCOLL, The Development of Supra-Provincial Administrative Regio in Communist China, 1949-60, Pacific Viewpoint, March, 1963, p 53-64. — U.S. DEPT. OF STATE, THE GEOGRAPHER, China-Hongko Boundary, International Boundary Study, No. 13, Washington, 19 — Idem, China-Korea Boundary, International Boundary Study N 17, Washington, 1962. — Idem, China-Laos Boundary, Int. Bounda Study No. 34, Washington, 1964. — Idem, China-Vietnam Boundar Int. Boundary Study No. 38, Washington, 1964. — Idem, Burma-Chi Boundary, Int. Boundary Study No. 42, Washington, 1964. — Ide China-Nepal Boundary, Int. Boundary Study No. 50, Washington, 19 — Idem, China-U.S.S.R. Boundary, Int. Boundary Study No. 6 Washington, 1966. — H. WIENS, China's North and Northwest Boun aries, in E. S. Kirby, ed., Contemporary China, V, 1961-62.

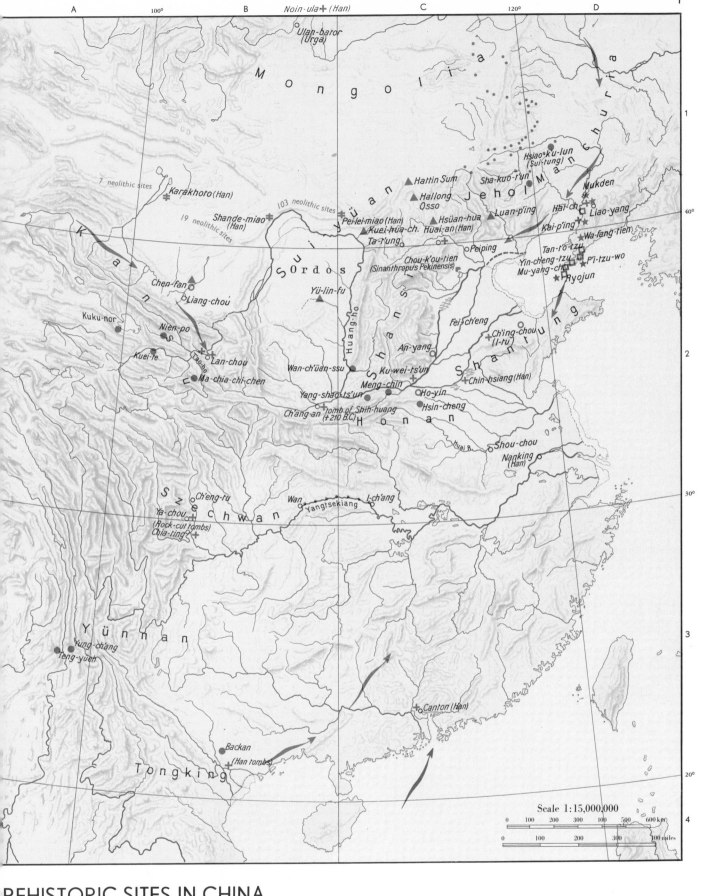

REHISTORIC SITES IN CHINA

Immigrations

Site or tomb of Neolithic Age

Other objects of Neolithic Age

Bronze Age site

Iron Age site

Iron Age tomb

Find of knife-money and spade-money

Han coins

Ordos bronzes (of Huns)

(Han) Period of the earlier Han Dynasty
(206 B.C. - 25 A.D.)

Scale 1:15,000,000

Map labels:

Noin-ula + (Han)

Ulan-bator (Urga)

M o n g o l i a

7 neolithic sites

Karakhoto (Han)

103 neolithic sites

Shande-miao (Han)

19 neolithic sites

S u i - y ü a n

Hattin Sum

Hallong Osso

J e h o l

Sha-kuo-t'un

Hsiao-ku-lun (Sui-tung)

Mukden

Pei-lei-miao (Han)

Kuei-hua-ch.

Ta-t'ung

Hsüan-hua

Huai-an (Han)

Luan-p'ing

Hai-ch

Liao-yang

Kai-p'ing

Wa-fang-tien

K a n s u

Chen-fan

Liang-chou

S o r d o s

Yü-lin-fu

Chou-k'ou-tien (Sinanthropus Pekinensis)

Peiping

Tan-t'o-tzu

Yin-ch'eng-tzu

Mu-yang-ch'

P'i-tzu-wo

Ryojun

Kuku-nor

Nien-po

Kuei-te

Lan-chou

Tao-ho

Ma-chia-chi-chen

Wan-ch'üan-ssu

Ku-wei-ts'un

Meng-chin

Yang-shao-ts'un

Ch'ang-an

tomb of Shih-huang (+210 B.C.)

An-yang

Fei-ch'eng

Ch'ing-chou (I-tu)

Chin-hsiang (Han)

Ho-yin

Hsin-cheng

H o n a n

S h a n s i

S h a n t u n g

M a n c h u r i a

Huai R.

Shou-chou

Nanking (Han)

S z e c h w a n

Ch'eng-tu

Ya-chou (Rock-cut tombs)

Chia-ting

Wan

Yangtsekiang

I-ch'ang

Y ü n n a n

Yung-chang

Teng-yüeh

Backan (Han tombs)

T o n g k i n g

Canton (Han)

A   100°   B   C   120°   D

2

THE BEGINNINGS OF ANCIENT CHINA, 1900-1300 B.C.

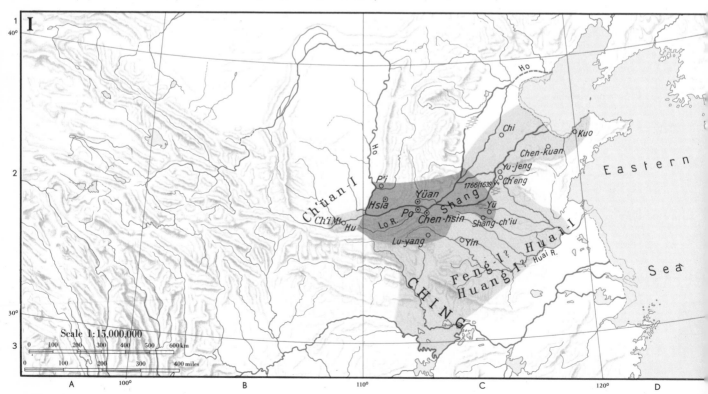

I

Scale 1:15,000,000

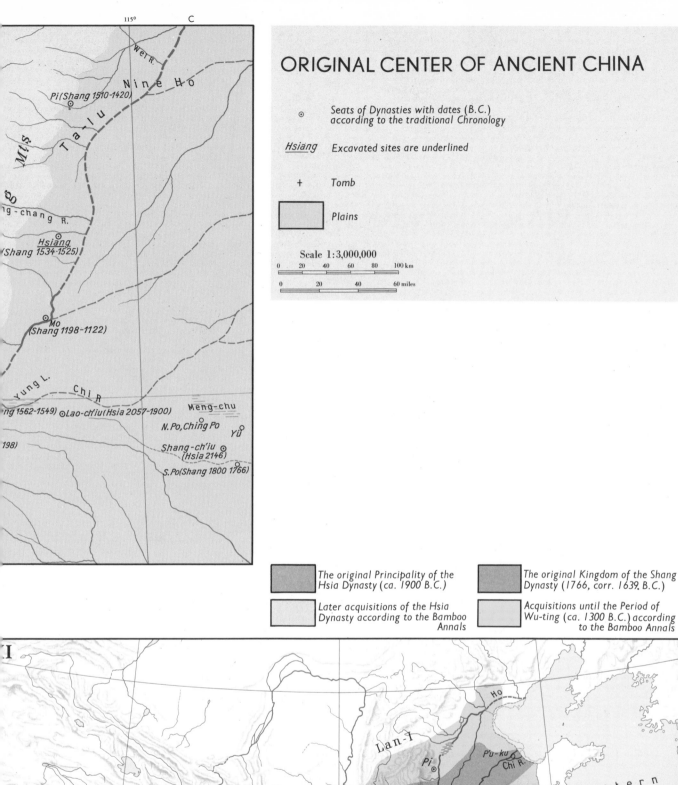

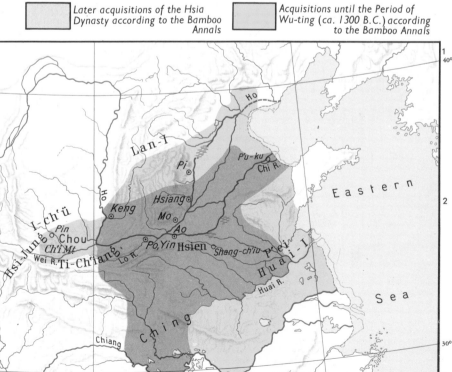

ORIGINAL CENTER OF ANCIENT CHINA

⊙ Seats of Dynasties with dates (B.C.)
    according to the traditional Chronology

Hsiang Excavated sites are underlined

+ Tomb

☐ Plains

Scale 1:3,000,000

|0 20 40 60 80 100 km|

|0   20   40   60 miles|

The original Principality of the
Hsia Dynasty (ca. 1900 B.C.)

The original Kingdom of the Shang
Dynasty (1766, corr. 1639, B.C.)

Later acquisitions of the Hsia
Dynasty according to the Bamboo
Annals

Acquisitions until the Period of
Wu-ting (ca. 1300 B.C.) according
to the Bamboo Annals

Left map labels:

Wei R.

Nine Ho

T a i l u

Mts

Pi (Shang 1510-1420)

ng-chang R.

Hsiang
(Shang 1534-1525)

⊙ Mo
(Shang 1198-1122)

Yung L.   Chi R.

ng 1562-1549) ⊙ Lao-ch'iu (Hsia 2057-1900)

Meng-chu

N. Po, Ching Po   Yü

198)

Shang-ch'iu
(Hsia 2146)

S. Po (Shang 1800 1766)

Bottom map labels:

Ho

Lan-i

Pi

Pu-ku

Chi R.

Eastern

Hsiang

Keng

Mo

Ao

I-ch'ü

Pin

Chou

Po, Yin Hsien Shang-ch'iu P'ei

Ch'i Mt.

Hsi-Jung

Wei R. Ti-Ch'iang Lo R.

Hu-i-I

Huai R.

Ching

Sea

Chiang

Scale 1:15,000,000

|100 200 300 400 500 600 km|

|100   200   300   400 miles|

A   100°   B   110°   C   120°   D

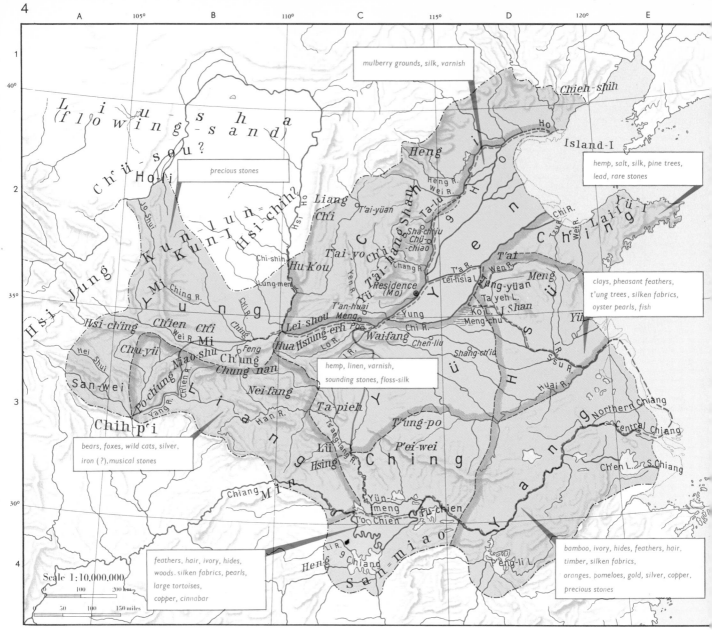

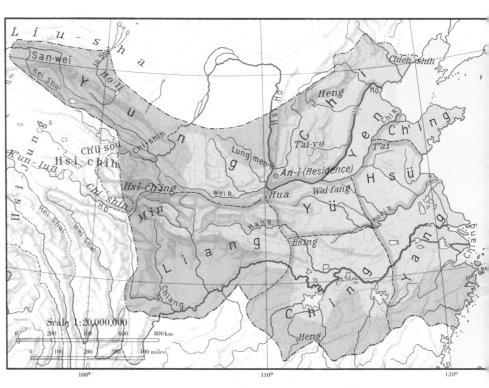

THE SHANG OR YIN DYNASTY,
CA. 1110 B.C.

———— Highways
       to the Royal Residence

– – – – Waterways
       to the Royal Residence

The 9 Provinces (chou) with their
Tributes according to the Geography
of the Tribute of Yü (Yü-kung),
dating from 1125 B.C.
     (according to A. Herrmann)

Other data
     according to the Bamboo Annals

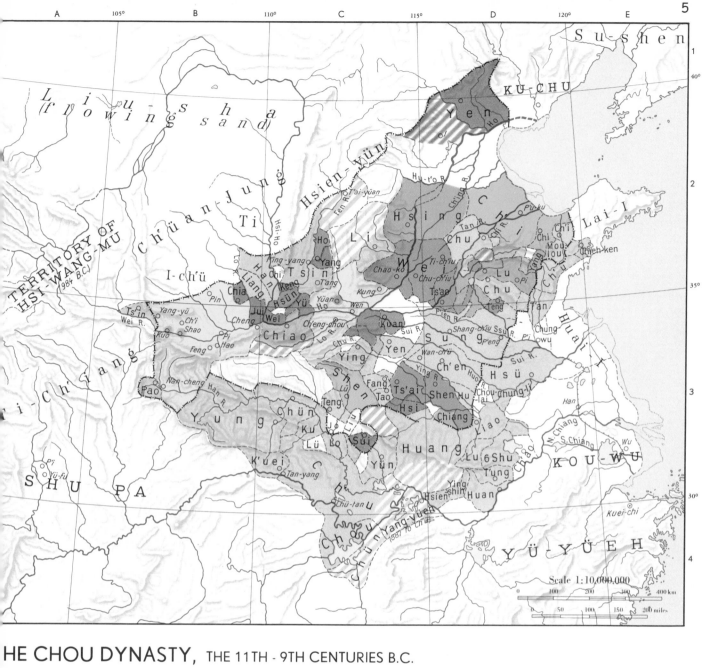

HE CHOU DYNASTY, THE 11TH - 9TH CENTURIES B.C.

Royal domain

┣━┅━┫ Boundary of China under Ch'eng-wang (ca. 1100 B.C.)

╌╌╌╌ Boundaries under Hsüan-wang (827-782)

fs bestowed on:

sons of Wen-wang

sons of Wu-wang

sons of Chou Wen-kung

other lines of the royal king

members of the family Chiang

members of other families

ncerning the barbarian tribes see also page 6/7

cording to G. Haloun and others

HE GEOGRAPHY OF THE YÜ-KUNG

ccording to the Confucian tradition, dating from 2200 B.C., and displacing the western boundary as far as Tibet and eastern Turkestan

Territories mistakenly annexed by commentators

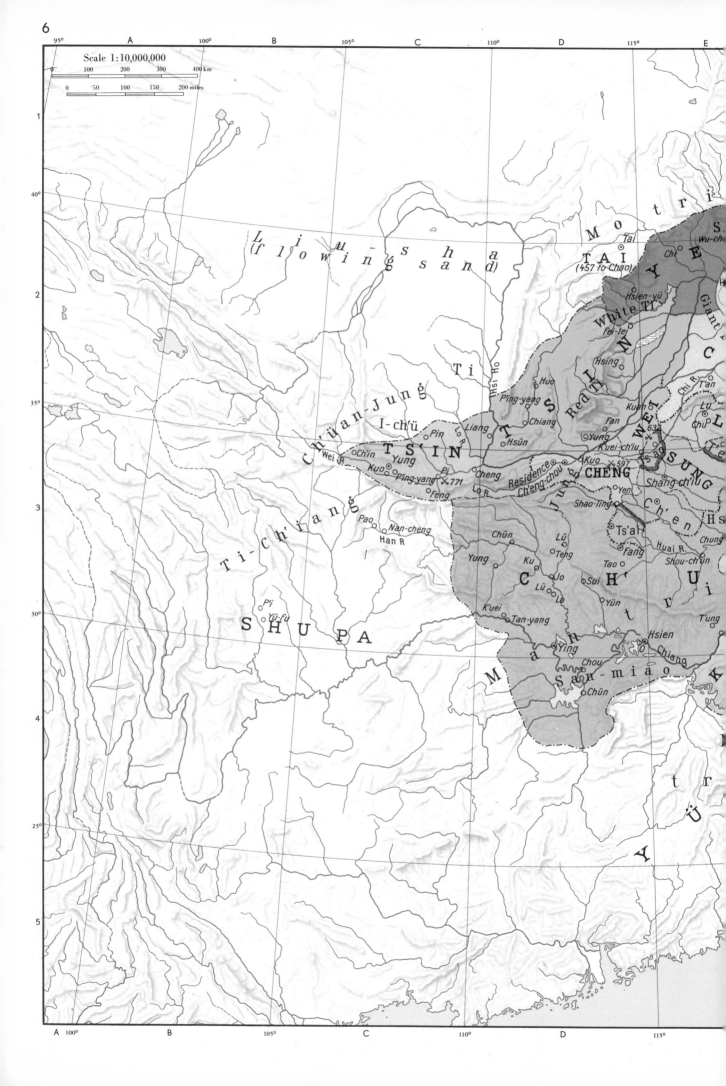

6

Scale 1:10,000,000

100   200   300   400 km
0   50   100   150   200 miles

95°   A   100°   B   105°   C   110°   D   115°   E

1

40°

35°

L   i   u   -   s   h   a
(f l o w i n g   s a n d)

Ti

Hsi Ho

M o t r i

Tai

TAI
(457 to Chao)

Chi

Wu-ch

S

E

Hsien-yü

White Ti

Giant T

Fei-lei

Hsing

Huo

Kueh

Chi R.

T'an

Lu

Chü

Ping-yang

Ch'üan-Jung

I-ch'ü

Pin

Lo R.

Liang

Chiang

Red Ti

WEI

Fan

632

Te

TS'IN

Yung

Hsün

Yung

K'uei-ch'iu

597

SUNG

Wei

Ch'in

Kuo

Ping-yang

Pi
×771

Cheng

Lo R.

Residence

Kuo

CHENG

Shang-ch'iu

Feng

Ch'eng-chou

Yen

Shao-ling

Ch'en

Hs

Pao

Chün

Lü

Ts'ai

Chung

Nan-cheng

Teng

Fang

Huai R.

Han R.

Yung

Ku

Tao

Sui

Shou-ch'un

Lü

Uo

Yün

T'ung

K'uei

Le

Lü

Pi

Yü-fu

SHU

PA

Tan-yang

Hsien

Ying

Chiang

Chou

Man

t   r   i

San-miao

Chün

K

30°

25°

Ü

Y

t   r

A   100°   B   105°   C   110°   D   115°

CH'UN-CH'IU PERIOD,
722 - 481 B.C.

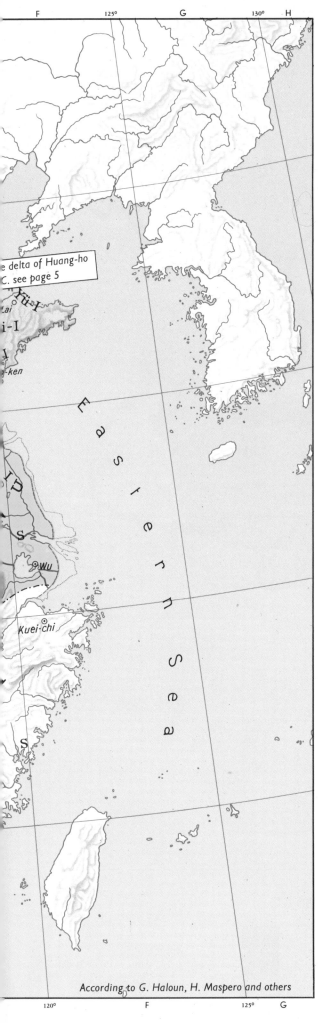

the delta of Huang-ho
C. see page 5

Eastern Sea

Kuei-chi

According to G. Haloun, H. Maspero and others

☐ Royal Domain

·–·+·–·+· Boundary between the Outer and the Inner States

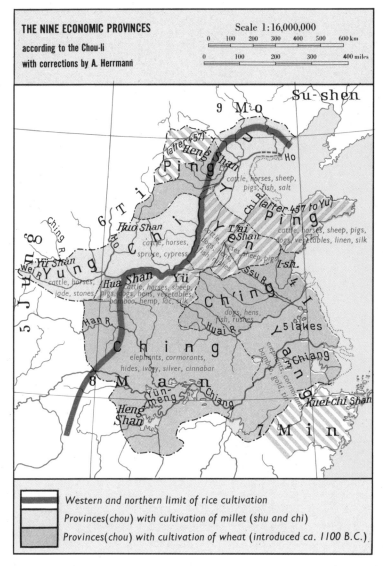

THE NINE ECONOMIC PROVINCES

according to the Chou-li
with corrections by A. Herrmann

Scale 1:16,000,000

0 100 200 300 400 500 600 km

0 100 200 300 400 miles

Su-shen

9 Mo

cattle, horses, sheep, pigs, fish, salt

cattle, horses, sheep, pigs, dogs, vegetables, linen, silk

cattle, horses, spruce, cypress

cattle, horses, jade, stones

cattle, horses, sheep, pigs, dogs, hens, vegetables, bamboo, hemp, lac, silk

dogs, hens, fish, rushes

5 lakes

elephants, cormorants, hides, ivory, silver, cinnabar

8 Man

7 Min

6 Yü

Yen

Ching

Chiang

══ Western and northern limit of rice cultivation

☐ Provinces(chou) with cultivation of millet (shu and chi)

▨ Provinces(chou) with cultivation of wheat (introduced ca. 1100 B.C.)

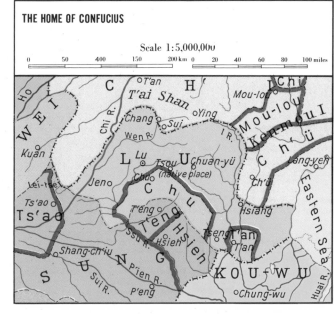

THE HOME OF CONFUCIUS

Scale 1:5,000,000

0 50 400 150 200 km   0 20 40 60 80 100 miles

WEI

T'ai Shan

Lu

Tsou
(native place)

Ts'ao

Chu

Teng

SUNG

KOU-WU

Eastern Sea

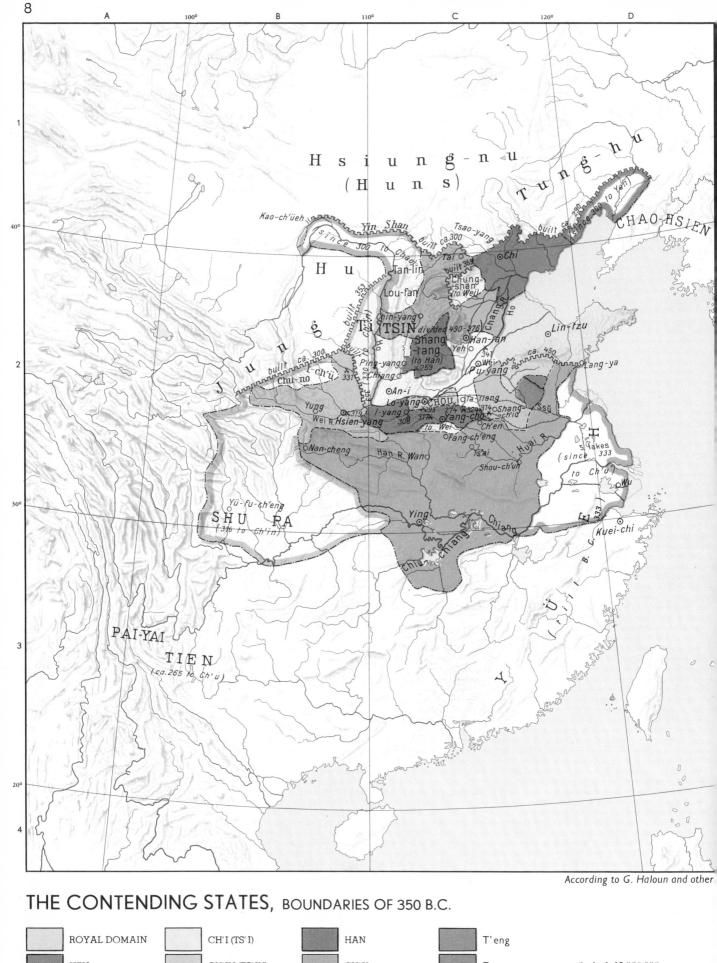

8

THE CONTENDING STATES, BOUNDARIES OF 350 B.C.

ROYAL DOMAIN	CH'I (TS'I)	HAN	T'eng
YEN	CH'IN (TS'IN)	CH'U	Tsou
CHAO	WEI	Sung	Lu

Scale 1:15,000,000

0 100 200 300 400 500 600 km

0 100 200 300 400 mile

Map labels: Hsiung-nu (Huns), Tung-hu, CHAO-HSIEN, Kao-ch'üeh, Yin Shan, built ca.300, Tsao-yang, built ca.230 (since 300 to Yen), Chi, Hu, since 300 to Chao, Tan-lin, Tai, built 369, Lou-fan, Chung-shan (to Wei), Lin-tzu, J u n g, built 353, Chin-yang, TI TSIN, divided 490-376, Shang-tang, Han-tan, Yeh, ca.450, built ca.300, Ho, Ping-yang, Wei, Pu-yang, Lang-ya, Chiu-no, T-ch'ü, built 331, Chiang, An-i, Lo-yang, CHOU, Ta-liang, Ssŭ, Yung, I-yang, Yang-ch'eng, Ch'en, H, Wei R. Hsien-yang, Fang-ch'eng, Ts'ai, 5 Lakes (since 333 to Ch'u), Nan-cheng, Han R. Wan, Shou-ch'un, Wu, SHU, PA, Yü-fu-ch'eng (316 to Ch'in), Ying, Chiang, Kuei-chi, Ü (till B.C. 333), PAI-YAI, TIEN (ca.265 to Ch'u), Chiang, Y

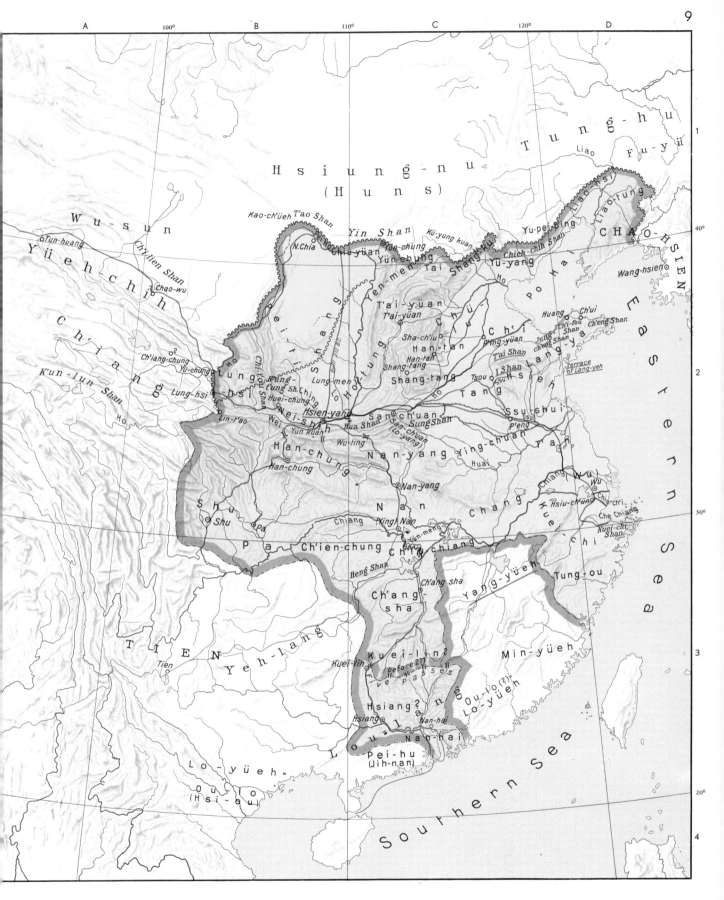

A 100° **B** 110° **C** 120° **D**

Wu-sun

Hsiung-nu
(Huns)

Tung-hu

Liao Fu-yü

Tun-huang
Chi-lien Shan
Chao-wu

Kao-ch'üeh T'ao Shan
N.Chia Pei Ho Chiu-yüan
Yin Shan
Yün-chung
Kü-yung kuan
Shang-ku
Yu-pei-ping
Lao-hsi
Liaotung
CHAO-
HSIEN

Yün-chung
Yen-men
Tai
Shang-ku
Yu-yang
Chieh-chih Shan
Po Hai
Wang-hsien

Yüeh-chih

Ch'iang-chung
Yü-chung
Lung-hsi
T'ai-yüan
T'ai-yüan
Chü-
lu
Ch'i
Huang Ch'ui
Chih-fou Shan
Ch'eng Shan
Jung-ch'eng Shan

K'un-lun Shan
Ch'i-lou Shan
Fung-ch'ing
Sha-ch'iu
Han-tan
Ping-yüan
T'ai Shan
Terrace of Lang-yeh

Ch'iang
Huei-chung
Han-tan
Shang-tang
Tsou
I Shan
Lang-yeh

Lin-t'ao
Wei Yün kuan
Wei-shih
Hsien-yang
Hua Shan
San-ch'uan
Sung Shan
Shang-tang
Tang
Ssu Hsieh
Ssu shui

Han-chung
Wu-ling
San-ch'uan
(Lo-yang)
Nan-yang
Ying-ch'uan
Tang
p'eng

Han-chung
Huai
Nan-yang
Chang
Wu
Wu
Hsiu-ch'un
Chu-chi
Che Chiang

Shu
Shu
Pa
Chiang
(Ying) Nan
Nan
Chang
Kuei-chi
Kuei-chi Shan

P a
Ch'ien-chung
Ch'ien chiang
Yün-meng

Heng Shan
Yang-yüeh
Tung-ou

Ch'ang sha
Ch'ang-sha

Tien
Yeh-lang
Kuei-lin
Kuei-lin
Min-yüeh

Tien
Kuei-lin
before 211
Five Passes
Ou-lo (?)
Lo-yüeh

Hsiang ?
Hsiang
Nan-hai
Nan-hai
Pei-hu
(Jih-nan)

Lo-yüeh
Ou-lo
(Hsi-ou)

Eastern Sea

Southern Sea

THE TS'IN DYNASTY, 255-206 B.C.

⊙   *Capital of province*

1 Shan   *Mountains with inscription set by Emperor Shih-huang, 219-210 B.C.*

——   *Highways*

Scale 1:15.000.000

0   100   200   300   400   500   600 km

0   100   200   300   400 miles

I

MACEDONIA

Pontus Euxinus
Byzantium
BITHYNIA
Sinope
Trapezus
PERGAMUM
GALATIA
PONTUS
CAPPADOCIA
Antioch
Alexandria
Egypt
Damascus
Sidon
ARABIA
Euphrates
Tigris
Babylon
Seleucia
Susa
ELYMAIS
Ecbatana
MEDIA ATROPATENE
R.SELEUCIDARUM
ARMENIA
Albani
Cyrus
Caucasus Mts
Tanais
Panticapaeum
Siraces
Aorsi
Caspian Sea
Apasiacae
Chorasmii
Parni
PARTHIA
HYRCANIA
Arsace
Hecatompylos
SOGDIANA
Maracanda
Antiokhia
Bactra
R.BACTRIANUM
ARIA
Alexandria
Cabura
ARACHOSIA
PERSIS
CARMANIA
GEDROSIA
SHEN-TU = INDIA
Oxus
Jaxartes
Taguri
Yüeh-chih ca.150 B.C.
Wu-sun ca.160 B.C.
Hsin-li
Ko-k'un
Ting-ling
Hu-chien
26 Kingdoms
Lou-la
Indus
ca.160 B.C.

II

MACEDONIA
Pontus Euxinus
Byzantium
Bithynia
Sinope
ASIA
GALATIA
Pontus Trapezus
CAPPADOCIA
Antioch
Alexandria
Egypt
ARABIA
Euphrates
Tigris
Seleucia
Susa
ELYMAIS
MESENE
R.SELEUCID
MEDIA ATROPATENE
ARMENIA
Albani
Cyrus
Caucasus Mts
Tanais
Panticapaeum
R.BOSPORANUM
Siraces Aorsi = Yeh-ts'ai
Huns 1.cent.A.D. and 375 A.D. Chien-k'un
Huns since ca.45 B.C.
Caspian Sea
Chorasmia
Hsin-li
Ting-ling
Hu-chien
Residence of Chih-chih ca.40-36
KANG-CHÜ
I-lieh
Wu-sun
Kutsi
Lun-t'ai
Chü-
Su-hsieh
TA-YÜAN
Maracanda = Kang = Wei
Oxus
PARTHIA = Aria
HYRCANIA
IL-KAN
Arsace
Hecatompylos
Bactra
Yüeh-chih 127 B.C.
Lan-shih
TA-HSIA
Cabura
Han-mi Yü-t'ien
36 B.C.
Indus
ARACHOSIA
Persis
Carmania
GEDROSIA
SHEN-TU = INDIA
Jaxartes
Alexandria

THE HSIUNG-NU
OR HUNS
IN CENTRAL ASIA,
176 B.C.

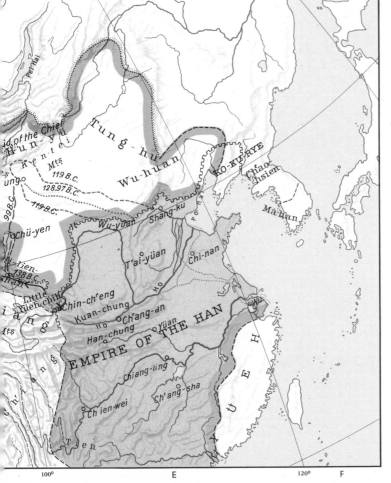

Scale 1:30,000,000

0   200   400   600   800   1000 km

0   200   400   600 miles

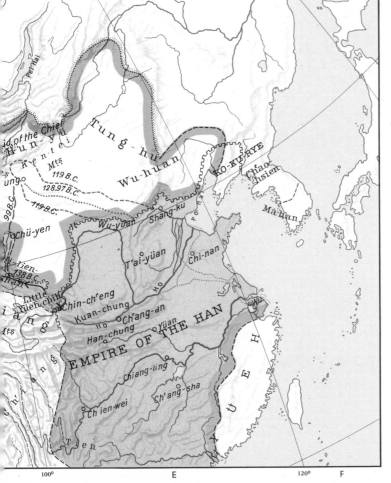

	Northern border of the steppe
	Original country
	Conquests of the Huns
	Under Mao-tun 210 - 174 B.C.
←---	Migrations of other peoples

128 - 36 B.C.

	Northern border of the steppe
	Power of the Huns about 100 B.C.
←	Later migrations to the West
	Empire of the Han about 100 B.C. (beginning of the direct relations with western civilization)
←	Mission of Chang Ch'ien to the Yüeh-chih 138 - 126 B.C., twice prisoner of the Huns

Campaigns against the Huns:

.... Wei Ch'ing 128 B.C.

------- Ho Ch'ü-ping and Wei Ch'ing 119 B.C.

——— Li Ling 99 B.C.

.... Li Kuang-li 92 B.C.

——— Ch'en T'ang with two army expeditions 36 B.C.

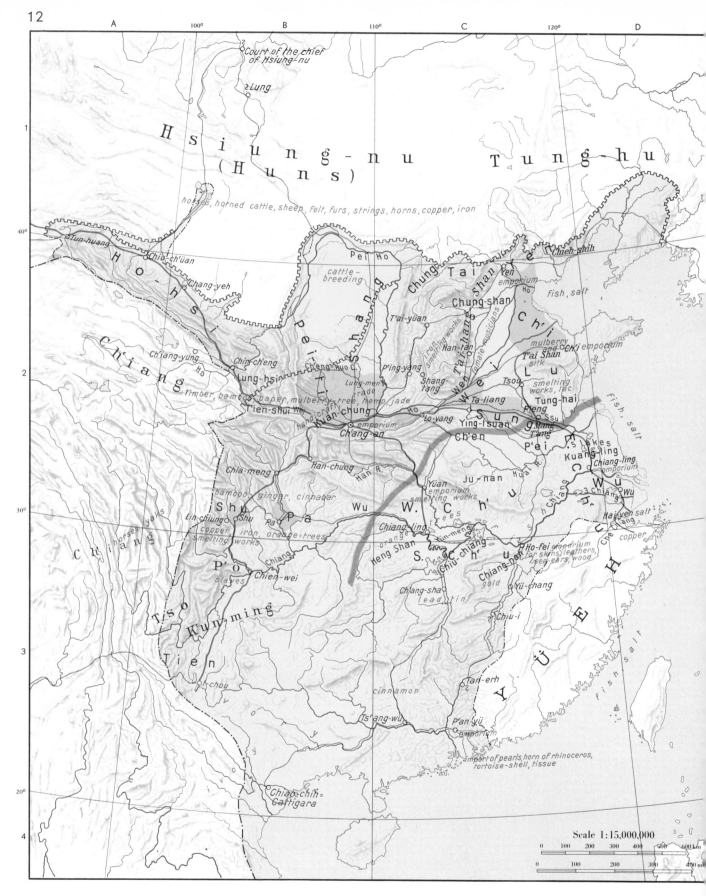

ECONOMIC DEVELOPMENT UNDER THE EARLIER HAN DYNASTY, CA. 100 B

Intensive agriculture

West and north boundary of rice cultivation

Highways

The economic data according to Shih-chi of Ssu-ma Ch'
chapt. 29 (translated by E. Chavann
and 129 (translated by Fr. Jä

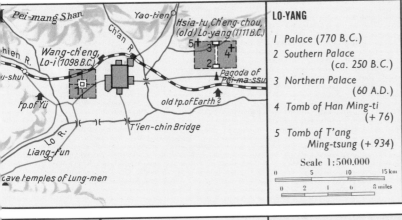

LO-YANG

1 Palace (770 B.C.)
2 Southern Palace (ca. 250 B.C.)
3 Northern Palace (60 A.D.)
4 Tomb of Han Ming-ti (+ 76)
5 Tomb of T'ang Ming-tsung (+ 934)

Scale 1:500,000

0   5   10   15 km
0   2   4   6   8 miles

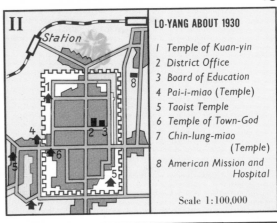

II

LO-YANG ABOUT 1930

1 Temple of Kuan-yin
2 District Office
3 Board of Education
4 Pai-i-miao (Temple)
5 Taoist Temple
6 Temple of Town-God
7 Chin-lung-miao (Temple)
8 American Mission and Hospital

Scale 1:100,000

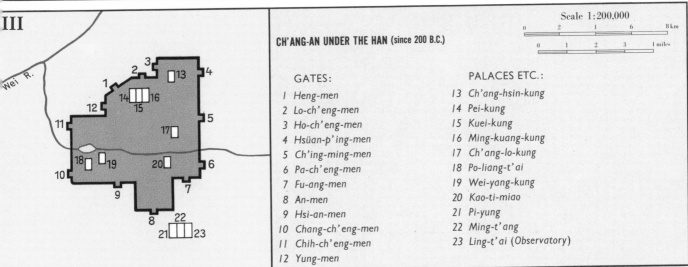

III

CH'ANG-AN UNDER THE HAN (since 200 B.C.)

Scale 1:200,000

0   2   4   6   8 km
0   1   2   3   1 miles

GATES:

1 Heng-men
2 Lo-ch'eng-men
3 Ho-ch'eng-men
4 Hsüan-p'ing-men
5 Ch'ing-ming-men
6 Pa-ch'eng-men
7 Fu-ang-men
8 An-men
9 Hsi-an-men
10 Chang-ch'eng-men
11 Chih-ch'eng-men
12 Yung-men

PALACES ETC.:

13 Ch'ang-hsin-kung
14 Pei-kung
15 Kuei-kung
16 Ming-kuang-kung
17 Ch'ang-lo-kung
18 Po-liang-t'ai
19 Wei-yang-kung
20 Kao-ti-miao
21 Pi-yung
22 Ming-t'ang
23 Ling-t'ai (Observatory)

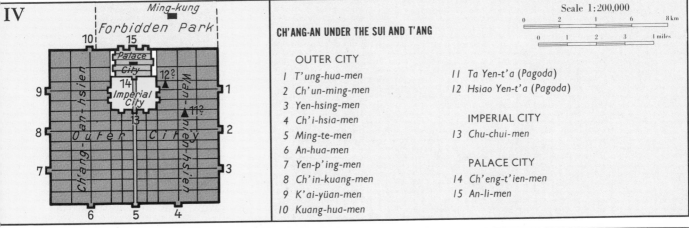

IV

CH'ANG-AN UNDER THE SUI AND T'ANG

Scale 1:200,000

0   2   4   6   8 km
0   1   2   3   1 miles

OUTER CITY

1 T'ung-hua-men
2 Ch'un-ming-men
3 Yen-hsing-men
4 Ch'i-hsia-men
5 Ming-te-men
6 An-hua-men
7 Yen-p'ing-men
8 Ch'in-kuang-men
9 K'ai-yüan-men
10 Kuang-hua-men
11 Ta Yen-t'a (Pagoda)
12 Hsiao Yen-t'a (Pagoda)

IMPERIAL CITY

13 Chu-chui-men

PALACE CITY

14 Ch'eng-t'ien-men
15 An-li-men

V   Scale 1:500,000

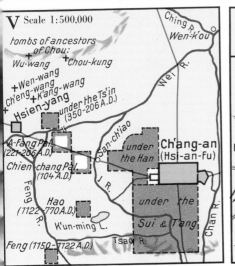

CH'ANG-AN ABOUT 1930   Scale 1:100,000

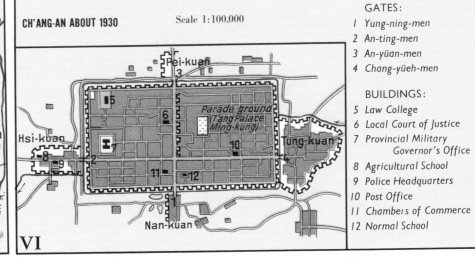

GATES:

1 Yung-ning-men
2 An-ting-men
3 An-yüan-men
4 Chang-yüeh-men

BUILDINGS:

5 Law College
6 Local Court of Justice
7 Provincial Military Governor's Office
8 Agricultural School
9 Police Headquarters
10 Post Office
11 Chambers of Commerce
12 Normal School

14

A 95° B 100° 105° D 110° E

N. Hsiung-nu

Western Region

Chü-mi E.

T z u - l u

Salt Lakes
Chü-yen

Lou-lan

Yü-men Kuan,
Daxata

Shan-shan

Yang Kuan

Yün-huang,
Throana

Jo R.

Black R.

S. Hsiung

Kao-ch'üeh

Yin Shan
Po-tao-ling

Lin-ho Pei Ho Yün-chung Ming-hsiang
Wu-yüan Chin-yüan Yen-men

Hsi-ho

Sho-fang

Shang-ho **Ping**

Hsi Ho T'ai-yüan

Shang

Chin-ch'üan, Drosakhe

the Green Ti

Chang-yeh,
Thogara

Ssu-chih

Hsi Hai

W. Ch'iang

Mien

Chir-shih Ho

built 113-112 B.C.

Wu-wei,
Sera

Little Yüeh-chih

Yen-chih Mts

Wu-li

T'ien Shan Mts

Hsi-hai

(Huang-chung)

Ho-kuan Tao R.

Ta-hsia Lung-hsi

Ling-chü ?

the White Horses Ti

Chin-ch'eng

Pei-ti

An-ting

Tien-shui

the White Ti
Jan Ti

Lin-t'ao Wei R.

Yellow Cattle
Ch'iang

Wu-fu the White
Horses Ti

Lung-men

Yu-fu-feng Tso-feng

Hung-nung

Ching-chao
(Ch'ang-an)

Wu-ling

Ho-tung Ho-nei

Ho-nan
(Lo-yang)

Shang-tang

S s u i

Nan-yang

Min Shan

Han-chung

Han R.

Chia-ming

Min-shan

C h ' i a n g

Chu R.

Ch'iang Kuang-han

Mao-niu Shu(Ch'eng-tu)

P'o

I (chou)

Ssu

Wu

Yüan

i n d e p e n d e n t t r i b e s

Nan, Lin-ch

Yün meng

Chiang

Pa

Tso

Chien-wei

Man

Jan

Kuei-yang

Wu-ling

Heng Shan

Jo R. Yüeh-sui

Ch'en-li

Sui

K'un-ming

Tsang-k'e

Ch'ar

Yen R.

Yeh-yü

Pai-yai

Yung-ch'ang

PAI TZU

CHIEN-NING

T I E N

Ling-ling

Ts'ang-wu

I-chou
(Ch'eng-chiang)

ü

Yü-lin

Nan

Chiao-chih,
Cattigara

South

Hop'u

Hsü-wen

B 100° C 105°

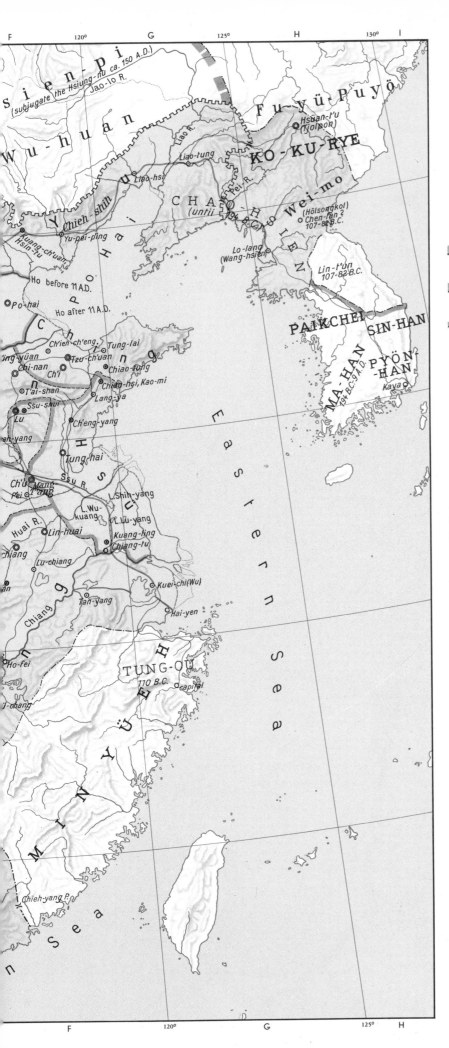

CHINA UNDER THE EARLIER AND LATER HAN DYNASTIES,

206 B.C. - 220 A.D.

Boundary under the Western Han, 1st Century B.C.

Boundary under the Eastern Han, about 100 A.D.

Boundaries of chou (provinces) under the Eastern Han

◎ Capitals of chün (commanderies) with more than 100,000 inhabitants

○ Capitals of chün (commanderies) with less than 100,000 inhabitants

◉ Capitals of kuo (principalities) with more than 100,000 inhabitants

• Capitals of kuo (principalities) with less than 100,000 inhabitants

After the Western Han, kuo became chün, several with other names

Special names of capitals in parentheses

———— Trade routes or highways

Scale 1:10,000,000

0   100   200   300   400 km

0   50   100   150   200 miles

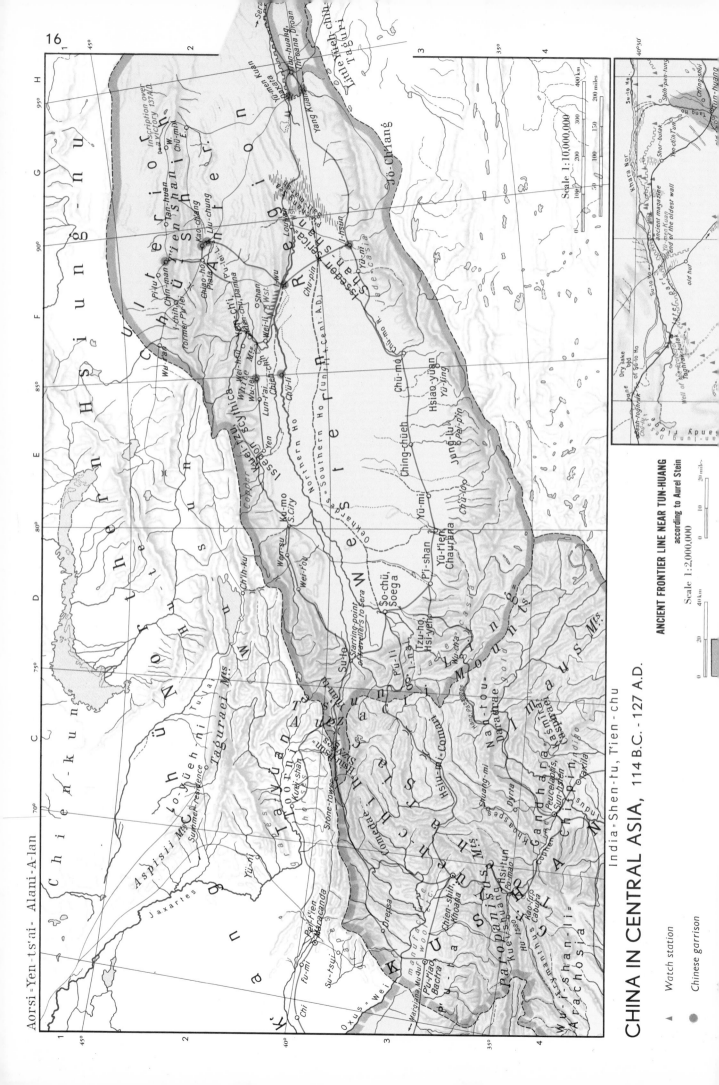

CHINA IN CENTRAL ASIA, 114 B.C. - 127 A.D.

India = Shen-tu, T'ien-chu

Aorsi = Yen-ts'ai = Alani-A-lan

Wu-i-shan-li = Arachosia

ANCIENT FRONTIER LINE NEAR TUN-HUANG

according to Aurel Stein

Scale 1:2,000,000

Scale 1:10,000,000

▲ Watch station

● Chinese garrison

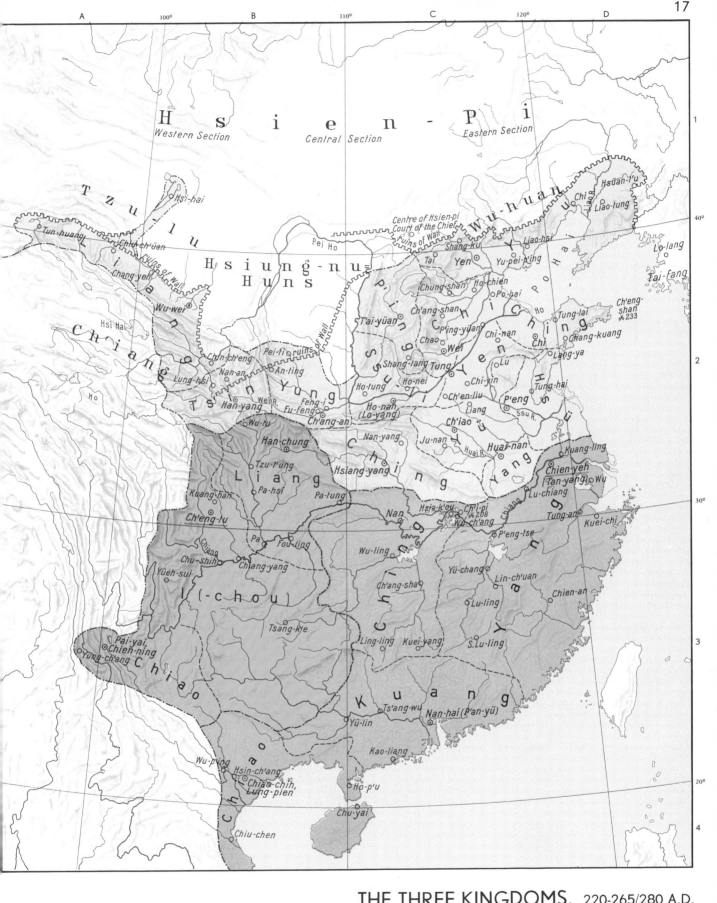

The following labels appear on the map:

Grid coordinates: A, 100°, B, 110°, C, 120°, D (top), 1, 2, 3, 4 (right side), 40°, 30°, 20° (right side)

Major regions:
H s i e n - p i
Western Section · Central Section · Eastern Section
T z u - l u
Hsiung-nu Huns
Wu-huan

Place names (north to south):
Hsi-hai, Tun-huang, Chiu-ch'üan, Liang, Chang-yeh, Hsi Hai, Wu-wei, Chün-ch'eng, Pei-ti, ruins of Wall, Pei Ho, Centre of Hsien-pi, Court of the Chief, Ruins of Wall, Shang-ku, Tai, Yen, Yu-pei-p'ing, Liao-hsi, Liao-tung, Hsüan-t'u, Chi, Lo-lang, Tai-fang

Chiang, Tsin, Yung, Nan-an, An-ting, Lung-hsi, Ssu, P'ing, Tai-yüan, Chao, Wei, Ch'ang-shan, Ho-chien, Po-hai, Chi-nan, Chi, Tung-lai, Ch'eng-shan ☆233, Ch'ing, Chiang-kuang, Lang-ya, Tung-hai

Han-yang, Wei R., Feng-i, Fu-feng, Ch'ang-an, Ho-tung, Shang-tang, Tung, Ho-nei, Lu, Ch'i-yin, Ch'en-liu, P'eng, Ssu R., Yen, Ho-nan (Lo-yang), Wu-tu, Nan-yang, Liang, Ch'iao, Ju-nan, Huai R., Huai-nan, Yü

Han-chung, Hsiang-yang, Ch'ing, Kuang-ling, Chien-yeh (Tan-yang), Wu, Tzu-t'ung, Pa-hsi, Pa-tung, Lu-chiang, Liang, Kuang-han, Pa, Nan, Hsia-k'ou, Chi-pi ☆208, Wu-ch'ang, Tung-an, Kuei-chi, Ch'eng-tu, Fou-ling, Yang, P'eng-tse, Chiang, Chu-shih, Chiang-yang, Wu-ling, Yü-chang, Lin-ch'uan, Chien-an, Yüeh-sui, I (-chou), Tsang-k'e, Ch'ang-sha, Lu-ling

Pai-yai, Chien-ning, Ling-ling, Kuei-yang, S. Lu-ling, Yung-ch'ang, Chiao, Kuang, Ts'ang-wu, Nan-hai (P'an-yü), Yü-lin, Kao-liang, Wu-p'ing, Hsin-ch'ang, Chiao-chih, Lung-pien, Ho-p'u, Chu-yai, Chiu-chen

THE THREE KINGDOMS, 220-265/280 A.D.

Wei dynasty

Wu dynasty

Shu or Minor Han dynasty

- - - - - - Boundaries of chou (provinces)

Scale 1:15,000,000

0 100 200 300 400 500 600 km

0 100 200 300 400 miles

A 20° B 40° C 60° D 80° E

Gau Scandiae Fel ii
Alg. Sueb Ocea amber
Trevi Colonia Germany Aestii Venedae
Lugdun Mogontiacum Sarmata Rha=
Mediolan Rhaetia Vistula Lianum Chien-kun
Genoa Pataun Bastarnae Metropolis Alani = A-lan Iastae Tyras Tiang-ling Northern
Ravenna nia gold Borysth Khuni Iazyges Tanais corn Maeotis Panticapaeum
Puteoli Naissus Dacia Drobi Thrace Olbia Northern Wu-sun copper
Rome Brundisium Thessalonica Bosporus Kingd. Pontus Euxinus Sinope Kucha Ching-chüeh
silver copper Byzantium Trapezus Phasis Harmozica Mts Caucasus Mts Ta-yüan bunch of grapes Ho So-chü Yü-fien
red corals Athens Asia minor Ancyra Armenia Artaxata Caspian Sea Dahae Chorasmia Jaxartes Maracanda Kang-chü Su-lo jade
Cyrene Crete Pergamum Taurus Mts Antioch Sinus Dahae Chorasmia Oxus Maracanda chih Chien shih S gold
Rhodes Ephesus Cyprus Syria Nisibis Mesopotamia Arbela Hyrcania Li-kien Antiokhia Margiana, Mu-lu Bactra Tokhari line of wool Purushapura indigo
Alexandria glass,manufact. slaves manufact Palmyra Damascus Euphrates Tigris Ctesiphon Ecbatana, A-man Hecatompylos, Ho-fu Cabura Alexandria gold
EGYPT of silk, purple Tyrus Gaza storax balsam Seleucia Ssu-lo Su-pin Alexandria Taxila
Memphis Petra gold silver Hirah Yü-lo Alexandria, Wu-shan-li
Thebes Myos Hormos Leucos limen Kharax Paraetacene P'ai-chin Manasa-Sarovara
Syene Coptos Persian Gulf Taocene, T Tao-chih Jonaca, An-ku Harmozia Indabara Emodus
Berenice Nilus Deuce come lathrippa Gerrha Omana Gedrosia Modura Diamuna Magadh sugar
ROMAN Macoraba ARABIA FELIX = TA TS'IN stage I Barbaricum Minnagara cotton Ozene Vindius Mts Palimbothra Ganges Gaya
Meroë Ptolemais theron Carna Minaei myrrh alabaster C. Didymi Syrastrene cotton Tamralip
Adule Axum Mariaba Sabatha Sarapidis I. Barygaza Andhra Maesolia
Aethiopia Ivory,horn of rhinoceros Homeritae aromatics,incense Saphar Adramitae = Lü-fen Moscha stage I stage II Simylla Paithana Tagara Alosygni
Muza Cane C. Syagrus stage III cotton, indigo, aromatics, precious stones Kerala Dimyric diamants
Qcelis Adane Dioscoridis I. Kola Sopatma
Auallies Malao Mosyllon Aromata stage IV sandal-wood Poduce
Barbarica myrrh, cassia, incense Opone Muziris Pandiones Camara
Azania (to Arabia Felix) Sarapium Nicon stage IV Nelcynda Madura Cottiara pepper,nard, malaba thrum C.Comara pearls Taprobane Salice precious stones tortoise-shell
ERYTHRAEAN Atoe Is. Palaesimundus

C 40° D 60° 80°

ASIA,
ca. 100 A.D.

The four stages refer to Pliny's description of sea routes in Book VI of his Natural History.

sic Alexandri classis navigavit; postea ab Syagro Arabiae promunturio Patalen favonio, quem Hippalum ibi vocant, peti certissimum videbatur XIII XXXII p. aestimatione, secuta aetas propiorem cursum tutioremque iudicavit si ab eodem promunturio Sigerum portum Indiae peteret, diuque ita navigatum est, donec conpendia invenit mercator, lucroque India admota est... nec pigebit totum cursum ab Ægypto exponere nunc primum certa notitia patescente...

(I) Such was the route followed by the fleet of Alexander; (II) but subsequently it was thought that the safest line was to take departure from Cape Syagrus in Arabia (= Ras Fartak) with the west wind, which is there known as Hippalus, and to set course for Patale, a distance reckoned as 1332 miles. (III) The following period considered it a shorter and safer route, setting out from the same cape, to steer for the Indian harbour of Sigerus, and for a long time this was the course followed, until a merchant discovered a shorter route, and the desire for gain brought India nearer...(IV) And it will not be amiss to set out the whole voyage from Egypt, now that reliable knowledge of it is for the first time available...

Scale 1:30,000,000

0   200   100   600   800   1000 km

0   200   100   600 miles

Han Hai

I-lou

Hsien-Pei

Fu-yü

Wu-huan

Hsiung-nu

graves with Chinese, Scythian, Hellenistic objects

Court of the chief of Hsiung-nu

Kuan huang

Chü-yen

Kao-chüeh

Chang-yeh, Thogara Sera metropolis, Wu-wei

Chin-yang

Chin-ch'eng

Chang-an

Lo-yang, Saraga Thinae

Li-yang

Chiang

Shu

Pa

Chang-sha

Min-yüeh

Kuei-yang

Chien-wei

Kuang-hsin

Nan-hai

yung-ch'ang

Chiao-chih

Ho-pu

Chu-yai

Cattigara

Jih-nan

Hsiang-lin

Cinnamon

copper

Cottiaris

Tên-yüeh

Besynga

Agimoetha

Acadra

Tomara

Cocconagara

Fu-nan

Pagrasa

Great Gulf

Zabae

Balonga

Great C.

Cocconagara

Tacola

Coli

C. Maleicolon

Palanda

Sabana

Sindae

tortoise-shell

Sabadivae I.

Chryse Chers.

Barussae I.

Chryse Iabadiu-Yen-kiao gold, tortoise-shell

Chi

Po-hai

Hsüan-tu

Huang-kou Jolpon

Ko-ku-rye

Lo-yang

Wang-hsien

Silla

Paikche

Mimana

Kashibara Kingd. founded about 17 B.C.

Wo

Eastern Sea

Sericus Oceanus

R I A

C

A

S E R

Court of the chief

Han Hai

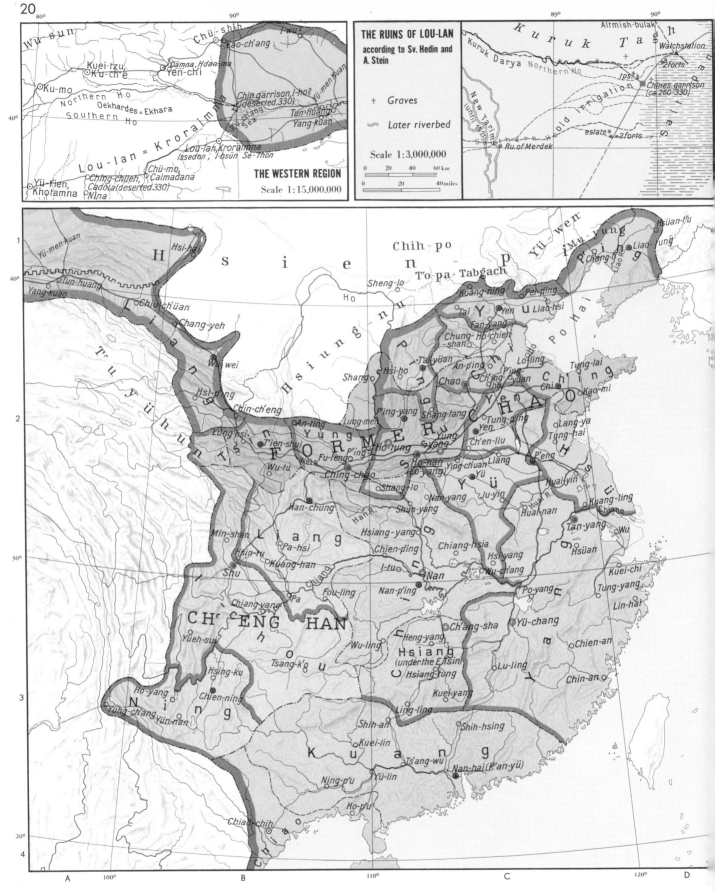

THE RUINS OF LOU-LAN
according to Sv. Hedin and
A. Stein

+ Graves

〜 Later riverbed

Scale 1:3,000,000

0   20   40   60 km

0   20   40 miles

THE WESTERN REGION
Scale 1:15,000,000

THE WESTERN TSIN DYNASTY, 265 - 316 A.D.

◉   *Capitals of chou (provinces) with more than 100,000 inhabitants*

●   *Capitals of chou (provinces) with less than 100,000 inhabitants*

◎   *Other places with more than 100,000 inhabitants*

○   *Other places with less than 100,000 inhabitants*

Regarding the states Han or Former Chao (304-329) and Ch'eng Han (304-347) see also p.

Scale 1:15,000,000

0   100   200   300   400   500   600 k

0   100   200   300   400

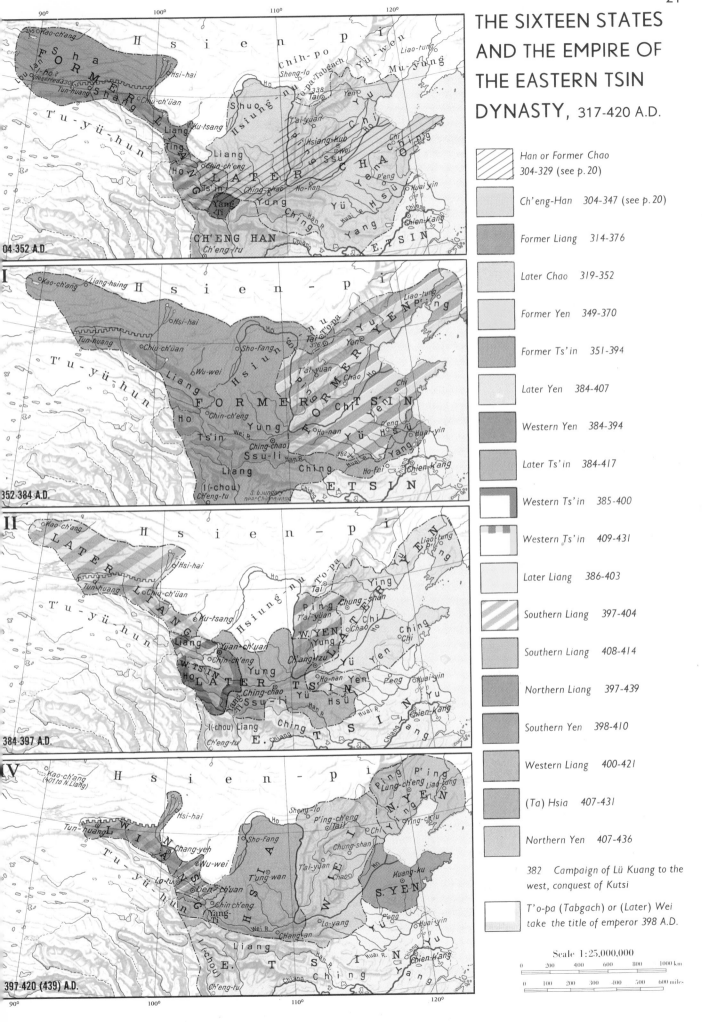

THE SIXTEEN STATES AND THE EMPIRE OF THE EASTERN TSIN DYNASTY, 317-420 A.D.

Han or Former Chao	304-329 (see p. 20)
Ch'eng-Han	304-347 (see p. 20)
Former Liang	314-376
Later Chao	319-352
Former Yen	349-370
Former Ts'in	351-394
Later Yen	384-407
Western Yen	384-394
Later Ts'in	384-417
Western Ts'in	385-400
Western Ts'in	409-431
Later Liang	386-403
Southern Liang	397-404
Southern Liang	408-414
Northern Liang	397-439
Southern Yen	398-410
Western Liang	400-421
(Ta) Hsia	407-431
Northern Yen	407-436

382 Campaign of Lü Kuang to the west, conquest of Kutsi

T'o-pa (Tabgach) or (Later) Wei take the title of emperor 398 A.D.

Scale 1:25.000.000

0	200	400	600	800	1000 km

0	100	200	300	400	500	600 miles

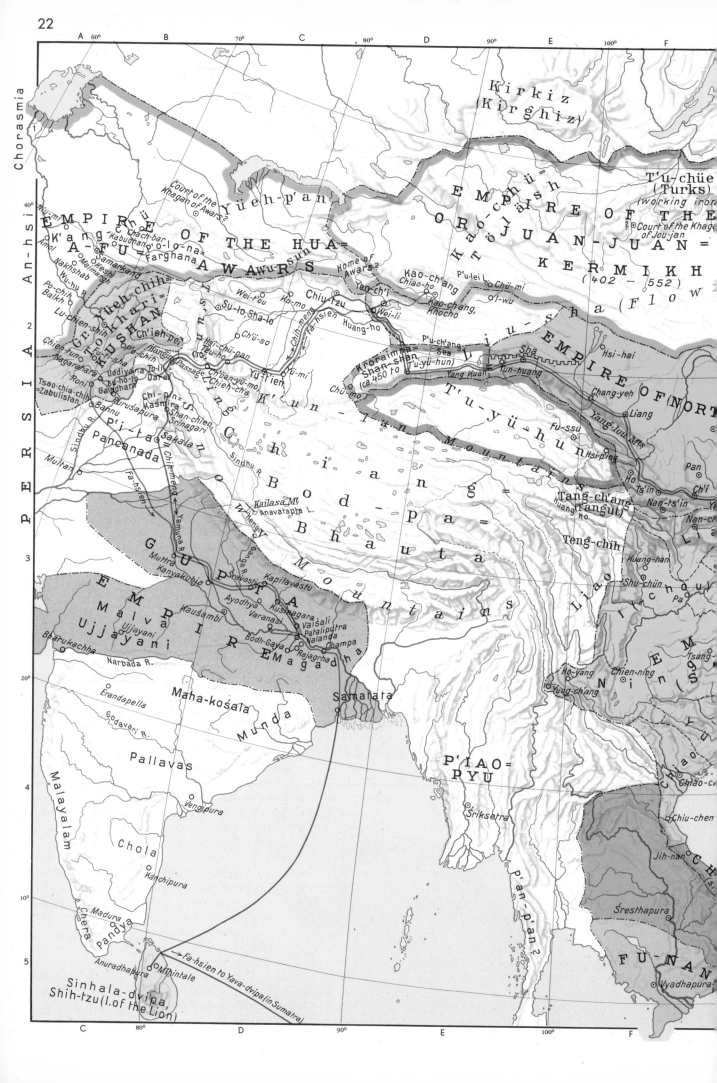

22

A 60° B 70° C 80° D 90° E 100° F

Chorasmia

An-hsi

Kirkiz
(Kirghiz)

Yüeh-p'an

T'u-chüe
(Turks)
(working iron

Court of the
Khagan of Awars?

EMPIRE OF THE HUA=

Ö-chü=
äsh

Court of the Khagan
of Jou-jan

EMPIRE OF THE
OR JUAN-JUAN=

40°

K'ang A-FU=Farghana AWARS

Ärö-jan?

KERMIKH
(402 — 552)

Chach-bar-lo-na

Habudhan-po-lo-na

Kao-ch'ang

Chü-mi

Sunu

Kao-chang,
Khocho

Samarkand

Maimargh

P E R S I A

K'ash

Amol

Nakhshab

Su-lo-Sha-lo

Wei-t'ou

Ho-mo

Chiu-tzu

Yen-ch'i

Chiao-ho

I-wu

Wu-hu R

Po-chih

Lu-chien-shih

Chü-so

Chih-meng

Fa-hsien

Wei-li

Gr. Yüeh-chih=

Tukhari=

KUSHAN

Ch'ieh-pei

Huang-ho

P'u-ch'ang
Sea

Ha (Flow

Balkh

Chien-t'uo=

Nagarahara

Liang-
Passage

Hsi-chü-pan

Yü-t'ien

Mi-mi

Ch'üan-yü-mo

Yü-t'ien

Chü-mo

Kroraimna=
Shan-shan
(ca 450 ro T'u-yü-hun)

P E R S I A   2

Lu-chien-shih

To-li

Darel

Chih-pin=U-

Chieh-cha

Yang Kuan

Tun-huang

EMPIRE OF (NORT

Hsi-hai

Roni

Uddiyana

Gandhara

Kashmira=
Shan-chien=

T'u-Yü-hun

Sha

Fu-ssu

Chang-yeh

Hsi-ping

Liang

An-hsi

Tsao-chia-chih
=Zabulistan

Bannu

Purushapura

Srinagari

Sakala

Su Chih-meng

K'un-lun

Mountains

Hsi-ping

Pan

Ch'i

Pi-ta=

Pancanada

Multan

Sindhu R

Fa-hsien

Yamuna R

Kailasa Mt.

Anavatapta L.

Ho

Ts'in

Nan-ts'in

Nan-ch

Tang-ch'ang
(Tangut)

Huang Ho

Li

G U P T A

Muttra

Kanyakubja

Sravasti

Srinagari

Kapilavastu

Teng-chih

Li-

Kuang-han

Shu-chün

Pa

M

Chien-ning

Tsang

3

E M P I R E

Malva

Ayodhya

Vaisali

Kusinagara

Kausambi

Varanasi

Pataliputra

Nalanda

N

Ujjayani

Ujjayani

Bodh-Gaya

Rajagrdha

Champa

Ho-yang

Yung-chang

Bharukachha

Narbada R.

Maha-kosala

Munda

Magadha

20°

Yung-chang

Erandapella

Samatata

P'IAO=
PYU

Śriksetra

Godavari R.

Pallavas

Vengipura

Chiu-chen

Malayalam

Chola

Kanchipura

Jih-nan

10°

Chera

Madura

Pandya

Anuradhapura Mihintale

Fa-hsien to Yava-dvipa(in Sumatra)

Śresthapura

5

Sinhala-dvipa,
Shih-tzu(I.of the Lion)

FU-NAN

Vyadhapura

C 80° D 90° E 100° F

EASTERN, CENTRAL
AND
SOUTHERN ASIA,
ca. 440 A.D.

ROUTES OF BUDDHIST PILGRIMS:

———————— *Fa-hsien from Ch'ang-an to India*

and homeward by sea, 399 - 414 A.D.

(Concerning the political states

in China see page 21 IV)

———————— *Chih-meng from Ch'ang-an to Pataliputra*

and back by the same route, 404 - 424 A.D.

- - - - - - - *Gunavarnam from Kashmir by sea*

to Nanking, 397 - 431 A.D.

Lo-yang   *In China Residencies are underlined*

⊙   *Capitals of chou(provinces)*

in the Northern State with the same name

as the corresponding chou

Scale 1:20,000,000

0   200   400   600   800 km.

0   100   200   300   400 miles

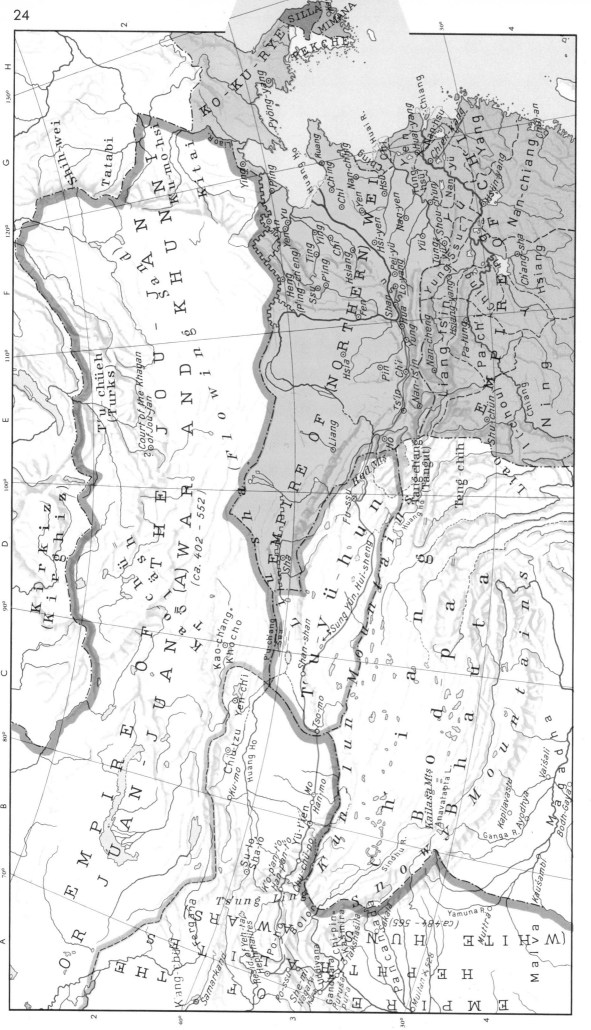

24

THE SOUTHERN CH'I AND THE NORTHERN WEI DYNASTIES, BOUNDARIES OF 500 A.D.

In China Residencies are underlined

⊙ Capitals of chou (provinces), in the northern state with the same name as the corresponding chou; concerning the southernmost chou, see page 22/23

Scale 1:20,000,000

0   200   400   600   800 Km

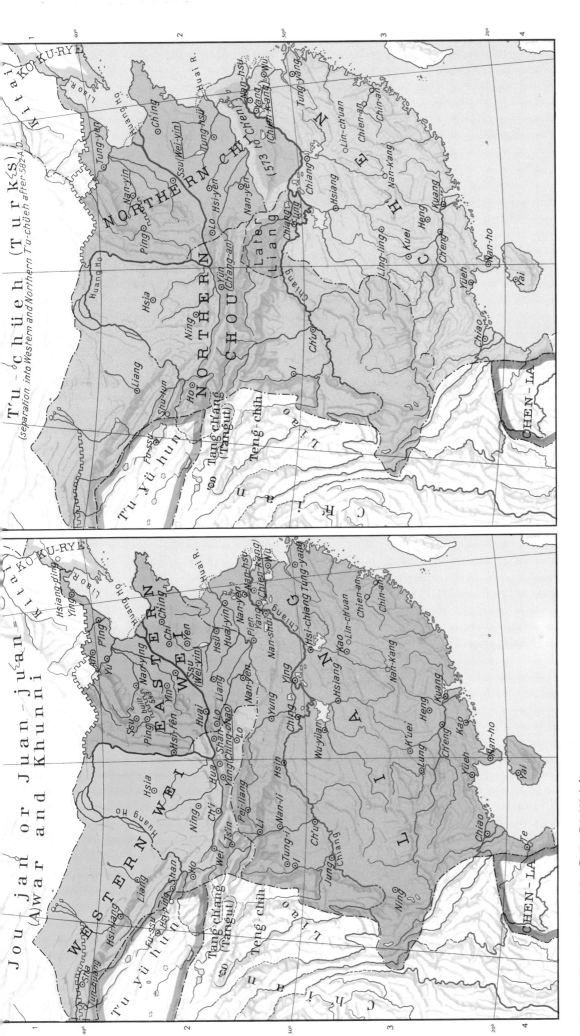

THE DIVISIONS OF CHINA, 535-560 A.D.

Scale 1:20,000,000

In China Residencies are underlined

Capitals of chou (provinces) with the same name as the corresponding chou; capitals with other than chou names in parentheses

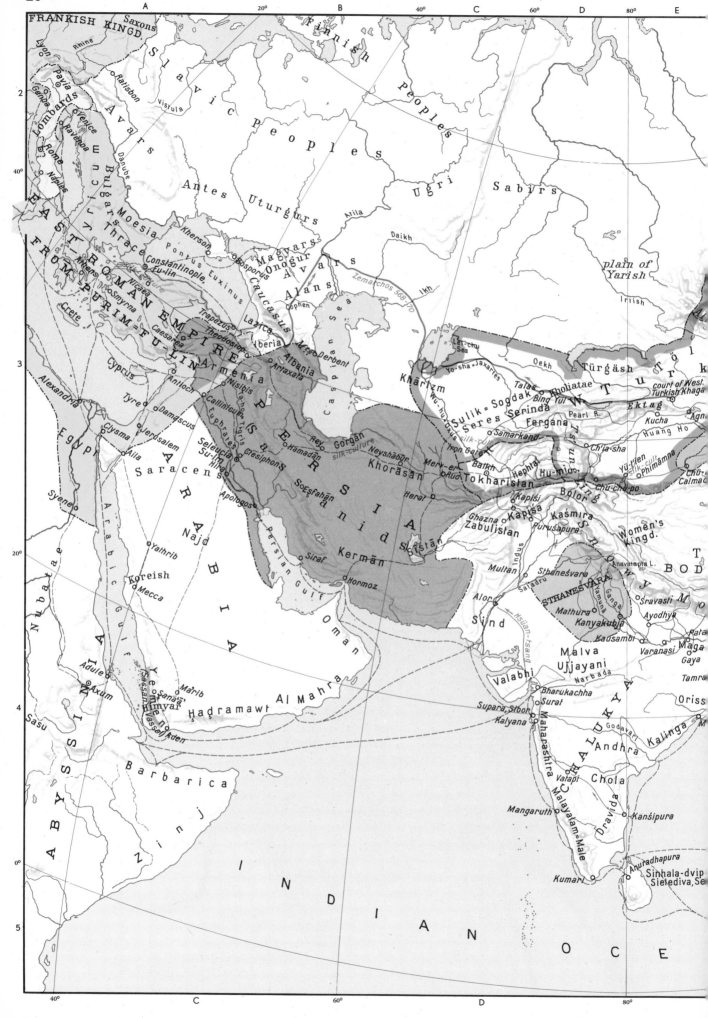

26

ASIA,
ca. 610 A.D

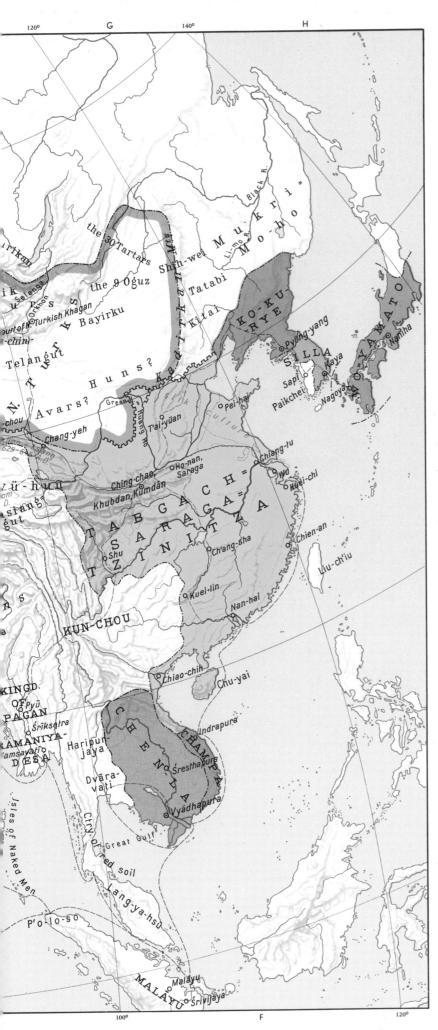

ROUTES OF TRAVELLERS:

──────── *Byzantine ambassador Zemarchos,*

568 - 570 A.D.

──────── *Chinese pilgrim Hsüan-tsang,*

629 - 645 A.D.

- - - - - *Other routes*

120°   G   140°   H

the 30 Tartars

Orkhon
the 9 Oguz

Selenga
court of the Turkish Khagan
Bayirku

Telanġut

N. T'u-küe

Avars? Huns?

-chou

Chang-yeh

-chin-

Shih-wei

Mukri=

Mo-ho

Li-mo-R.

Black R.

Kadirkir Kitai

KO-KU-RYE

Pyöng-yang

SILLA

Sapi

Kaya

Paikchei

YAMATO

Naniha

Nagoya?

Green...

Hwang ho

T'ai-yüan

o Pei-hai

Culture

Chiang-tu

Ho-nan,
Saraga

Wu

Kuei-chi

Ching-chao

Khubdan, Kumdan

TABGACH=
SARAGA=
TZINITZA

Ch'ang-sha

Chien-an

Shu

Liu-ch'iu

Kuei-lin

Nan-hai

tü-hun

sian

gut

KUN-CHOU

Chiao-chih

Chu-yai

KINGD.
OF
PAGAN

Pyū

Srīksetra

RAMANIYA-
DESA

amsavati

Haripun-
jaya

Dvāra-
vati

CHEN-LA

Undrapura

CHAMPA

Sresthapura

Vyādhapura

Isles of Naked Men

City of red soil

Great Gulf

Lang-ya-hsü

P'o-lo-so

MALAYU

Malayu

Srivijaya

100°   F   120°

Scale 1:30,000,000

0   200   400   600   800   1000 km

0   200   400   600 miles

A 100° B 110° C Shih-wei D

Court of
N. Turkish
Ötükän (Tu-chin) Mts Khagan

N o r t h e r n (E a s t e r n)
T'u - c h ü e h (T u r k s)

Kadirkan Mts Tatabi
Kitan
Hsi KO-KU-RY

Yü-men Kuan Shih-chang
Tun-huang Pei Ho Yü-lin renewed 423 A.D. Liao-hsi
Yen Chang-yeh Ying-hsiang Che Yü-yang Pei-p'ing
Chih-wu-wei Mts Ma-i Ying-men Shang-ku
T'u-yü-hun Ling-wu built Lou-fan Po-ling Ho-chien
585 A.D. Sho-fang Hêng-shan Po-hai
Ho-yüan Hsi-p'ing Yen-ch'uan Li-shih Tai-yüan Hsin-tu Yüan Tung-lai
Hsi-hai Chin-ch'eng Tiao-yin Hsi-ho Chao Hsiang-kuo Ch'ing-ho Chi Pei-hai
Chiao-ho P'ing-liang Hung-hua Lung-ch'üan Wu-an Wei Chi Lu Kao-mi
Fou-han Pei-ti Shang Lin-fen Shang- Lang-ya
Ho Lung-hsi An-ting P'ing-i Feng Wen-ch'eng tang Ho-nei Tung Ch'i- Tung-hai
Lin-t'ao Tang- Han-yang Fu-feng Ho- Ho-nan yin
chang Ho-ch'ih (Ch'ang-an) Ching-chao tung Ho-nan Liang Hsia-p'ei
Wu-tu Shun-cheng Fang-ling Hung-nung Hsiang- Jung-yang Ying-ch'uan Yün Ho
P'ing-wu I-ch'eng Han-ch'uan Hsi-yang ch'eng Yüyang Ü Shui Chung-Li
P'u-an Min-shan Ch'ing-hua Hsi-ch'eng Nan-yang Ju-nan Huai R. Ju-yin Li-yang
Chin-shan Shui T'ung-ch'uan Pa-hsi Pa-tung Hsiang-yang Ch'un-ling Han-tung I-yang Huai-nan Tan-yang P'i-ling
Lin-ch'iung Hsin-ch'eng I-ling Ching-ling An-lu Lu-chiang Wu
(Ch'eng-tu) Sui-neng Ch'ing-chiang Nan Chiang-hsia Yung-an Ch'i-ch'un Yü-hang Kuei-chi
Yin-shan Tzu-yang Fou-ling Li-yang Pa-ling Chiu-chiang Sui-an
Mei-shan Lu-ch'uan Chien-an Wu-ling Hsin-an Tung-yang
Yüeh-sui Chien-wei Tsang-k'e Ch'ang-sha Yü-chang Yung-chia
Hêng-shan I-ch'un Lin-ch'uan Chien-an
Ling-ling Kuei-yang Lu-ling
KUN-CHOU Ch'eng-chiang Chih-an Nan-k'ang
(NAN-CHAO) Chih-an Yü Ling Liu-ch'iu
Hsi-p'ing
Ts'ang-wu Hsin-an
Yu-lin Yung-hsi Lung-chou
Chiao-chih Yung-p'ing Nan-hai I-an
Kao-ping
Ho-p'u
Chu-yai
Chiu-chen

THE SUI DYNASTY, 581-618 A.D.

◎   *Capitals of chün (commandery) with more than 100,000 inhabitants*

○   *Capitals of chün (commandery) with less than 100,000 inhabitants*

——   *Highways*

Scale 1:15,000,000

0   100   200   300   400   500   600 km

0   100   200   300   400 m

A 100° B 110° C 120° D

Uigurs

Syr-
Tardush

Ö-ÿükän (Tu-chin) Mts.

Han-hai,
An-pei 663-714

Orghun
court of
N. Turkish Khagan

Tu-wei-chien Mts.

Bayirku

Telangut

Pu-ku

Northern (Eastern)
T'u-chüeh (Turks)

Huns?

Avars?

Hsi-ch'eng

Chung-shou-chiang,
An-pei 714-722

Shan-yü
650-663

Yen-jan,Yün-chung,
Shan-yü 663-698

Hsin-ch'eng,
An-tung 677-714

PO-HAI

Liao-tung
An-tung 676-677

Hsi-an-p'ing
(668-677 to China)

40°

Tun-huang

Su

Kan

Lung-yu

Liang

Shan

Huang Ho

Lan

Ya-lei

Wei

Ching

Ling

Yu

Kuan-nei

Hui

Lin

Hsia

Yüan

Ch'ing

Yen

Hsi

Lung

Lan

Lin

Wei

Ch'in

Fang

T'ung

Ho-chung

Huai

Hsia

Ho-nan

Lu-chi

Lo-yang

Wei

Feng

Ching-chi

Ch'ing-chao
(Ch'ang-an)

Tai-yüan

Fên

Liao

Chin

T'e

Ming

Pei
Wei

Hsiang

Huang

Ts'ao

Che

Ting

Shen

Ying

P'ing-lu

Yen

Tu-li

Wu-hu I.

Teng

Lai

Ching

Mi

Tai Shan

Yün

Hai

Shan-nan

(-hsi)   (-tung)

Li

Sung

Lung

Mao

Che

Kuo

Wan

Kuei

Hsiang

Feng

Pi

Teng

Han R.

Ch'in

Kuang

An

Chiang-ling

Wu

Huang

Chi

Ch'ih

Shu

Hsüan

Huai-nan

Sheng

Ch'ang

N.Chiang

S.Chiang

K'an-pu

Su

Jun

Yang

Chien-nan

Ch'eng-fu

Ya

Ch'ang

Chang

Shih

Ch'ien

Lang

Feng

Yao

T'an

Hung

Fu

Yüan

Ming

Yüeh

Hang

T'ai

Leng

Wu

Ch'u

Ch'ü

Jung

Lu

Ch'en

Ssu

Heng

Mien

Yung

Yü

Ch'u

Chi

Hsin

 Hien-chung)

Chiang-nan

(-hsi)   (-tung)

Chien

Fu

Ting

Ch'üan

Chün

Sui

Yao

712 to 755

Lung-yü
(cap. after 650)

NAN-NING, LIU-CHAO
(NAN-CHAO)

Shan-shan-fu

Ch'eng-chiang

Huan

Kuei

Tao

Shao

Lien

Chang

Ch'ao

T'ien

Wu

Tuan

Kuang

Hsün

Ling-nan

Yung

Chin

Jang

Hsin

Lien

Feng

Chiao
An-nan 681-757

Lei

Yai

Ch'iung

Chang

Tan

Wan-an

Ch'en

Ai

Huan

20°

Scale 1:15,000,000

0 100 200 300 400 500 600 km

0 100 200 300 400 miles

THE T'ANG DYNASTY, 618-906 A.D. - BOUNDARIES OF 700 A.D.

◎   Capitals of fu and chou (prefecture) with more than 100,000 inhabitants

◉   Capitals of fu and chou (prefecture) with less than 100,000 inhabitants

●   Capitals of tu-hu-fu (protectorate)

○   Other places

(Tu-chi) = New province from the division of 734-906

Capitals of provinces and protectorates are underlined

FRANKISH KINGD.
Saxons

Baltic Sea

S L A V I C

Rhine
Geroa
ONaples
Rome
Lombards
Bavaria
Venice
Oder
Vistul
Yumne

A v a r s

Serbs
Danube

Bulgars

P e o p l e s

F i n n i s h

P e o p l e s

Kiev, Kutabah

OBolgar

Bashkir

Smelling Country
Sallam 842-844

Samrik

Sisian
Kimäk

Adkas

EAST-ROMAN EMPIRE
GREATER = FU-LIN

Constantinople

Black
Bulgars

Magyars

Alans

Kherson
Bosporus
Pontus Euxinus

O Nicaea

Crete
Cyprus

Trapezus
Tarsus

Iberia
Caucasus Mts.
Armenia
Tiflis
Shirvan

Sea

Tarkhan
Derbent

Khamlydj
842
Itil

Khazars

G h o z

Sallam
842

Urgench

Khärizm

Saynun R.
Chash

Talas
751
Fergana
Suj-ab

Suj-ab

Talas K A R L U K
(715-766 to China)

An-hsi
Chia-sha

Ammonia
Mts.

Agni

To Ao-s

Antioch
Acco
Jerusalem
Fostat
paper 800
Aidab
Alexandria
Smaller

E-AL JAZIRA
O Damascus
Frat

Al Mawsil
(Mosul)

Tabriz
Azurbäijan
Samarra
(836-882)
porcelain
Resid.749-762

Baghdad Fu-ta,
Ta-ts'in
paper 793

Gilan
Tabaristan
Rey

Neyshabur

Gorgan

Merv
er-Rud

Balkh

Samarkand
paper 751

Il Jayhun R.
Khuttal

Sughd
Shighnan

Bolor
Bru-sa

Shnn-zing

The Four Ga
Hor (to Fu-Tan 670
to China 692

Yü-t'ien
O-don

silk

AlKufah
Resid. 749-762
Ahuaz
AlBasrah

Cotsfahan

K h o r a s a n
Tokharistan

Kapisa
Zabulistan
Gandhara
Kashmir
Purusapura
Ghazna

Kingd.of
Women T'u

Yar

Anavatapta L.

Misr

Taymā

Najd

Medina

Bahr

Bahrain

Kishfars

Shiraz
Siraf

F a r s

Kuhistan
Herat

Kermān

Hormoz

Sistān
Zaranj

Mokrān

Sthanesvara
Multan

Ganga
Kanyakubja

Palali

Kingd. of PAL

Gaya

T'u

Mo
Nepa

Nahr Mihran
Daybul

Oman

Masquat

Mecca
Jiddah

EMPIRE
= TA-SHIH

A L I h
C A J I K

Malva

Valab
Narbada R.

Nasika

Tamralı

KINGD OF RASTRAKUTA

C o u n t r y

of B r a h m a n s

ABYSSINIA
OAxum

Yemen
Sanā
Al Mukhā
Aden

Hadramawt Al Mahrah
Al Mukallā

Barbarica

Kumari

Kūlam-Male
Mo-lai
Calicut

PALLAVA
Chola
Kanšipura

Anuradhapura
Sinhala-d
Shih-tzu

Z i n j

G
R E E N S

ASIA,

ca. 750 A.D.

ROUTES OF TRAVELLERS:

_____ Chinese pilgrim I-ching,

689 - 695 A.D.

- - - - - Chinese pilgrim Wu-k'ung,

751 - 790 A.D.

_____ Other routes

● Arab settlement

Kurikan Han Hai
Chü-chieh Shih Wei Yü-chih
Tartars Mukri=
Fu-kuei the 9 Oguz Mo-ho
Selengao Orkhon R. Chief Resid. Shuai-pin-fu
capital of
Uigurs Bayirku PO-HAI
Altai Mts u r z g h u z Kitai
→Wu-k'ung Hsi Liao-yang (755-935
(789-90) Huns Shan-yü vo Silla) Ho-an
T o h u z Yu-chou SILLA= (cap.794-1868) Nara
(747- SILA Kaya (cap.709-794)
840) Teng-chou WO
Sukchau Han-chou Paikchei
I-k'ung 75 Wei-chou Nagoya Nagasaki
Khamchau silk
N Pien-Ho embroideries
u-yü-hun Chih-ling salt copper articles
-fan Lo-yang Yang-chou fish salt
Tang-hsiang (783-860) Ch'ang-an, Kantu
Khamdan Ming-chou
Li-niu R. tea Hang-chou
Sumpa= Chang-ling camphor I-ching 689-695
E.Kingd. porcelain
of Women Ch'eng-tu copper Chüan-chou Liu-ch'iu
articles Janju
silk
Kuang-chou P
Ta-ho Khanfu A
NAN-CHAO Mt T'un-men C
I
An-nan, Chiu-chou rocks F
PYU Lung-pien silk, porcelain, aloe,
Pagan Lukin tea, camphor, saddles I
Srikṣetra sable-furs C
Pi-ching Elephant rock
CH E N Huan- Mt Chan-pu-lao S
OF LAND OL wang E
802 = KHMER SEA Indrapura Mt Ling A
Dvaravati Men-tu CHAMPA precious stones, gold, pearls,
Phnomkulen Kauthara ivory, horn of rhinoceros, tortoise-shell
(cap.802) Pan- Vyadhapura Pandu- aromatics, drugs
P'an ranga Mt Chün-t'u-lung
Kakola
Ligor
Kalah Kila,
p'o-lu= Ko-lo K
Balus U N
Rami(ni) L U N = D V I P A N T A R A
WAKWAK Strait
of Chih
lan ŚRIVIJAYA=
Malāyu Resid. ance
(SHIH-LI-)FO-SHIH=
SRIBUZA=ZABAG

Scale 1:30,000,000

0   200   400   600   800   1000 km

0   200   400   600 miles

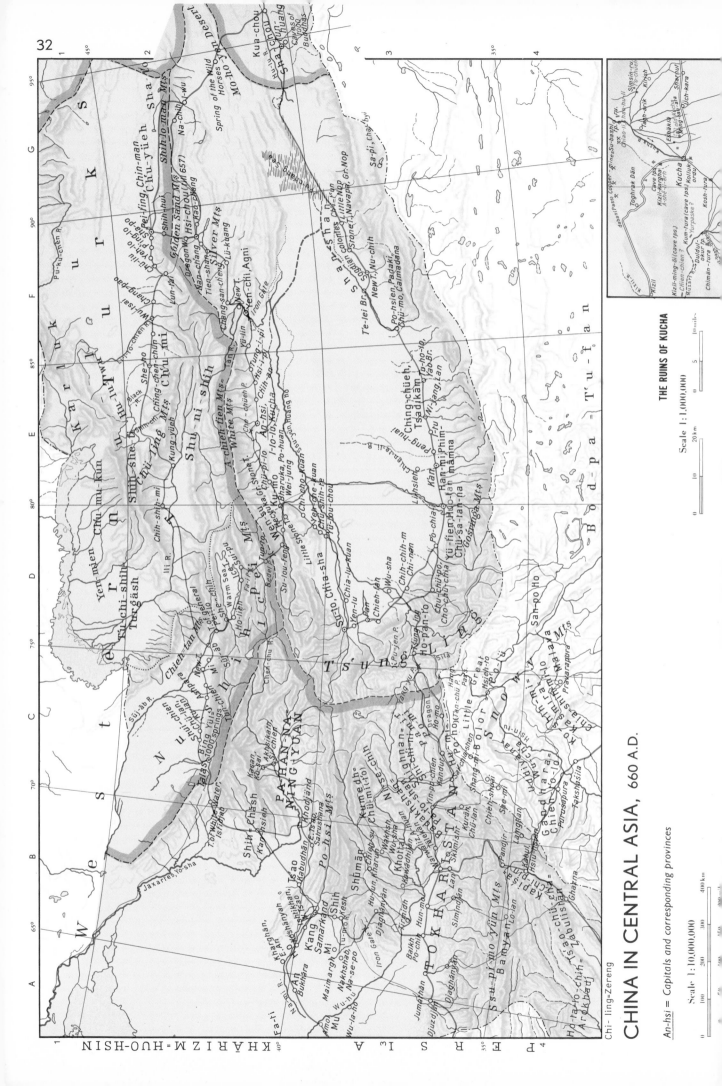

CHINA IN CENTRAL ASIA, 660 A.D.

An-hsi = Capitals and corresponding provinces

Chi- ling-Zereng

Scale 1:10,000,000

THE RUINS OF KUCHA

Scale 1:1,000,000

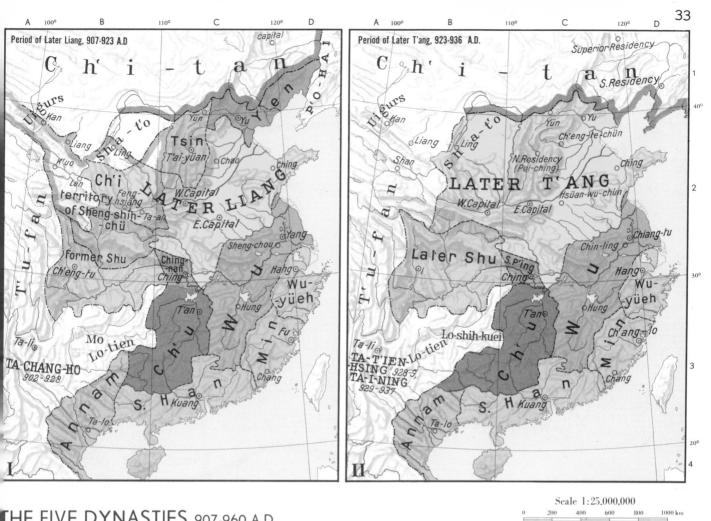

THE FIVE DYNASTIES, 907-960 A.D.

Scale 1:25,000,000

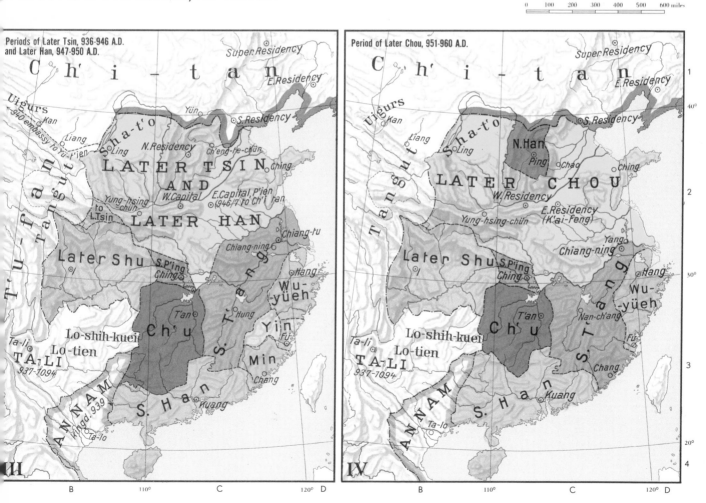

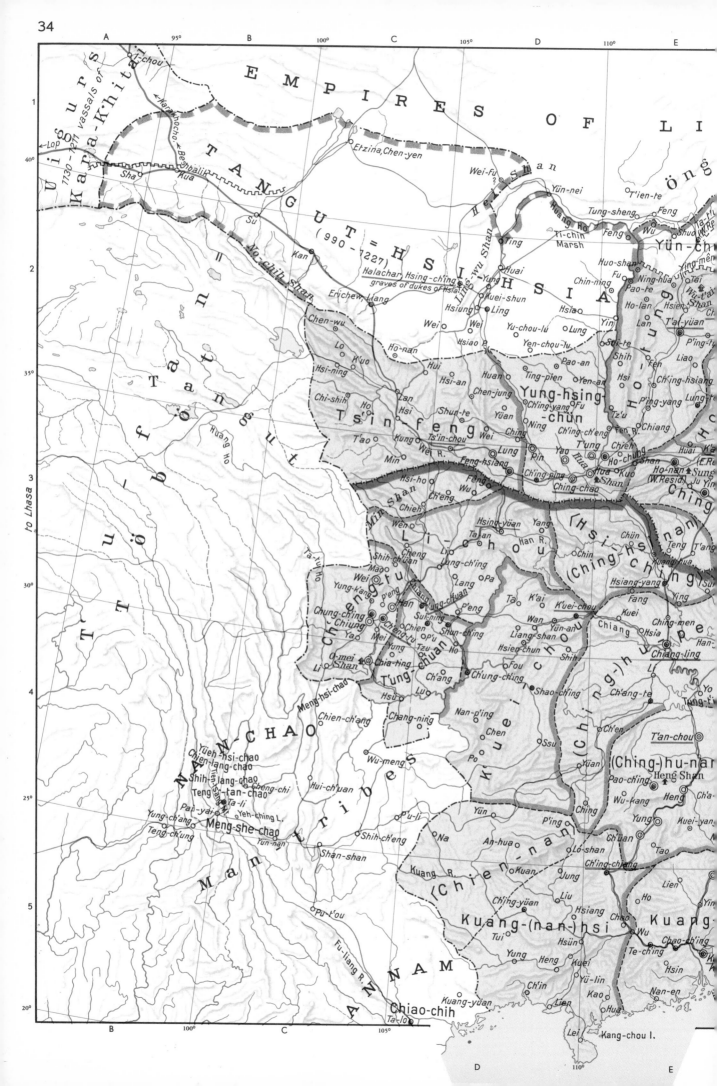

THE SUNG, LIAO AND CHIN DYNASTIES,
960-1280 A.D.

IN THE COUNTRIES OF SUNG AND HSI-HSIA:

- Capitals of *fu* (superior prefectures) with more than 100,000 inhabitants
- Capitals of *fu* (superior prefectures) with less than 100,000 inhabitants
- Capitals of *chün* (prefectures) with more than 100,000 inhabitants
- Capitals of *chün* (prefectures) with less than 100,000 inhabitants
- Capitals of *chou* (superior districts) with more than 100,000 inhabitants
- Capitals of *chou* (superior districts) with less than 100,000 inhabitants
- Capitals of other countries with more than 100,000 inhabitants
- Capitals of other countries with less than 100,000 inhabitants
- Boundary between Southern Sung (1127-1279) and Chin (after 1234 Yüan)

(nan-) = omitted under Southern Sung

⟨Che-hsi⟩ = added under Southern Sung

- ♠ The five holy old-Chinese mountains
- ⚑ The four holy Buddhist mountains

Scale 1:10,000,000

| 0 | 100 | 200 | 300 | 400 km |

| 0 | 50 | 100 | 150 | 200 miles |

THE YANGTZE DELTA
Scale 1:5,000,000

Names of Marco Polo (1272-90) in parentheses

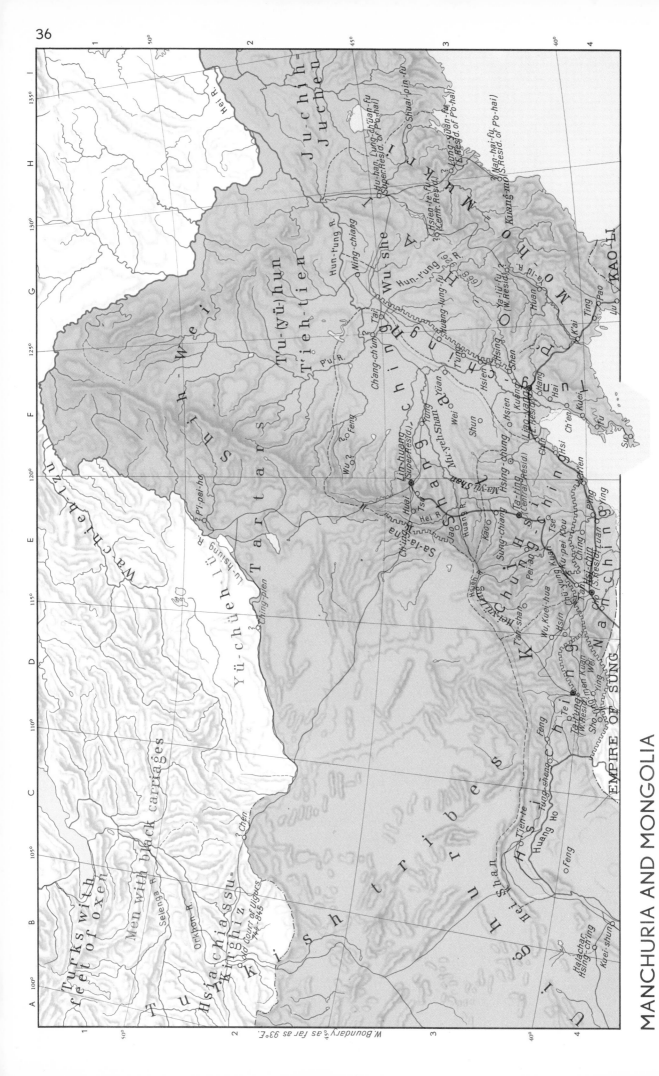

MANCHURIA AND MONGOLIA
UNDER THE LIAO (KITAN) DYNASTY, 937-1125 A.D.

In the 5 provinces of Liao:

Scale 1:10,000,000

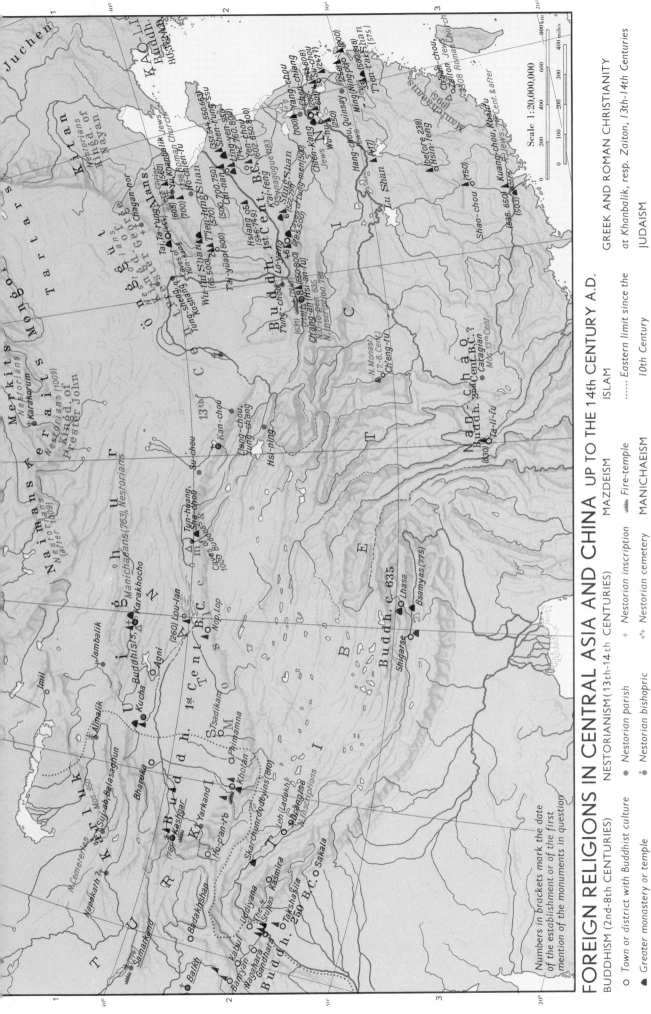

FOREIGN RELIGIONS IN CENTRAL ASIA AND CHINA UP TO THE 14th CENTURY A.D.

BUDDHISM (2nd-8th CENTURIES)

o Town or district with Buddhist culture

▲ Greater monastery or temple

▲ Greater stupa, pagoda or rock-Buddha

(The pagodas according to E. Boerschmann)

Numbers in brackets mark the date of the establishment or of the first mention of the monuments in question

NESTORIANISM (13th-14th CENTURIES)

● Nestorian parish

✝ Nestorian bishopric

✚ Nestorian archbishopric

▲ Nestorian monastery

MAZDEISM

+ Nestorian inscription

✚ Nestorian cemetery

N. Nestorians

Districts with Nestorians in the 7th Century are underlined

🔥 Fire-temple

ISLAM

...... Eastern limit since the

MANICHAEISM

△ Manichaean parish   Mos. Moslems

GREEK AND ROMAN CHRISTIANITY

at Khanbalik, resp. Zaiton, 13th-14th Centuries

JUDAISM

since the 1st Century (?), later at K'ai-feng

Scale 1:20,000,000

A · 60° · B · 70° · C · 80° · D · 90° · E · 100° · F

KHĀRIZM

Kirghiz Oirats

K i m a k

N a i m a n's

Merkit

Selenga R.

Orkhon R.

Tola R.

Shash R. Isfidjab

Jaihun R.

(Vassals

Talas

Bukhara

Osrushana

Shash

Balasaghun

Almalik

Jambalik

K e r a i t s
KINGD. OF PRESTER JOHN

Tirmidh

Samarkand

1141*

1141 (–1208)

Akhsikath

Fergana

(75.6

K A R A K H I T A I

Barskhan

Bakhuan

Beshbalik,
Pei-t'ing

Solmi

S h a - m o (D

Balkh

Eilumedh

Uch-birman?

Kashgar

(1130–1211)

Ugu-Kusan

Kucha

Karakhocho

Komul

Etsina

Shighnan

Yarkand,
Satinh?

Uighur

(847–1218)

Sha

H S I - H S I A

3 · Wakhan

Bamyan

Kabul

Bolor

Yü-t'ien,
Khotan

Hsien

Desert Chien Ta-t'un, Tatran

Chung-yung

Su

(1031–1227)

Kan

Hua

SALJUK
SULTA-
NATE

Han-chou

An-chiu-chou

H T A N G U T = L

Liang

Halacha

Ghazna

GHAZNEVID
SULTANATE OF

KASMIRA,
S(e)(Leh)

Parasara

Pravarapura,

ZANGS Ladakh,

DKAR

Nunti

Guge

Pu-hrangs

Kailasa Mt.

Anavatapta L.
Mapham L.

T' U Ö' B Ö Y U T

Rma-chu

Hsi-ning

Lan

Lin-t'ao

Lin-chao

Ping

Ch'ing-
yüan

Feng-
hsiang

Feng-hsiang

Ling

E M

Hsir

Sindhu

Lahore

Sutlej R.

Sthanesvary

Dbus

Gtsang

Khams

Ch'eng-tu

Shang-chou

Ch'ung-ch'ing

OF

Rajput

Delhi

Ajmer

Muttra

Gwalior

Jamna R.

Kanauj

Agra

Kalinjar

Ganga R.

Prayaga

Zhikatse

Lhasa

R A J P U T S N

N E P A L A D

Anhalvara

Gujerat

M a l w a

Ujjain

Cambay

Surat

Thana

Deogarh

C h e l a

Kanauj

M a g a d h a

Tamralipti

L

NAN CHAO

Ta-li

Yün-nan

Ch'ing-yüa

fu-liang R.

A

Arimaddanapura

P'U-KAN=
PAGAN

Sriksetra

Chiao-chih

Nan-

Chi-y

A n d a m a n   I s.

Hamsavati

Haripun-
jaya

M

C H E N

Lopburi

K A M E

Amara

Indrapura

Sresthapura

Dvaravati

Yasodarapura

Teng-liu-mei?

Lorek

New
Cha

A

C · 80° · D · 90° · E F

ESAN-FO-CH'I = ŚRĪVIJAYA

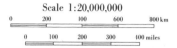

EASTERN, CENTRAL AND SOUTHERN ASIA,
1141 A.D.

Scale 1:20,000,000

0   200   100   600   800 km

0   100   200   300   400 miles

Wa-chieh-tzu

Tartars
(...t)

Wu-ti-kai
Wu-kuo
P'u-hsing
Hui-ning
Wan-hung
Lin-huang
Shang-ching
Ch'ing
Hsü-p'in
Ta-ting
Hsien-ping
Shen
Liao-yang
Tung-ching
Ho-lai
P'ing-jang
K'ai-ching
KAO-LI
Ho-chien
Tung-ping
Shan-tung-hsi-tung
K'ai-feng
Hsü
Shou
Chen-chiang
Chiang-ning
Lin-an Quinsay
Lung-hsing
Chien-ch'ang
Shui-an
Nan-chien
Fu-chou
Kan
Ch'üan, Zayton
Liu-ch'iu
Visaya
P'eng-hu I.
T'an-ma-yen I.
Pai-p'u-yen-Babuyan I.
Liu-hsin, Luzon
+Wan-li rocks
P'u-li-lu, Polillo I.
Li-chin-tung?
Li-han? Lubang
Pa-chi-lung
Chia-ma-yen, Calamian
Pa-lao-yu-Palawan
MA-I

Hun-tung R. Hei R.
built 1138:1200
K pei-ching
Hsing-chung
Cheung-...
Ta-hsing
Pei-... Tung-ping
Ta-...ming
K'ai-feng
...ching
...g-ling
RE...HERN
HG
NG
Osaka Hei-an
Nara
Shikoku
Kyushu
JIH O PEN
N ...chen
Ch...
Mu k'...
F...

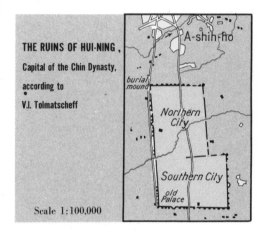

THE RUINS OF HUI-NING,
Capital of the Chin Dynasty,
according to
V.I. Tolmatscheff

A-shih-ho
burial mound
Northern City
Southern City
old Palace

Scale 1:100,000

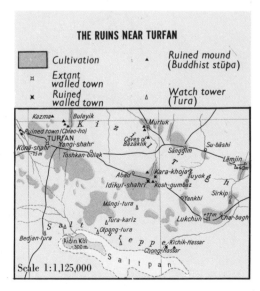

THE RUINS NEAR TURFAN

Cultivation
Extant walled town
Ruined walled town
Ruined mound (Buddhist stūpa)
Watch tower (Tura)

Kazma   Bulayik
Kiz
Ruined town (Chiao-ho)   Murtuk
TURFAN
Yangi-shahr   Caves of Bazaklik
Kōna-shahri ~15m   Su-bāshi
Toshkan-bulak   Sänggim   Lämjin
Abad   Kara-khoja   Tuyok   ~40m
Idikut-shahri   Kosh-gumbaz   Sirkip
Mängi-tura   Yankhi
Tura-kariz   Lukchun ~11m   Char-bagh
Olpang-tura   Kichik-Hassar
Bedjan-tura   Aidin Köl ~300m   Salt steppe   Chong-Hassar
Salt pan

Scale 1:1,125,000

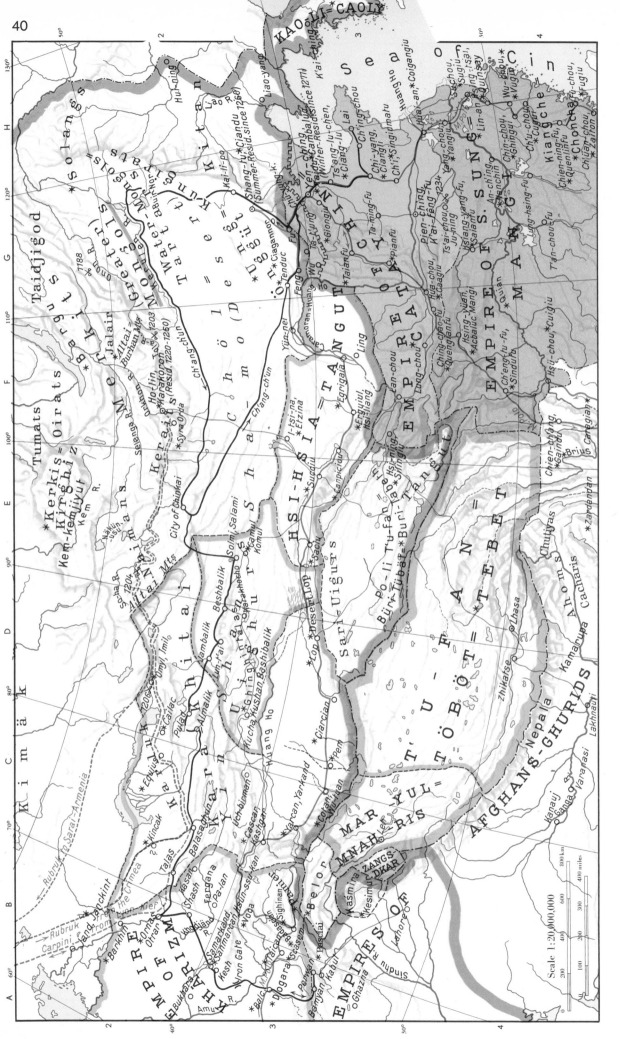

BEGINNINGS OF THE MONGOL EMPIRE · BOUNDARIES OF 1234 A.D.

Countries conquered by the Mongols, 1188–1233 A.D.

Chinese Taoist Ch'ang-ch'un,

Papal embassy of Piano de Carpini, 1245–1247 A.D.

Papal embassy of William of Rubruk,

Marco Polo, 1271–1295 A.D.

Other routes

Geographical names noted by European travellers are marked with a star *

Scale 1:20,000,000

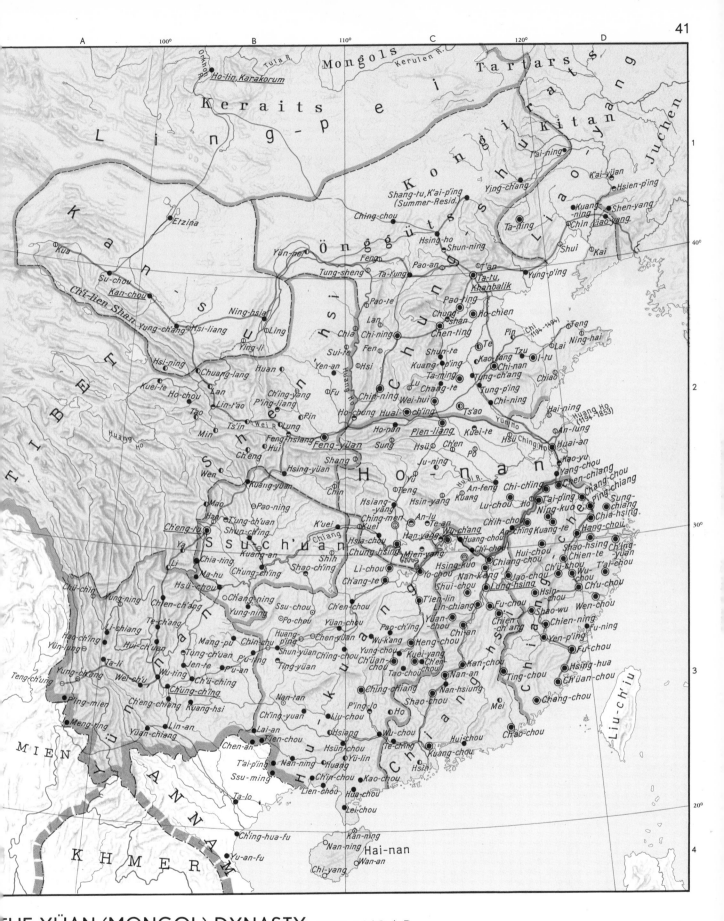

THE YÜAN (MONGOL) DYNASTY, 1280-1368 A.D.

◉	Capitals of lu with more than 100,000 inhabitants	◐	Capitals of chou, 1st class
●	Capitals of lu with less than 100,000 inhabitants	◑	Capitals of chou, 2nd class
◒	Capitals of fu, 1st class	◉	Capitals of an-fu-ssu
◓	Capitals of fu, 2nd class	○	Capitals of chün

Capitals of provinces are underlined

Scale 1:15,000,000

0   100   200   300   400   500   600 km

0   100   200   300   400 miles

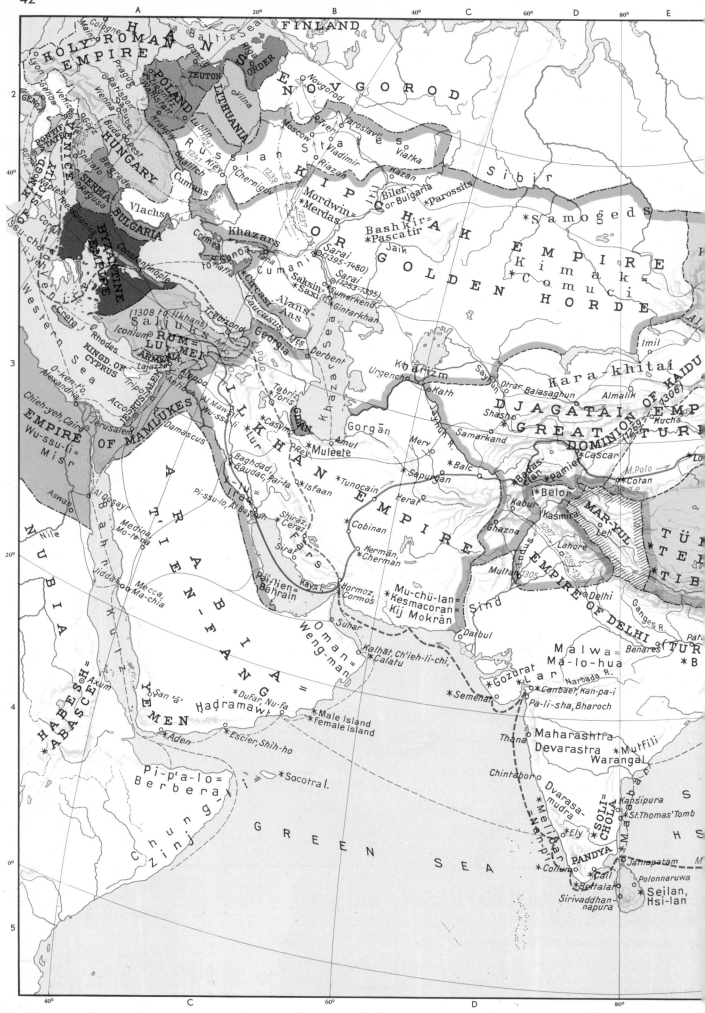

ASIA UNDER THE MONGOLS,
1290 A.D.

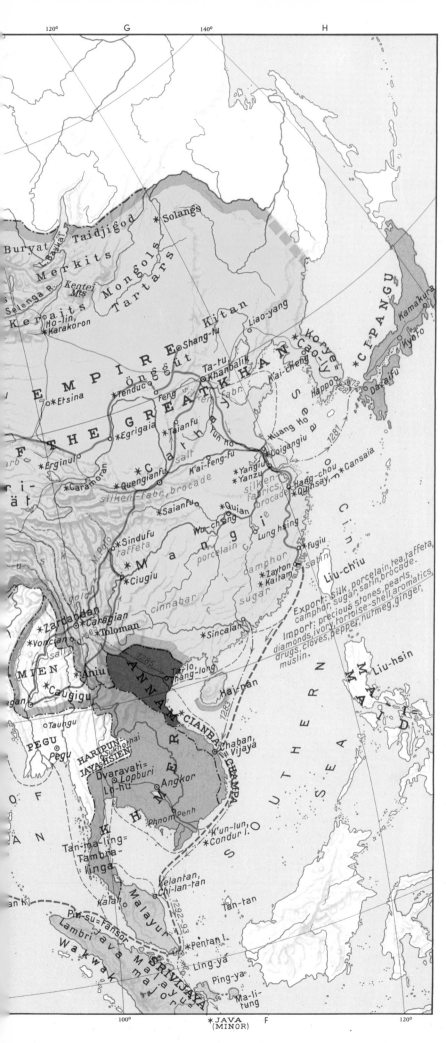

----·--->   Advances of Mongol hordes

━━━━━   Route of Marco Polo, 1271-1295 A.D.

━━━━━   Other routes

Geographical names of European travellers,
mostly of Marco Polo, are marked with a star ✳

Scale 1:30,000,000

| 0 | 200 | 100 | 600 | 800 | 1000 km |

| 0 | 200 | 400 | 600 miles |

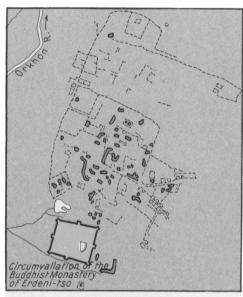

THE RUINS OF KARAKORUM
according to W. Radloff
Scale 1:50,000

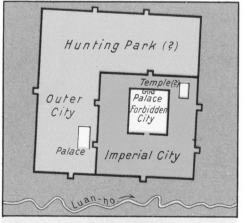

THE RUINS OF SHANG-TU
according to Lawrence Impey
Scale 1:50,000

44

A   100°   B   110°   C   120°   D

Dzasagtu-   Sain-noyan   Urga (1602 Resid. of   × 1388
Khoning,   Tu hetu R.   Hutuhtu Lama)   Buir Nor
Ho-lin, Karakorum   Tola R.   Kerulen R.   Khorchin
-khan   × 1409   Setsen-khan   (Oirat)
(1585 Lamaism)   H   a   l   h   a   -   M   o   n   g   o   l   s   Juchen

T'U-LU-FAN   S   h   a   KHANATE   Chien-chou
=TURFAN   OF CHAHAR
K'ai-p'ing   (1586 Lamaism)   Kuang-yang
Ta-ning   Liao-tung
40°   Chia-yü Kuan   KHANATE OF   Hai-chou   K'ai-chou
Su-chou   ORDOS   TUMET   built 1436   Hsüan-fu-wei   Ning-yüan   Shan-hai Kuan
Shan-hsia   (1572 Lamaism)   Tung-sheng   Pao-an   built 1436   Ku-yung Kuan   Ku-pei K'ou   Yung-p'ing
Kan-chou   built 1595   P'ien-t'ou K'ou   Ta-t'ung   Pao-t'ou   Tzu-ching Kou   Peking
Liang-chou   built 1595   built   Shun-t'ien-fu
Mongols   Ch'ing Hai   Urgai, Ning-hsia   Pao-te   Pao-ting   Ho-chien   Teng-chou   Ning-hai
Torgut (till 1616)   Ling   Chia   Yü-lin   Chen-ting   Lai-chou   Ch'ing-chou   Mi
(often under Mongols,   Ning-hsia-chung   Sui-te   T'ai-yüan-fu   Te   Pin   Kao-t'ang
1572 under Ordos Tümed)   Hsi-ning   Yen-an   Fen-chou   Shun-te   Chi-nan-fu   Tung-ch'ang
Ta-erh-ssu,(Lamaist   Gumbum,   Chuang-   P'ing-yang   Kuang-p'ing   Ta-ming   Ts'ao   Huang Ho
Monastery, 1562 AD)Ho-chou   lang   Lan   Ch'ing-yang   Lu-an   Yen-chou
Chaling Hu   T'ao-chou   Lin-t'ao   P'ing-liang   Pin   Ho-nan   K'ai-feng-fu   Kuei-te   Hsü
Odon-tala   Min-chou   Kung-ch'ang   Lung   T'ung   P'u   Ju   Hsü   Huai-an
TIBET-   Wei R.   Ho-nan   temporary branch   Feng-yang
To-kan-   Huang Ho   Ch'ieh   Feng-hsiang   Hsi-an-fu   Shang   Ju-ning   branch 1375)   Huai R.   Yang-chou
Do-kham   Sung-pan   Han-chung   Yün-yang   Nan-yang   Hsin-yang   An-ch'ing   Ch'u   Chen-chiang   Nan-ch'ing
Lung-an   Hsing-an   Han R.   Hsiang-yang   Te-an   Wu-ch'ang   Ying-t'ien-fu   Nan-ching
Tsa-ku   Ch'eng-tu-fu   Hsiang-yang   Ch'eng-t'ien   Wu-ch'ang   Lü-chou   T'ai-p'ing   Su-chou   Chang-chou   Sung-chiang
T'ung-ch'uan   K'uei-chou   Kuei Ching-chou   Han-yang   Hui-chou   Ning-kuo   Chia-hsing
30°   Ssu-ch'uan   Shun-ch'ing   Han-yang   Huang-chou   Ch'iu-   Hang-chou   Ning-po Liampo
Tien-chuan   Shih-chou   Shih-chu   Chiang   chiang   Shao-   (Port.1533-45)
Chia-ting   Chiang   Hsi-yang   Chang-te   Yao-chou   Che-chiang   hsing
Yüeh-sui   Hsü-chou   Ma-hu   Ch'en-chou   Nan-k'ang   Ch'ü-chou   T'ai-chou
Ning-fan   Ssu-ch'uan   Nan-ch'ang-fu   Kuang-hsin
Li-chiang   Chen-hsiung   Tsun-i   Ssu-nan   Ch'ang-sha   Lin-chiang   Fu-chou   Shao-wu   Wen-chou
Ta-li   Hao-ch'ing   Wu-meng   Wu-wei   Pi-chieh   Shih-ch'ien   Pao-ch'ing   Yüan-chou   Chien-ning
Yao-an   Meng-hua   Wu-ting   Chü   Ssu-chou   Li-p'ing   Chi-an   Ting-chou   Yen-p'ing   Hsing-hua   Fu-chou   Chi-lung
Teng-yüeh   Yung-   Hsün-nien   ching   Kuei-yang-fu   Tu-yün   Heng-chou   Kan-chou   Fu-chien
Shun-ning   ch'ang   Ch'u-hsiung   An-shun   P'u-an   Yung-chou   Nan-an   Ch'üan-chou
Ching-tung   Yün-nan-fu   Cheng-   Kuang-hsi An-lung   Li-p'ing   Nan-hsiung   Ch'ao-chou,   Tai-wan
Meng-ting   Chen-yüan   Yüan-   chiang   Kuei-lin-fu   Shao-chou   Cinceo (Port. 1547-49)
MIEN-TIEN   chiang   Fu-lang R.   Lin-an   Liu-chou   P'ing-lo   Pescadores
=AVA-   Lan-an   Kuang-tung   (Dutch 1622-24)
PEGU   Küang-nan   Ho-chih   Wu-chou   Kuang-chou-fu   Ch'ao-chou
Chen-an   Chao-ch'ing   Hui-chou
Kao-p'ing-chou   Hsün-chou   Kao-chou   Ao-men K'ou, Macao (Port.1557 ff)
LAO-CHUA-   Chiao-tu, Tung-tu   Nan-ning   Yü-lin   Shang-ch'uan I, Sancian (Port. 1550)
LAOTIEN   Ssu-ming   Lampacao (Port. 1554), Lang-pai Chau
(1404 vassal of China)   Muong Chwa   Lien-chou   T'ai-p'ing   Lei-chou
HSIEN-LO=   (absorbed Champa 1471)   Ch'ing-hua, Hsi-tu   Ch'iung-chou
SIAM   Yu-an   Tan   Hai-nan
Yai   Wan

THE MING DYNASTY, 1368-1644 A.D. - BOUNDARIES OF 1580 A.D.

• Capitals of sheng (provinces)   ⊙ Capitals of chou (districts)

◒ Capitals of fu (prefectures)   ⊠ Capitals of wei (guard-districts)

◐ Capitals of shu-chou (districts)

⊕ Capitals of ssu (districts)   —— Port. = Portuguese

Scale 1:15,000,000

0   100   200   300   400   500   600 km

0   100   200   300   400 m

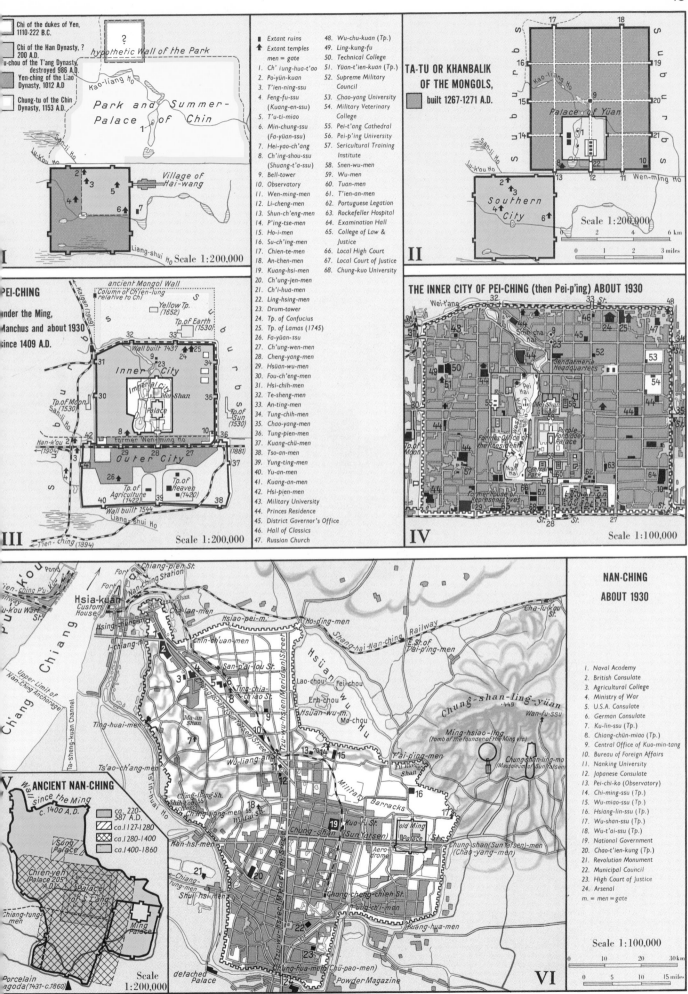

A 20° B 40° C 60° D 80° E

FRANCE
Lyon
GENOA
PONTIF-SEX.
Rome
Lu-mi
NAPLES
Rhine
HOLY ROMAN EMPIRE
Prague
Vienna
Buda Pest
HUNGARY
VENICE
Venice
Akhara
ALBANIA
SERBIA
BOSNIA
Ragusa
Crete
Rhodes
Baltic Sea
Berlin
Danzig
Riga
TEUTO NIC ORDER
Vilna
POLAND-LITHUANIA
Krakow
Kiev
Moldavia
Walachia
Bulgaria
OSMAN
EMPIRE
Adrianople
Brussa
K'u-ssu-tan, Constantinople
Ankuria
Lu-mi
Rum
KINGD. OF CYPRUS
Tarabuluz

NOVGOROD
Novgorod
Grand-duchy of Moscow
Moscow
Khanate of Kazan
Kazan
SIBIR
GOLDEN
Khanate of Crimea
to Genoa
Kaffa
Tana
Sarai
Itil
HORDE
Astrakhan
Khanate of White Horde
DOMINION AND DUGHLAT
Kokcha-Tengiz
Almalik
Yulduz
Bashibalik
Kucha
KHANATE OF DJAGHA
Kashgar
Khotan

ALEXANDRIA
Cairo
EMPIRE
OF
MAMLUKES
Misr
Aswan
NUBIA
Nile
Suakin
Jiddah
Mecca
Medina
Mo-te-na,
Y E N - B I A N
Trebizond
Armenia
Tabriz
Al Mawsil
Haleb
Damascus
Baghdad
'Iraq 'Arabi
Esfahan
Shiraz
Siraf
FARS
Kerman
Hormuz
Makran
Georgia
Azarbaijan
Mazandaran
Sultania
KINGD. OF KARA YUSUF
Caucasus Mts.
Alanse Aas
Sea of Baku
Derbent
Baku
Khanate of Uzbek
Jayhun R.
Kharizm
Bukhara
Merv
Herat
KINGDOM OF KHORASAN
Khorasan
SHAH RUKH
Sistan
Kandahar
Ghazni
Kabul
Balkh
Badak
Sihun R.
Otrar
Sairam
Shahrukkia
Samarkand (Resid. of Timur)
Tashkent
Andizhan
Balkh
Shiuk
Kasmira
Leh
Maryul
TI
Sindhu R.
Lahore
Agra
Jumna R.
Ganges R.
Delhi
KINGD. OF SAIYIDS
NEPAL
Db
Pat

ARABIA
Oman
Masquat
Kalhat
Jiddah
Tien-rang,
San'a'
Yemen
Aden
Hadramawt
Shihr
Djofar
Sind
Karachi
Rajputana
Chitorgarh
Malwa
Gujarat
Narbada R.
Broach
Fang-pai
Bombay
Daulatabad
BAHMANI KINGDOM
Wu-tieh
Orissa

HABASH
Sa-la, Zeila
Madadjan
Su-ma-li= Somalia
Adjam
Socotra
Hsu-wen-na, Vijayanagar
VIJAYANAGAR
Peng-chia-lo, Mangalore
Pan-chi-ni-na, Fandaraina
Ku-li-fo, Calicut
Ko-chih, Cochin
Ko-lan, Quilon
Meliapur
Sha-li-pa-tan, Seringapatam
Seng-ka-la, Hsi-lan, Sail
Kao-lang-pu, Colomb
Mt. of Gr. Buddh. Adam's Peak

Zinj
Ts'eng-ya-lo, Zanguebar
Mu-ku-tu-shu, Mogadisho
Pu-la-wa, Barawa
Chu-pu, Jubo
Ya-li, Galle
Liu Is, Tieh-kan Is

40° C 60° D 80°

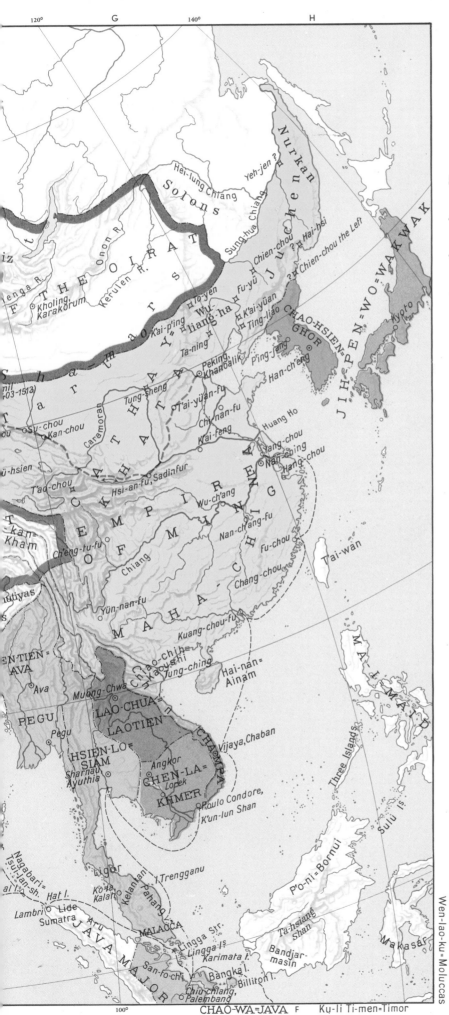

ASIA DURING THE MING DYNASTY –

BOUNDARIES OF 1415 A.D.

Boundary of the Empire of Timur at his death, 1405 A.D.

Embassy of Shahrukh from Herat to Peking, 1419-1420 A.D.

Homeward journey, 1421-1422 A.D.

Cruises of the admirals Ma Pin (1403 A.D.) and Cheng Ho (1405-07, 1408-11, 1412-15, 1417-19, 1421-22, 1424-25, 1431-33 A.D.) to the Indian Ocean

⌑ Seat of a Chinese guard district

Scale 1:30,000,000

0 200 100 600 800 1000 km

0 200 100 600 miles

THE NORTHWESTERN FRONTIER OF CHINA,

15th Century A.D.

Scale 1:15,000,000

Wen-lao-ku=Moluccas

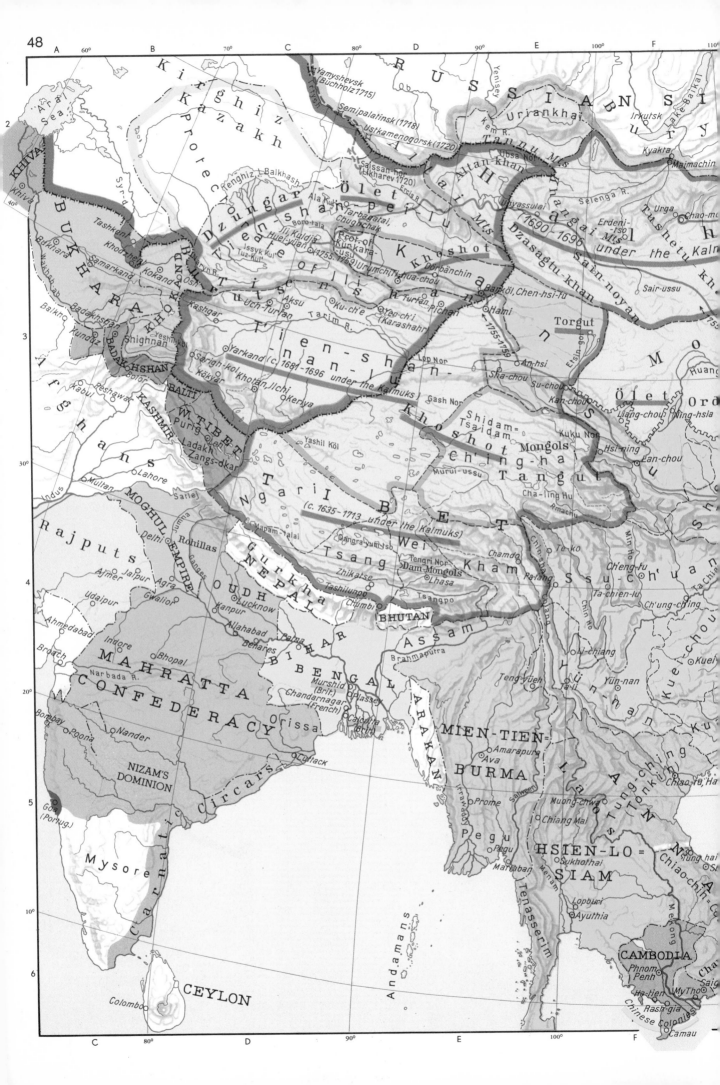

48

RUSSIAN SI
BERIA

Kirghiz
Kazakh
Protec
torate

Aral
Sea

KHIVA
Khiva

BUKHARA

KHOKAND

BADAKHSHAN
Afghans
Kabul
Peshawar
KASHMIR
BALTI
W. TIBET
Purig
Ladakh
Zangs-dkar

Dzungar
Ölet-peiliu
Tien-shan Protectorate of Ili
Prot. of Kurkara-usu (1755-1759)
Khoshot and
(1755-1759)

Tien-shan-
Yarkand (c 1681-1696) under the Kalmuks
Sarigh-kol Khotan, Ilchi
Kökyar Kerlya

Khoshot
Ching-hai
Tangut

Torgut

Ölet Ord

Mongols
Hsi-ning Lan-chou

Shidam = Tsaidam
Kuku Nor
Muru-ussu Cha-ling Hu

Rajputs
Delhi
Rohillas
Agra
Jaipur Ajmer
Udaipur Gwalior
Ahmedabad

MOGHUL EMPIRE
Jumna
Ganges

Lahore
Multan
Indus

GURKHA
NEPAL
OUDH
Lucknow
Kanpur
Allahabad
Patna
Benares
BIHAR
BENGAL
Murshid (Brit.)
Chandarnagar (French) Plassey
Calcutta (Brit.)
Orissa

Mapam-talai
Dangra yum tso
Tengri Nor
Zhikatse Dam-Mongols
Tashilunpo Lhasa
Chumbi Tsangpo
BHUTAN

Tari BET (c. 1635-1713 under the Kalmuks)
Ngari
Tsang Wei Kham
Chamdo

Assam
Brahmaputra

Ssu-ch'uan
Ch'eng-fu
Ch'ung-ching
Ta-chien-lu

MAHRATTA
CONFEDERACY
Narbada R.
Indore
Bhopal
Nander
Broach
Bombay
Poona

NIZAM'S DOMINION

Northern Circars

Carnatic

Mysore

Goa (Portug.)

CEYLON
Colombo

Cuttack

ARAKAN

MIEN-TIEN = BURMA
Amarapura
Ava
Prome
Pegu
Pegu
Martaban

Andamans

Irrawaddy
Salween

HSIEN-LO = SIAM
Chiang Mai
Muong-chwa
Sukhothai
Lopburi
Ayuthia
Menam

Tenasserim

Yün-nan
Teng-yüeh
Ta-li

Lai-chou

Tung-ching
Tonking

CAMBODIA
Phnom Penh
Ha-tien
Rach-gia
Camau
Saigon
My Tho
Chinese colonies

EASTERN CENTRAL AND SOUTHERN ASIA,
1760 A.D.

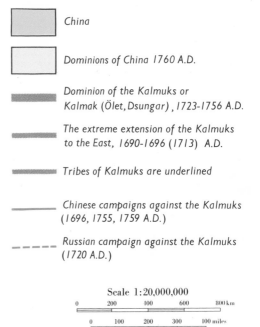

Legend:

▨	China
▨	Dominions of China 1760 A.D.
▬	Dominion of the Kalmuks or Kalmak (Ölet, Dsungar), 1723-1756 A.D.
▬	The extreme extension of the Kalmuks to the East, 1690-1696 (1713) A.D.
▬	Tribes of Kalmuks are underlined
▬	Chinese campaigns against the Kalmuks (1696, 1755, 1759 A.D.)
- - -	Russian campaign against the Kalmuks (1720 A.D.)

Scale 1:20,000,000

0   200   100   600   800 km

0   100   200   300   100 miles

Map labels:

120° H 130° I 140° J

Albazin, Amur, Sakhalin-ula, Hei-lung Chiang, Aigun, oMergen, Tsitsihar, Hailar, Buir Nor, Argun R., Ilka R., i-khan R., Khorchin, Betuna, Ninguta, Chi-lin, original seat of the Manchus, Shen-yang, Liao-yang, Ch'eng-te (Jehol) (Summer Resid.), Liao R., P'ing-jang, Shun-t'ien-fu, Peking, Teng-chou, Ching-ch'eng, Chi-nan, SHAN-tung, Huang Ho, Huang-ho, K'ai-feng, Chiang-nan, Chiang-ning, Nan-ching, Yangtze R., An-ch'ing, Hang-chou, Wu-ch'ang, Ning-po, Che-chiang, Wen-chou, Ch'ang-sha, Kiang-hsi, Fu-chien, Fu-chou, Hsia-men (Amoy), Chi-lung, Tai-pei, T'ai-chung, T'ai-wan, Formosa (Kingd. 1662-1683), Fort Zelandia (Dutch 1624-1662), Kuang-chou, Canton, Macao (Portug.), -tung

Tarrakei, Ol. in front of the mouth of Sakhalin, Karafuto, La Perouse Strait, Yezo, Ainu, Sea of Japan, Toyama, Edo, Kyoto, Osaka, JIHPEN=JAPAN, Shikoku, Kyushu, J. Hirado (Dutch 1609-1636), Nagasaki, J. Deshima (Portug. 1635-1639, Dutch Factory 1641-1854), Tanega, Liu-chiu Is

CHAO-HSIEN=KOREA, Protectorate of Chi-lin, Kyongheung, Masampho, Fusan, Yellow Sea

Mts Solons or Solons, Dahūr, Sung-hua, Daghestan

Luzon, PHILIPPINES (Spanish 1569-1762, 1764-1898, British 1762-1764), Manila, Batan Is, Babuyan Is, Palawan, Caracel Is

G 120° H 130°

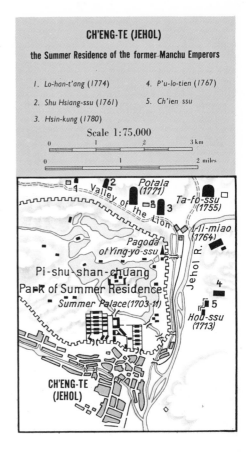

CH'ENG-TE (JEHOL)
the Summer Residence of the former Manchu Emperors

1. Lo-han-t'ang (1774)
2. Shu Hsiang-ssu (1761)
3. Hsin-kung (1780)
4. P'u-lo-tien (1767)
5. Ch'ien ssu

Scale 1:75,000

0   1   2   3 km

0   1   2 miles

Valley of the Lion, Potala (1771), Ta-fo-ssu (1755), I-li-miao (1764), Pagoda of Ying-yo-ssu, Pi-shu-shan-chuang, Park of Summer Residence, Summer Palace (1703-11), Jehol R., Hou-ssu (1713), CH'ENG-TE (JEHOL)

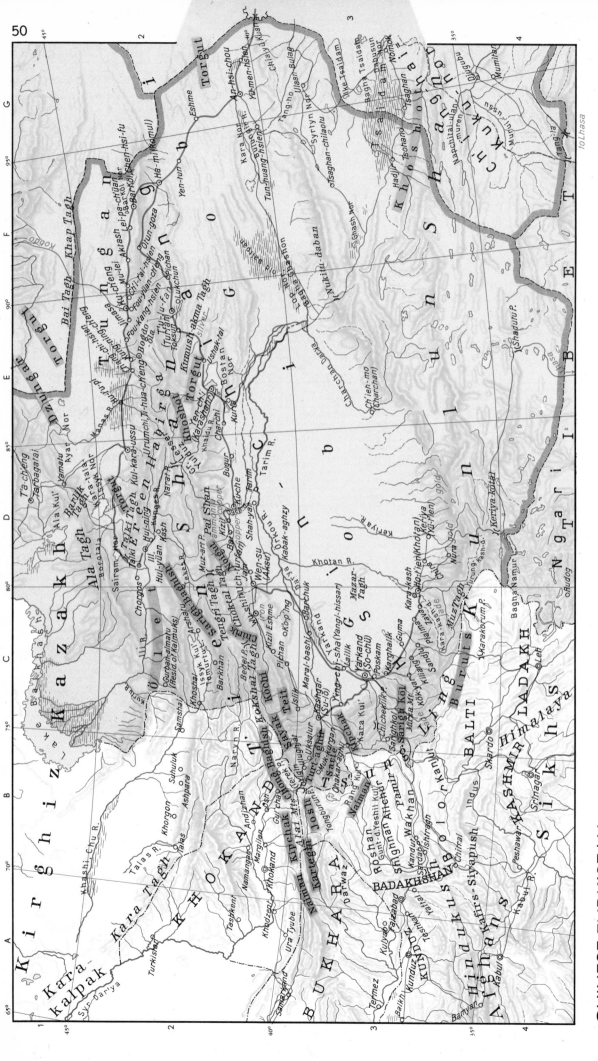

50

CHINESE TURKISTAN, 1820 A.D.

Scale 1:10,000,000

Nomadic tribes of Kalmuks (Kalmak)

Nomadic tribes of Buruts (Kara-Kirgiz)

Later appellations of towns are in parentheses

cheng (Chin.) = walled town

hsien (Chin.) = district town

Kul' (Turk.) = lake

Nor (Mong.) = lake

Tagh (Turk.) = mountain

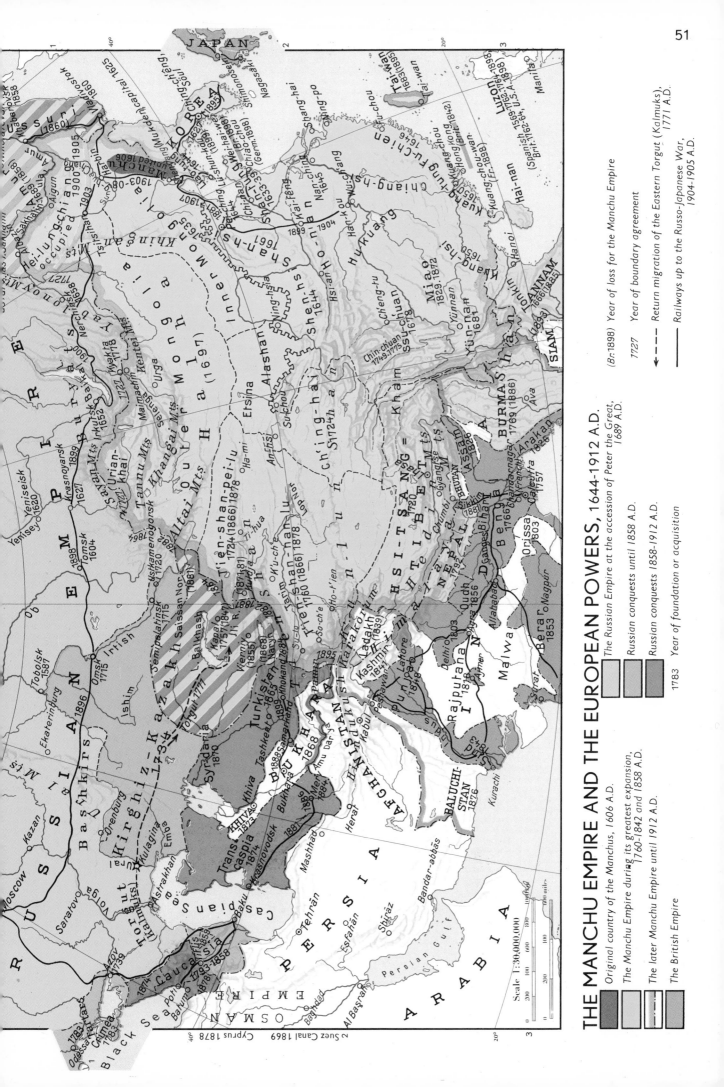

THE MANCHU EMPIRE AND THE EUROPEAN POWERS, 1644-1912 A.D.

Original country of the Manchus, 1606 A.D.

The Manchu Empire during its greatest expansion, 1760-1842 and 1858 A.D.

The later Manchu Empire until 1912 A.D.

The British Empire

The Russian Empire at the accession of Peter the Great, 1689 A.D.

Russian conquests until 1858 A.D.

Russian conquests 1858-1912 A.D.

1783   Year of foundation or acquisition

(Br.1898) Year of loss for the Manchu Empire

7727   Year of boundary agreement

- - - → Return migration of the Eastern Torgut (Kalmuks), 1771 A.D.

———   Railways up to the Russo-Japanese War, 1904-1905 A.D.

Scale 1:30,000,000

Map of China and surrounding regions

OUTER MONGOLIA

INNER MONGOLIA

Tsun-sünit

Mangan B.

Ude

Sudji

Shara-murun

Khobr

Durbot

Pei-ling-miao

Tsagan-chulutai

Wu-yüan

Kuei-hua-ch'eng

Sui-yüan

Pao-t'ou

Sho-ping

Ta-t'ung

Ottok

Ordos

Pao-te

Ning-wu

Yü-lin

Chia

T'ai-yüan

Hsin

P'ing-

Liao

Fen-chou

Ts'in

Ning-hsia

Hua-ma-ch'in

Yen-an

Hsi

Ho

Lu-an

Ling

Chung-wei

Huan

Fu

P'ing-yang

Chiang

Tse

P'ing-yüan

Hai-ch'eng

Ku-yüan

Ching-yang

Ning

Pin

P'u-chou

Chieh

Shan

Ho-nan

Huai-

Ts'in

Kai-

Yü

Etsina

Alashan Ölet

Torguta

Chü-yen L.

P'ing-shu-yüan

Mao-mu

Shande-miao

Huang Ho

Ting-k'ou

Kishi Baru

Ha-mi (Komul)

Hsing-hsing-hsia

An-hsi

Yü-men

Tun-huang

Syrtyn Nor

Oulanbulak

Chia yü-kuan

Su

Kao-t'ai

Kan-chou

Shan-tan

Chen-fan

Ting-yüan-ying

Yung-ch'ang

Liang-chou

Ku-lang

Kara Nor

Karluk

Tibetans

Tangut

Dulan-kitt

Ch'ing Hai Kuku Nor

Tenkar

Hsi-ning

P'ing-fan

Ching-yüan

Nien-po

Kuei-te

Ho

Ti-tao

Lan-chou

Ku-yüan

Gumbum

T'ao-chou

Hua-p'ing-ch'uan

Kung-ch'ang

Ch'ing-shui

Feng-hsiang

T'ung-chou

Han

Hsi-an

Tung-kuan

Shang

Hadjin

Tsohan

Barun-kureu

Dichu-rabdan

Chala-ling-hu

Djugubu

Mumian

Lama-tologoi

Mo-chu-ko-ch'i Ho

Sokpa

Kegudo

Chinosha Chiang

to Lhasa

Riuchi

Bargo

Chamdo

Darge-gonchen

Lan-tsang-chiang

Lhodjong

Ta-chin Chiang

Sung-pan

Min Ho

Wen

Chieh

Han-chung

Han Chiang

Yün-yang

Nan-yang

Hsing-an

Hsiang-yang

An-lu

CH'IEN-TSANG = ANTERIOR TIBET

Showa

Namcha-barwa

Kandse

Drango

Cucin

Mou-kung

Zanla

Li-fan

Mao

Mien

Pao-ning

Sui-ting

K'uei-chou

Wan

Ching-men

I-ch'ang (1877)

Ching-chou

Sha-shih (1896)

Pa-an

Batang

Lirang

Kang-ting

Ta-chien-lu

Tien-ch'uan

Ya-chou

Mei

Ch'eng-tu

Chiung

Shun-ch'ing

T'ung-ch'uan

Chung

Shih-nan

Hsien-feng

Mishmi

Drewa-gomba

Rima

Menkrong

Mo-s

Chung-kien

Wei-hsi

Li-chiang

A-lung

Hsü-chou

Ta Chiang

Lu

Tz'u

Ch'ung-ch'ing (1897)

Ch'ih-shui

Yu-yang

Ssu-nan

Sung-t'ao

Ch'en-chou

Yung-shun

Yu-sui

T'ung-t'ing

ASSAM

Sadiya

Dibrugarh

Kachin

Maingkwan

Myitkyina

Bhamo

Momein (1902)

Teng-yüeh

Yung-ning

Ning-yüan

Chao-t'ung

Chen-hsiung

Yung-ning

Pi-chieh

Tsun-i

T'ung-jen

Feng-huang

Yüan-chou

Huang-chou

Hunan

Hsiang-t'an (1904)

Ch'en

Pao-ch'ing

Heng-yang

MIEN-TIEN = BURMA (1886 to British India)

Ku-yung-chou

Yung-ch'ang

Meng-hua

Ta-li

YPE = MIN YÜN-NAN

Yung-pei

Hui-li

Tung-ch'uan

Ta-ting

Miao

An-shun

Kuei-yang

Tu-yün

P'ing-yüeh

Li-p'ing

Ching

Yung-chou

Ch'en

Hsiang

Mandalay

Shun-ning

Ching-tung

Chu-hsiung

Yün-nan

P'ing

Kuei

Tu-shan

Tu-yün

I-chia

Yao

Kuei-lin

Ho-lao

Yao

Wing-yüan

Shao-

Chen-yüan

Chen-pien

P'u-erh

Lin-an (1889)

Kuang-hsi

Kuang-nan

Ssu-ch'eng

Ch'ing-yüan

Liu-chou

Lien

P'ing-lo

Meng-lien

Meng-hun

Takuis

Meng-tzu (1889)

Yüan-chiang

K'ai-hua

Hsing-i

Po-se

Chen-an

Ssu-en

Hsün-chou

Wu-chou (1897)

San-shui (1897)

Kuang-chou (Canton)

Keng-tung

Ssu-mao (1892)

Ho-k'ou

Lao-kai

Kuei-shun

Lung-chou (1889)

Ta-p'ing

Nan-ning (1901)

Lo-ting

Kuei

Kuang-tung

So

Sorgkoiching

Liang-shan Langson

Shang-ssu

Ch'in

Lien-chou

Yü-lin

Kao-chou

Mekong

MANSIANG

Tung-iching = Tonkin (1885 to France)

LAOS

Ho-nei Hanoi

Pei-hai Pakhoi (1877)

Lei-chou

Kuang-chou-wan (1898 to France)

Hsiao-lao = Hoc-lo

Gulf of Tonkin

Ssu-Ch'uan

Kuei-chou

Kuang-hsi

Hsin-chiang

Hsin-kiang

Kansu

Shensi

Shansi

Honan

Hupei

to Lhasa

THE CH'ING (MANCHU) DYNASTY-
BOUNDARIES OF 1900 A.D.

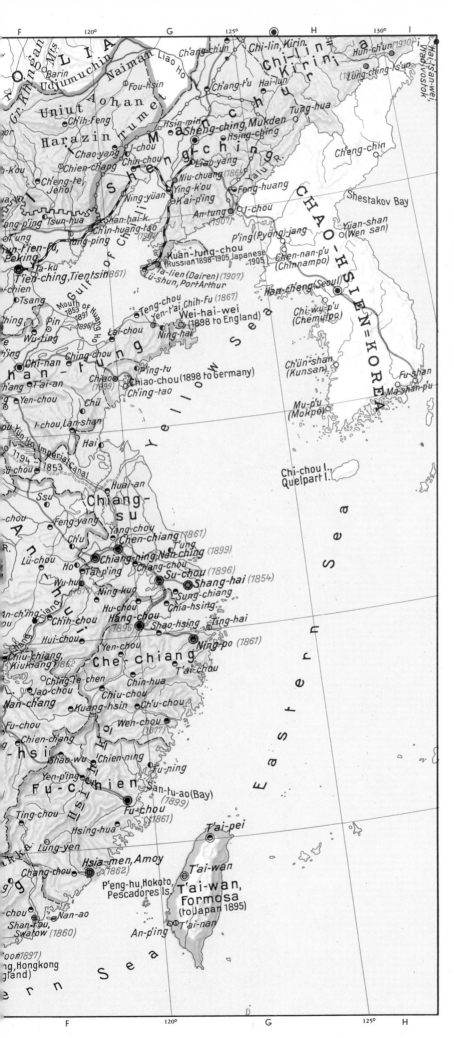

Legend:

	Tributary territory
	Ceded territory
◉	Treaty port with date of customs opening Chen-chiang *(1861)*
⟲	Lamaist monastery
Yao =	Half-independent aborigines of China
●	Capitals of sheng (provinces)
◓	Capitals of fu (prefectures)
◐	Capitals of chih-li-chou (districts)
◑	Capitals of chih-li-t'ing (districts)
◍	Capitals of hsien (subdistricts)
⊙	Capitals of chou (subdistricts)
⊖	Capitals of t'ing (subdistricts)
◎	Towns with more than 500,000 inhabitants
◎	Towns with more than 100,000 inhabitants

Map labels (selection):

Hsing-an Mts. — Gr. Khingan — Barin — Udjumuchin — Naiman — Liao Ho — Ch'ang-ch'un — Chi-lin, Kirin — Chi-lin, Kirin — Hun-ch'un (1910) — Hai-tsan-wei, Vladivostok — Aohan — Fou-hsin — Ch'ang-t'u — Hai-lun — Tung-hua — (Tung-ching-ts'un) — Uniut — Ch'ih-feng — Hsin-min — Sheng-ching, Mukden — Hsing-ching — Ch'eng-chin — Harazin — Chao-yang — I-chou — Chin-chou — Liao-yang — Chien-chang — Yalu R. — Chao-yang — Jehol — Ning-yüan — Niu-chuang (1864) — Ying-k'ou — Feng-huang — Shestakov Bay — Ch'eng-te — Ch'in-huang-tao (1901) — An-tung (1907) — I-chou — Yüan-shan (Wen san) — Tsun-hua — Shan-hai-k. — Kuan-tung-chou (Russian 1898-1905 Japanese 1905) — P'ing (Pyöng)-jang — Peking — Ta-lien (Dairen) (1907) — Chen-nan-p'u (Chinnampo) — Ta-ku — Lü-shun, Port Arthur — Tien-ching, Tientsin (1861) — Han-ch'eng (Seoul) — Teng-chou — Chih-fu (1867) — Chi-wu-p'u (Chemulpo) — Yen-t'ai — Mouth of Huang Ho 1853 — Wei-hai-wei (1898 to England) — Pin — Lai-chou — Ning-hai — Wu-ting — Ch'ün-shan (Kunsan) — Chi-nan — P'ing-tu — Fu-shan — Ma-shan-p'u — T'ai-an — Chiao-chou (1898 to Germany) — Mu-p'u (Mokpo) — Yen-chou — Ching-tao — Yellow Sea — CHAO-HSIEN=KOREA — Hai — Imperial Canal 1194-1853 — Chi-chou I., Quelpart I. — Chiang-su — Huai-an — Feng-yang — Yang-chou — Chen-chiang (1861) — Nan-ching (1899) — Ch'u — Chiang-ning, Nan-ching — Ch'iang-chou — Su-chou (1896) — Shang-hai (1854) — Ho — T'ai-p'ing — Wu-hu (1877) — Ning-kuo — Sung-chiang — Chia-hsing — Hu-chou — Hang-chou (1896) — Shao-hsing — Ting-hai — Hui-chou — Yen-chou — Ning-po (1867) — Chiu-chiang, Kiukiang (1862) — Che-chiang — T'ai-chou — Ching-te-chen — Chin-hua — Jao-chou — Chiu-chou — Nan-chang — Kuang-hsin — Ch'u-chou — Wen-chou (1877) — Chien-ch'ang — Shao-wu — Chien-ning — Fu-ning — Yen-p'ing — San-tu-ao (Bay) (1899) — Fu-chien — Ting-chou — Fu-chou (1861) — Hsing-hua — T'ai-pei — Lung-yen — Hsia-men, Amoy (1862) — P'eng-hu, Hokoto, Pescadores Is. — T'ai-wan — Chang-chou — Nan-ao — Shan-t'ou, Swatow (1860) — An-p'ing — T'ai-wan, Formosa (to Japan 1895) — T'ai-nan — (Kowloon 1897) — Hongkong (England) — Eastern Sea — Southern Sea — Gulf of Chih-li — Shan-tung — An-hui

Scale 1:10,000,000

0 — 100 — 200 — 300 — 400 km

0 — 50 — 100 — 150 — 200 miles

CHINA 1930

Scale 1:18,000,000

- – – – Provincial boundary   —— Railway
- ☐ Town with more than 500,000 inhabitants
- ◉ Town with 100,000 - 500,000 inhabitants
- ○ Town with less than 100,000 inhabitants

SOVIET UNION

CHOSEN

Hei-lung-chiang

Chi-lin

Liao-ning

Jehol

Chahar

Sui-yüan

Ning-hsia

MONGOLIA

SOVIET UNION

Hsin-chiang

Kan-su

Ch'ing-hai

Tibet

Hsi-k'ang

Ssu-ch'uan

Shen-hsi

Shan-hsi

Ho-pei

Shan-tung

Ho-nan

An-hui

Chiang-su

Che-chiang

Hu-pei

Hu-nan

Chiang-hsi

Fu-chien

Kuei-chou

Kuang-hsi

Kuang-tung

Yün-nan

Burma

NEPAL

BHUTAN

BRITISH INDIA

Hai-nan

Tonkin

Kuang-tung
Kuang-chou-wan (Fr.)

T'ai-wan (Jap.)

PEI-PING
TIEN-CHING
NAN-CHING
SHANG-HAI
WU (SU-CHOU)
HAN-K'OU
CH'ANG-SHA
CHUNG-CH'ING
CHENG-TU
KAI-FENG
PA

Semipalatinsk
Alma Ata
Frunze
Su-fu (Kashgar)
I-ning (Kuldja)
Wen-su
Kucha
Khotan
Yü-t'ien
Leh
Ha-mi
Ti-hua
Yü-men
Chü-yen
Kandse
Garlok
Shigatse
Gyang-tse
Lhasa
Sadiya
Bhamo
Paoshan
Meng-tzu
Yün-ning
K'un-ming
Ta-li
Pa-shan
Yu-shu
Ch'ang-tu
Ta-tsien-lu
Ya-an
Ts'an-wei
Li-chiang
Kuei-lin
Li-p'ing
Kan
Hengyang
Shao-yang
Ch'ang-te
Chir-an
Nan-ch'ang
Yü-shan
Ch'ien-yang
Swatow
Amoy
Fu-chou
Chao-an
Ta-i
Wang
I-pin
Lu
Fu-shun
Lo-shan
Kuei-yang
Kuei-ling
Yang-ting
Hsi-ning
Lan-chou (Lan-chou)
Kao-lan
Lin-hsia
Tsan-lan (Ning-hsia)
Chu-yen
Pao-tou
Pao-chi
Ning-hsia

Tainan
Taihoku
MIN-HOU (FU-CHOU)
FAN-YÜ (CANTON)

Khabarovsk
Vladivostok
Seoul
Mok-p'o
Pusan
Pyöngyang
An-tung
Mukden
Liaoyang
Yin-k'ou
Lü-shun (Port Arthur)
Ta-lien
Tsi-nan
Ch'ing-tao
Wei
Yen-t'ai
Chang-ch'un
Kirin
Tun-hua
Harbin
Ko-shan
Mergen
Hailar
Tsitsihar
Tao-nan
Ch'ang-t'u
Chao-yang
Ch'ih-feng
Ch'eng-te
Tsun-hua
Hsüan-hua
Chang-chia-k'ou
Wan-ch'uan
Pao-tou
Kuei-sui

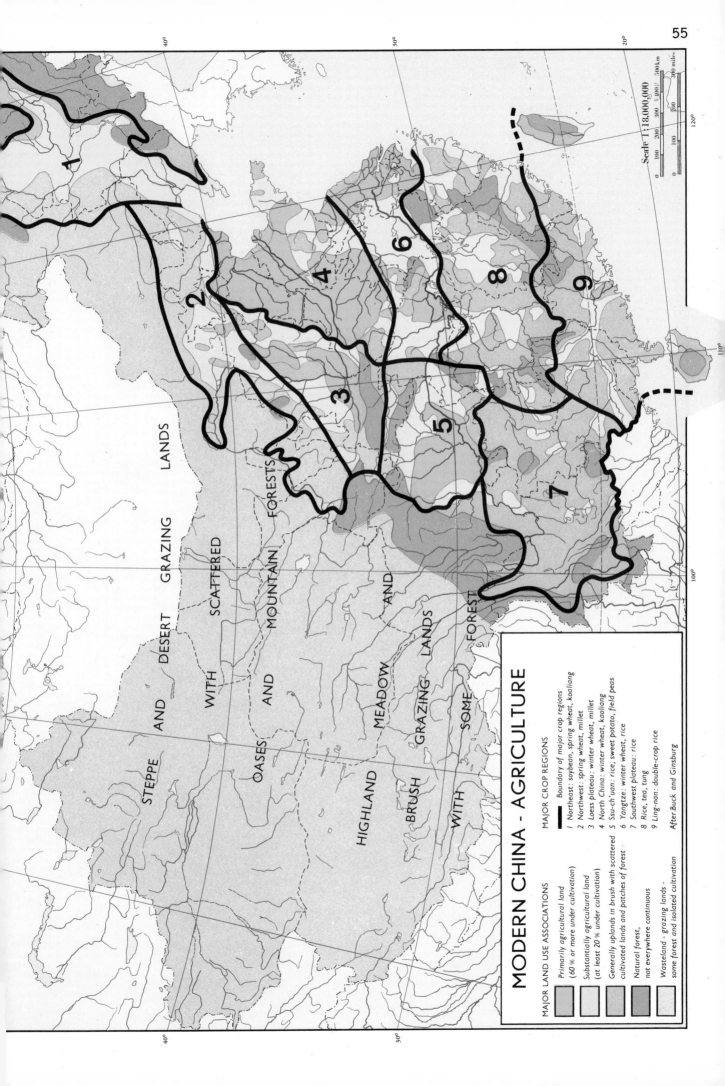

MAJOR LAND USE ASSOCIATIONS

MAJOR CROP REGIONS

Boundary of major crop regions

1 Northeast: soybean, spring wheat, kaoliang
2 Northwest: spring wheat, millet
3 Loess plateau: winter wheat, millet
4 North China: winter wheat, kaoliang
5 Ssu-ch'uan: rice, sweet potato, field peas
6 Yangtze: winter wheat, rice
7 Southwest plateau: rice
8 Rice, tea, tung
9 Ling-nan: double-crop rice

After Buck and Ginsburg

Primarily agricultural land
(60 % or more under cultivation)

Substantially agricultural land
(at least 20 % under cultivation)

Generally uplands in brush with scattered
cultivated lands and patches of forest

Natural forest,
not everywhere continuous

Wasteland - grazing lands -
some forest and isolated cultivation

MODERN CHINA - AGRICULTURE

Scale 1:18,000,000

STEPPE AND DESERT GRAZING LANDS

OASES WITH SCATTERED FORESTS

HIGHLAND MEADOW AND MOUNTAIN

BRUSH GRAZING LANDS

WITH SOME FORESTS

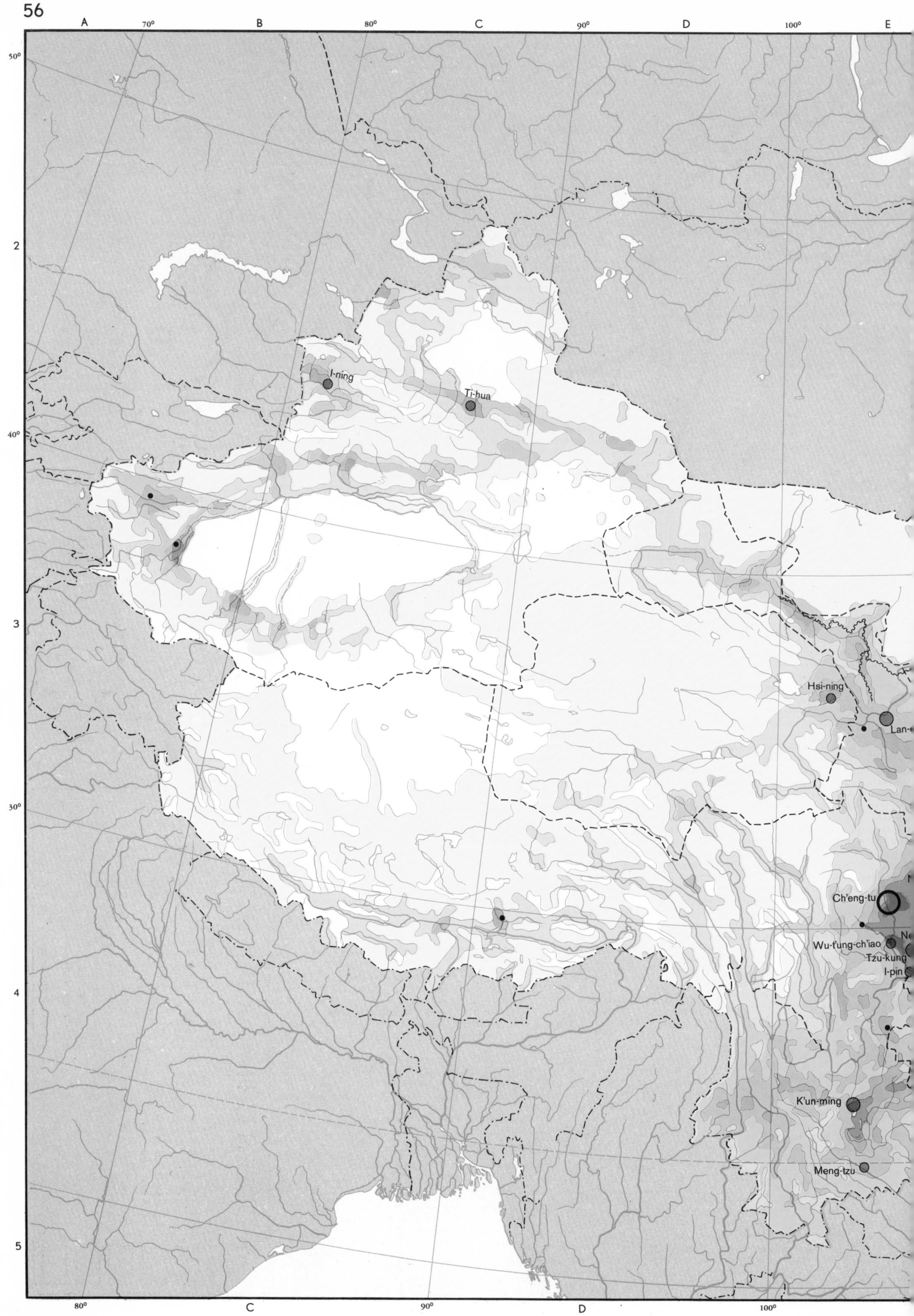

A 70° B 80° C 90° D 100° E

50°

2

40°

I-ning

Ti-hua

3

Hsi-ning

Lan-

30°

Ch'eng-tu

4

Wu-t'ung-ch'iao N
Tzu-kung
I-pin

K'un-ming

Meng-tzu

5

80° C 90° D 100°

MODERN CHINA - POPULATION
(after Atlas Narodov Mira)

TOWNS
Number of inhabitants

over 3,000,000

1,000,000- 3,000,000

300,000-1,000,000

100,000-300,000

50,000-100,000

DENSITY OF POPULATION

Inhabitants per sq. km
(sq. mile)

over 700
(over 1750)

200-700
(500-1750)

100-200
(250-500)

50-100
(125-250)

10-50
(25-125)

1-10
(2-25)

under 1
(under 2)

uninhabited

Scale 1:15,000,000

0 100 200 300 400 500 600 km

0 100 200 300 400 miles

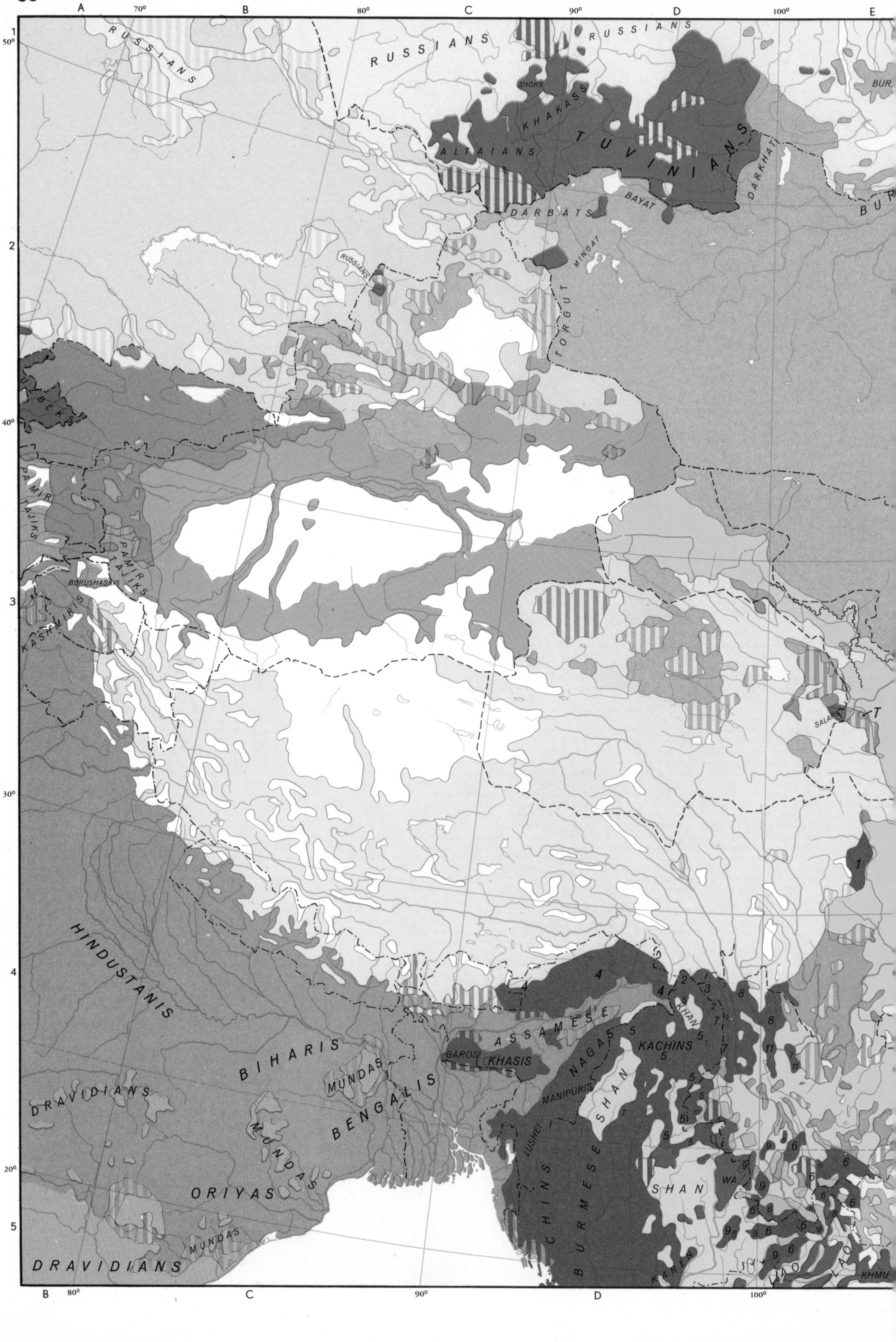

A 70° B 80° C 90° D 100° E

1
50°

RUSSIANS

RUSSIANS

RUSSIANS

BUR

SHORS

KHAKASS

TUVINIANS

DARKHAT

BUR

ALTAIANS

BAYAT

DARBATS

MINGAT

2

TORGUT

RUSSIANS

BEKS

40°

PAMIR TAJIKS

PAMIRS

TAJIKS

BURUSHASKIS

3

KASHMIRIS

SALARS

T

30°

1

HINDUSTANIS

4

4

4

3

2

8

KHAN

2

7

7

8

ASSAMESE

NAGAS

KACHINS

5

11

BIHARS

GAROS

KHASIS

MANIPURIS

5

5

MUNDAS

LUSHEI

5

BENGALIS

SHAN

7

DRAVIDIANS

MUNDAS

CHINS

BURMESE

5

9

6

20°

ORIYAS

SHAN

WA

9

6

6

MUNDAS

6

6

9

6

5

KAREN

6

9

6

5
DRAVIDIANS

LAO

KHMU

B 80° C 90° D 100°

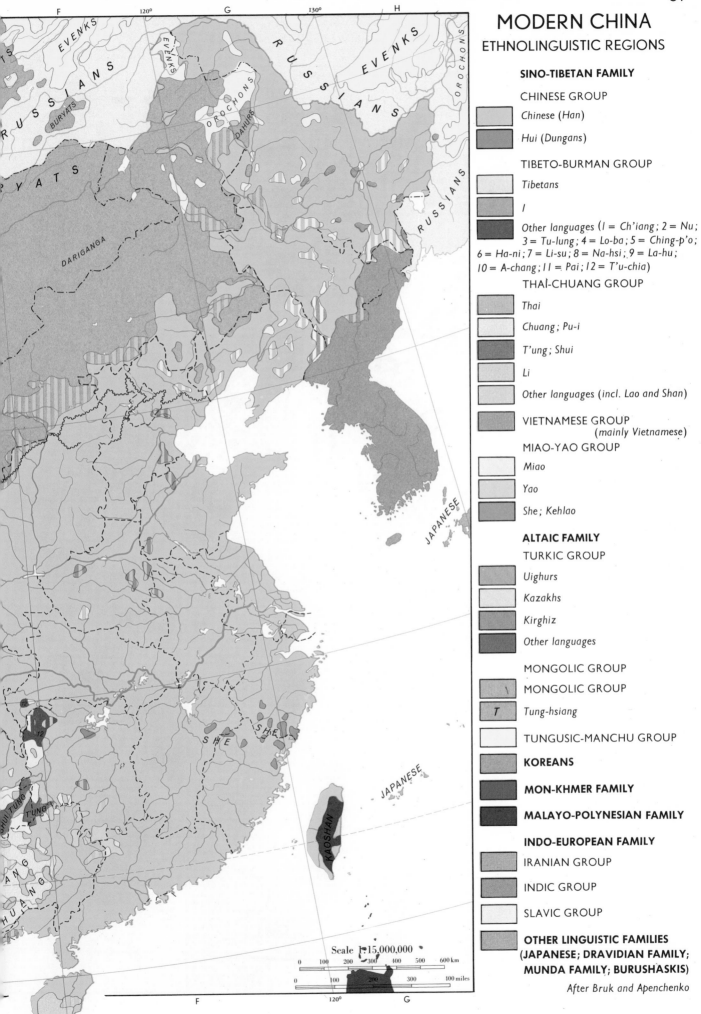

MODERN CHINA
ETHNOLINGUISTIC REGIONS

SINO-TIBETAN FAMILY

CHINESE GROUP

Chinese (Han)

Hui (Dungans)

TIBETO-BURMAN GROUP

Tibetans

I

Other languages (1 = Ch'iang; 2 = Nu; 3 = Tu-lung; 4 = Lo-ba; 5 = Ching-p'o; 6 = Ha-ni; 7 = Li-su; 8 = Na-hsi; 9 = La-hu; 10 = A-chang; 11 = Pai; 12 = T'u-chia)

THAI-CHUANG GROUP

Thai

Chuang; Pu-i

T'ung; Shui

Li

Other languages (incl. Lao and Shan)

VIETNAMESE GROUP
(mainly Vietnamese)

MIAO-YAO GROUP

Miao

Yao

She; Kehlao

ALTAIC FAMILY

TURKIC GROUP

Uighurs

Kazakhs

Kirghiz

Other languages

MONGOLIC GROUP

MONGOLIC GROUP

Tung-hsiang

TUNGUSIC-MANCHU GROUP

KOREANS

MON-KHMER FAMILY

MALAYO-POLYNESIAN FAMILY

INDO-EUROPEAN FAMILY

IRANIAN GROUP

INDIC GROUP

SLAVIC GROUP

**OTHER LINGUISTIC FAMILIES
(JAPANESE; DRAVIDIAN FAMILY;
MUNDA FAMILY; BURUSHASKIS)**

After Bruk and Apenchenko

Scale 1:15,000,000

0   100   200   300   400   500   600 km

0   100   200   300   100 miles

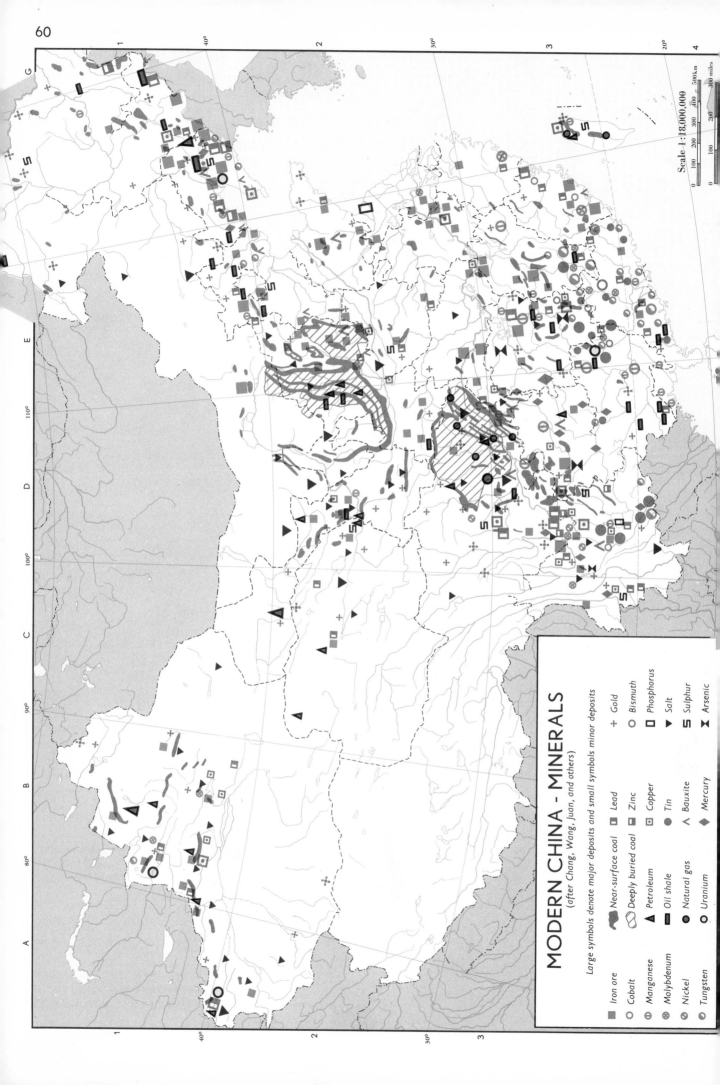

MODERN CHINA - MINERALS
(after Chang, Wang, Juan, and others)

Large symbols denote major deposits and small symbols minor deposits

▪ Iron ore		Near-surface coal	▫ Lead	+ Gold	○ Bismuth
○ Cobalt		Deeply buried coal	▫ Zinc	○ Phosphorus	
◐ Manganese		Petroleum	▣ Copper	◨ Salt	
⊗ Molybdenum		Oil shale	● Tin	▼ Sulphur	
⊗ Nickel		Natural gas	⋀ Bauxite	◛ Sulphur	
○ Tungsten		Uranium	◆ Mercury	⋈ Arsenic	

Scale 1:18,000,000

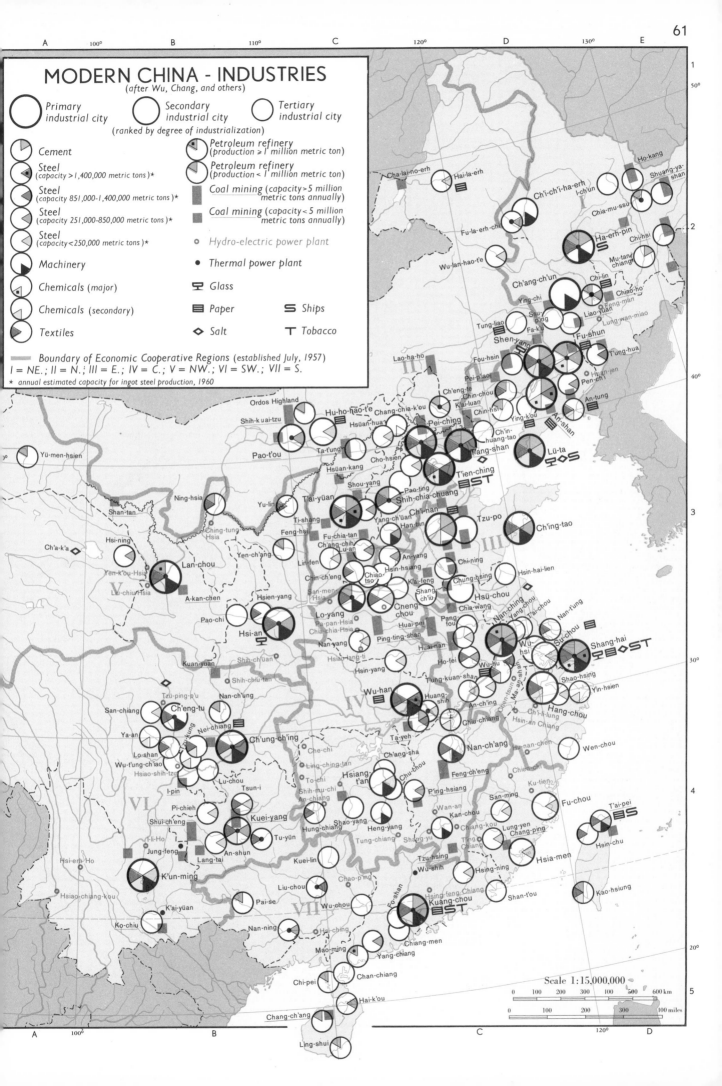

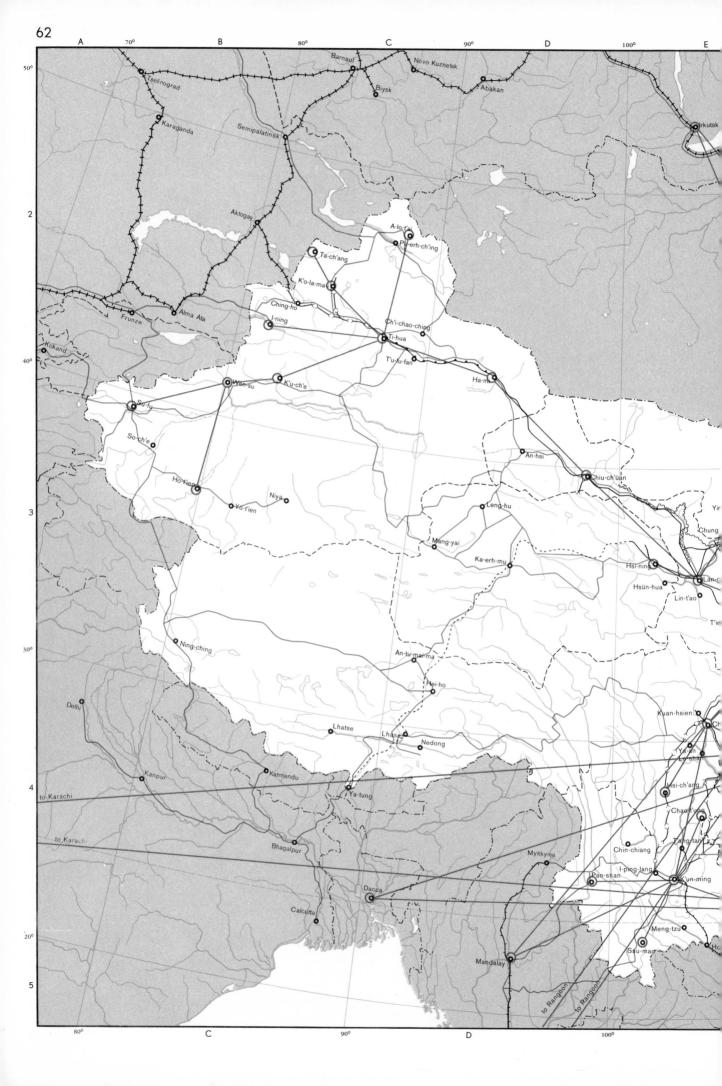

MODERN CHINA - TRANSPORTATION

RAILROADS

——————— *Single track, regular gauge*

—×—×— *Single track, regular gauge, under construction*

----------- *Single track, regular gauge, projected*

══════ *Double track*

+++++ *Broad gauge*

▲▲▲▲▲ *Temporary commercial line*

⊥⊥⊥⊥⊥ *Narrow gauge*

⊤⊤⊤⊤⊤ *Narrow gauge, under construction*

⊔⊔⊔⊔⊔ *Cape gauge*

—II— *Ferry point*

ROADS

——————— *Main motor routes*

AIR ROUTES

——————— *Air routes*

○ *Airports*

NAVIGABLE INLAND WATERWAYS

▓▓▓ *Ocean-going steamers*

▒▒▒ *Medium steamers*

░░░ *Small steamers*

——— *Junks and rafts*

·········· *Grand Canal in process of renovation*

Scale 1:15,000,000

0 100 200 300 400 500 600 km

0 100 200 300 100 miles

64

THE CHINESE IN SOUTHEAST ASIA

AND THE PRINCIPAL PLACES OF THEIR ORIGIN IN CHINA
(after Purcell)

Main areas of Chinese concentration

Other areas of Chinese concentration

TRIBES IN CHINA:

Hokkien
Cantonese
Hakka
Teochiu
Hainanese

Kwongsai
Hokchiu
Hokchia
Henghua

Scale 1:22,500,000

800 km

600

300

200

100 miles

INDIA

EAST PAKISTAN

Dacca

BURMA

Mandalay

Chiengmai

Prome

Rangoon

Moulmein

Tavoy

Phuket

YUNNAN

Kun-ming

KUEI-CHOU

KUANG-HSI

Nan-ning

Kuei-lin

Liu-chou

AUT. REGION

CHIANG-HSI

HUNAN

FU-CHIEN

T'ai-pei

TAIWAN

Fu-chou

Ch'üan-chou

Hsia-men (Amoy)

Shan-t'ou (Swatow)

Cheng-chou

Wu-chou

Chan-chiang

Ch'iung-shan

HAI-NAN

KUANG-TUNG

Kuang-chou (Canton)

Hong Kong (Br.)

Macao (Port.)

NORTH VIETNAM

Hanoi

Haiphong

Huê

Da Nang

Binh Dinh

SOUTH VIETNAM

Saigon-Cholon

CAMBODIA

Phnom Penh

Battambang

LAOS

Vientiane

THAILAND

Uttaradit

Nakhon Sawan

Bangkok

Nakhon Ratchasima

Suratthani

ISTHMUS OF KRA

MALAYA

Kota Bharu

Kuala Trengganu

George Town

Ipoh

Kuala Lumpur

Malacca

Johore Bharu

SINGAPORE

RIAU ARCH.

SUMATERA

Kutaradja

Medan

Sibolga

Padang

Djambi

Rengat

Palembang

Telukbetung

BANGKA

BELITUNG

Singkawang

Pontianak

KALIMANTAN

Sibu

Kuching

SARAWAK

BRUNEI

SABAH

Jesselton

Sandakan

Tarakan

Balikpapan

Samarinda

Bandjarmasin

DJAWA

Djakarta

Tjirebon

Bandung

Semarang

Surabaja

BALI

LOMBOK

SUMBAWA

SULAWESI

Makasar

Manado

Gorontalo

FLORES

HALMAHERA

Ternate

MALUKU

Ambon

IRIAN BARAT

Kotabaru

PHILIPPINES

LUZON

Aparri

Laoag

Lingayén

Manila

MINDORO

PANAY

Iloilo

NEGROS

Cebu

LEYTE

SAMAR

Catbalogan

Legaspi

Surigao

MINDANAO

Davao

Zamboanga

PALAWAN

Index of Geographical and Proper Names

General Remarks

The headings in the Index refer to the geographical and personal names in the Atlas. Variant spellings, as well as explanations or locations, follow in parentheses.

The figures and letters following the name indicate the page number and quadrangle on the map in which the place or proper name is to be found. Small letters indicate insert maps. Where only a page number is given, the name will be found either in the title or in the legend. In the case of Chinese names a number follows in square brackets, which refers not to the maps, but to the Index of Chinese Characters.

Transcription and Pronunciation of Chinese names

For the most part, Chinese place names are transcribed according to the Wade-Giles system (with hyphen). On some maps, the common, familiar spellings appear alongside the Wade-Giles romanization. The same system is followed in this index. According to this system vowels are spoken as in German or Italian, consonants as in English; k', p', t' are aspirated k, p, and t; ch, somewhat nearer a soft g, and ch' like the English ch as in church, include also the ts or ts' used in some other systems. An exception is made in the inclusion of the forms tsin and ts'in, which are written thus to differentiate from chin and ch'in (only regarding the names of dynasties). Widely varying spellings found in the "China Postal Album" are added in square brackets with the prefix P.

Transcription and Pronunciation of Other Oriental Names

Other oriental names appear on the maps in simplified usual form, while diacritical marks are reserved for the index:

ch as in Engl. church (cf. ch' in Chinese)
gh with a guttural accompaniment sh as in Engl. shoe
h sharply guttural d t supradental d t (in Sanscr.)
j as in Engl. pigeon y as in Engl. yellow
q deeply guttural z as in Engl. zone

Abbreviations

Ctry.	= Country	Loc.	= Locality
Distr.	= District	R.	= River
Dyn.	= Dynasty	Tn.	= Town
I(s).	= Island(s)	Tr.	= Tribe
La.	= Lake		

Index of Geographical and Proper Names

Appearing on the Historic Maps (1–53). For names appearing on the maps of Modern China, see special index on page 83.

Index of Geographical and Proper Names

Appearing on the Maps of Modern China (I–II, 54–64, III–IV)

Shao-kuan IV F4
Shao-pien IV F4
Shao-pien Yao A.H. IV F4 (75)
Shao-yang IV F4
Sha-shih IV F3
She 59 FG4
Shen-hsi IV EF3
Shen-si 54 D3
Shen-yang (Mukden) IV G2
Shigatse 54 B4
Shih-chia-chuang 63 F3
Shih-chiu-tan 61 B3
Shih-ch'üan 61 B3
Shih-kuai-tzu 63 F2
Shih-lu 63 E5
Shih-men IV F3
Shih-men 63 F4
Shih-ming-tzu 63 E3
Shih-mu-chi 61 C4
Shih-p'ing 63 E4
Shih-wan-ta Shan II E4
Shih-wei 63 FG1
Shors 58 C1
Shou-yang 61 C3
Shuang-ch'eng IV G2
Shuang-ya-shan 63 H2
Shui 59 E4
Shui-ch'eng 61 B4
Shu-yang IV F3
Sialkot III B3
Sian IV E3
Sibolga 64 B6
Sibu 64 E6
Sih-k'o-tse (Zhikatse) III C4′
Sihote Alin Khrebet II H2
Sikkim III C4
Silinhot 63 F2
Singapore 64 C6
Singkawang 64 D6
Sinuiju IV G3
So-ch'e (Yarkand) III B3
So-chu 54 A3
Son R. I C4
Soochow IV G3
South China Sea IV F4
South Korea IV G3
South Vietnam 64 D4
Soviet Union III,IV AH1/2
Srinagar III B3
Ssu-ch'uan III,IV E3
Ssu-mao 63 E4
Ssu-nan 63 E4
Ssu-p'ing IV G2
Su-chou IV G3
Su-fu III B3
Su-hsien IV F3
Sui-fen-ho 63 H2
Sui-hua 63 G2
Sui-ning III E3
Sui-yüan 54 DE2
Sulawesi 64 FG7
Sumatera 64 BC6/7
Sumba 64 F8
Sumbawa 64 F8
Su-nan Yü-ku III D3
Su-nan Yü-ku A.H. III D3 (10)
Sungari Res. II C2
Sungari R. II GH 2
Sung-hua Chiang (Sungari R.) II GH2
Sung-t'ao IV E4
Sung-t'ao Miao A.H. IV E4 (60)
Su-pei III D3
Su-pei Mongol A.H. III D3 (9)
Surabaja 64 E8
Suratthani 64 B5
Surigao 64 H5
Sutlej R. III B3
Su-zo 63 G4
Svobodnyy IV G1
Swatou 54 E4
Swatow see Shan-tou
Sze-chwan see Ssu-ch'uan

Ta 54 D3
Ta-ch'ang 62 C2
Ta-ch'ang IV F3
Ta-ch'ang Hui A.H. IV F2/3 (24)

Taegu IV G3
Ta-hsien IV E3
Ta-hsing-an Ling II FG 1/2
Ta-hsüeh Shan I E3/4
Ta-hu-erh IV G2
Ta-hu-erh (Daghur) A.Ch'i IV G2 (17)
T'ai-an IV F3
T'ai-chou IV FG3
T'ai-hang Shan II F3
Taihoku 54 F4
Tai Hu II FG3
Tailagein Khara I E2
Tainan see T'ai-nan
T'ai-nan IV G4
T'ai-pei IV G4
T'ai Shan II F3
T'ai-tung 63 G4
Taiwan see T'ai-wan
T'ai-wan (Formosa) IV G4
T'ai-yüan IV F3
Takla Makan I BC3
Ta-li III E3
Ta-li 54 C4
Ta-lien 54 F3
T'a-li-mu Ho (Tarim) III C2
Ta-li Pai A.C. III DE4 (45)
Ta-liang Shan I E4
T'a-li-mu Ho (Tarim) I C2
Ta-lou Shan II E4
Ta-miao-shan IV E4
Ta-miao-shan Miao A.H. IV E4 (70)
T'ang La I C4
Tangla Pass I D3
T'ang-shan IV F3
T'ang-tan 62 E4
T'ao-nan IV G2
Ta-pa Shan II EF3
Ta-pieh Shan II F3
Tarakan 64 F6
Tarim III C2
Tarim Basin I C3
Tashi Chho Dzong III C4
T'a-shih-k'u-erh-kan (Tash Kurghan) Tadzhik A.H. III B3 (1)
Tash Kurgan III B3
Ta-t'ung IV F2/3
Ta-yao-shan IV F4
Ta-yao-shan Yao A.H. IV EF4 (69)
Ta-yeh 61 C4
Te-hung Thai and Ching-P'o A.C. III D4 (44)
Telukbetung 64 D8
Tengri Khan I BC2
Ternate 64 H6
Thai 58–59 DE4/5
Thailand 64 C3
Thanglhari I CD3
Tibet, Plateau of I CD3
Tibet Autonomous Region III C3
Tibetans 58–59 BC3/4
Ti-ch'ing Tibetan A.C. III D4 (40)
T'ieh-ling IV G2
T'ien-ching (Tientsin) IV F3
T'ien-chu III E3
T'ien-chu Tibetan A.H. III E3 (11)
T'ien Shan I BC2
T'ien-shui III E3
Tientsin IV F3
T'ien-tu 63 E5
Ti-hua (Urumchi) III C2
Timor 64 GH8
T'ing Chiang 61 C4
Ting-hsien IV F3
Ti-shang 61 C3
Tjirebon 64 D8
To-chi 61 BC4
Tonkin 54 D4
Tonkin, Gulf of II E4/5
Torgut 58 D2
Trans-Himalaya I C3/4
Triangle, the I D4
Tsang 54 E3
Ts'ang-hsien IV F3
Tsangpo (Brahmaputra) III C4
Ts'ang-wu 54 E4

Ts'ang-yüan III D4
T'sang-yüan K'awa A.H. III D4 (51)
Tsan-lan 54 D3
Tsingtao IV G3
Tsitsihar 54 F2
Tsun-hua 54 E2
Tsun-i IV E4
Tu-an IV E4
Tu-an Yao A.H. IV E4 (68)
T'u-chia 59 EF4
Tu-erh-po-t'e IV G2
Tu-erh-po-t'e Mongol A.H. IV G2 (18f)
T'u-lu-fan (Turfan) III C2
Tu-lung 58 D5
Tu-men Chiang IV G2
T'un-ch'i IV F4
T'ung 59 E4
Tung-chiang 61 C4
T'ung-chiang 63 H2
T'ung-ch'uan 63 E3
Tung-hai 54 E3
Tung-hsiang III E3
Tung-hsiang 58 D3
Tung-hsiang A.H. III E3 (12a)
Tung-hsing IV E4
Tung-hsing Multinational A.H. IV E4 (77)
T'ung-hua IV G2
T'ung-jen III E3
T'ung-kuan 63 F3
T'ung-kuan 63 F4
Tung-kuan-shan 61 C3
T'ung-liao 63 G2
Tung-shih IV E5
T'ung-tao IV E4
T'ung-tao T'ung A.H. IV E4 (63)
Tung-t'ing Hu IV F4
Tungusic-Manchu group 59 EH1/2
Tun-hua 54 F2
Turfan III C2
Tuvinians 58 D1
Tu-yün IV E4
Tzu-ch'iu 63 F3
Tzu-hsing 61 C4
Tzu-kung III E4
Tzü-ping-p'u 61 B3
Tzu-po IV F3

Uighur 58 BD 2/3
Ulaan Baatar III E2
Ulaan Goom III D2
Ulanhoto IV G2
Ulan-Ude III,IV E1
Urumchi III C2
Urungu I C2
Ussuri R. IV H2
Ussuriysk IV H2
Ust' Kamenogorsk III C1
Uttaradit 64 C3
Uzbeks 58 B2

Varanasi III C4
Vientiane 64 C3
Vietnam 64 CD 2–4
Vitim R. II F1
Vladivostok IV H2

Wa 58 D4
Wan 54 D3
Wan-an 61 C4
Wan-chüan 54 E2
Wan-hsien IV E3
Wei 54 E4
Wei-hai-wei IV G3
Wei Ho I,II E3
Wei-hsien IV F3
Wei-nan IV E3
Wei-ning III E4
Wei-ning I, Hui, and Miao A.H. III E4 (57)
Wei-shan III E4
Wei-shan Hu II F3
Wei-shan I A.H. III E4 (45b)
Wen-chou 61 D4
Wen-ch'üan 63 FG2
Wen-shan III E4
Wen-shan Chuang and Miao A.C.

III E4 (56)
Wen-su (Aksu) III C2
Wu 54 F3
Wu Chiang II E4
Wu-ch'iao Ling I E3
Wu-chih Shan II E5
Wu-chou 63 F4
Wu-han IV F3
Wu-hsi IV G3
Wu-hsing IV FG3
Wu-hu IV F3
Wu-i Shan II F4
Wu-kung Shan II F4
Wu-lan-hao-t'e (Ulanhoto) IV G2
Wu-liang Shan I E4
Wu-shih 61 C4
Wu-t'ung-ch'iao III E4

Ya-an III E3
Yablonovyy Khrebet II F1
Ya-k'o-shih 63 G2
Ya-lu Chiang IV G2
Yamdrog Tsho I D4
Yang-chiao-kou 63 F3
Yang-chou IV F3
Yang-ch'ü 54 E3
Yang-ch'üan IV F3
Yang-ch'un 61 C4
Yang-ch'un-k'ao 63 F4
Yangtze R. III DE3
Yao 58–59 EF4
Yarkand III B3
Ya-tung 62 C4
Yellow River IV EF2/3
Yellow Sea II G3
Yen-ch'ang 61 B3
Yench'eng IV G3
Yen-ch'i III C2
Yen-chi IV G2
Yen-ch'i Hui A.H. III C2 (6a)
Yenisey R. III D1
Yen-kou-Hsia 61 B3
Yen-pien Korean A.C. IV G2 (21)
Yen-t'ai (Chefoo) IV G3
Yin (Ning-p'o) 54 F3/4
Yin-ch'uan III,IV E3
Ying-chi 61 D2
Ying-chi-sha III B3
Ying-k'ou IV G2
Ying-t'an 64 F3
Yinge-te 63 F4
Yin-hsien IV G3/4
Yin Shan II F2
Yüan-p'ing 63 F3
Yüan R. II F4
Yu Chiang II E4
Yu-lin 61 B3
Yü-men III D2
Yü-men-hsien 61 A2
Yün-ching-hung III E4
Yung-an 63 F4
Yung-chia IV G4
Yung-chien III E4
Yung-chien Hui A.H. III DE4 (45a)
Yung-ning 54 D4
Yung-ting Ho II F2/3
Yün Ho (Grand Canal) IV F3
Yün-ling Shan I D4
Yün-nan III E4
Yün-nan Plateau I E4
Yü-shan 63 F4
Yü-shu 63 G2
Yü-shu III D3
Yü-shu Tibetan A.C. III D3 (33)
Yü-t'ien III C3
Yü-tu 63 F4
Yü-tz'u IV F3

Zamboanga 64 G5
Zhikatse III C4

潘1540 柳1541 六1542 柳1543 瀊1544 家 榴1545 柳1546 中 六1547 分 子 六1548 合 流1549 新 琉1550 璃 廠 留1551 垻 六1552 盤 流1553 沙 六1554 順 柳1555 樹 屯 劉1556 公 瀏1557 陽 歷1558 陽 溧1559 陽 羅1560 欒1561 洛1562 灤1563 樂1564 至 樂1565 清 洛1566 川 羅1567 斛 樂1568 會 洛1569

邑 羅1570 爛 樂1571 浪 玀1572 玀 雒1573 洛1574 寧 蘿1575 蘆1576 羅1577 施 鬼 羅1578 甸 羅1579 田 羅1580 定 樂1581 亭 樂1582 都 羅1583 次 樓1584 蘭 洛1585 陽 羅1586 源 樂1587 越 匿 雒1588 容 纑1589 魯1590 淥1591 瀘1592 呂1593 旅1594 灤1595 瀘1596 溪 盧1597 盧1598 監 氏 陸1599 川

鹽1600 分 陸1601 豐 祿1602 豐 矑1603 朐 鑪1604 霍 鹿1605 邑 路1606 呂1607 光 陸1608 涼 呂1609 梁 廬1610 陵 露1611 路 蘆1612 眉 魯1613 迷 龍1614 隴1615 隆1616 昌1617 龍1618 鎮 龍1619 龍1620 溪 龍1621 龍1622 井 龍1623 川 龍1624 泉 驛1625 龍1626 駒 寨 隆1627 化 龍1628 里 龍1629 茗

龍1630 編 龍1631 勝 隆1632 德 龍1633 王 塘 龍1634 游 龍1635 原 龍1636 潭 隆1637 德 龍1638 巖 輪1639 臺 鑪1640 盧1641 氏 旅1642 順 魯1643 甸 瀘1644 定 魯1645 倉 魯1646 陽 澳1647 麻1648 麻1649 嘉 馬1650 家 集 鎮 馬1651 蹟 馬1652 韓 麻1653 逸 馬1654 麻1655 囉 華 巒1656

芒1657 莽1658 里 蠻1659 耗 茂1660 茂1661 名 毛1662 目 旄1663 牛 冒1664 頓 馬1665 邊 麻1666 陽 馬1667 孟 郿1668 梅1669 梅1670 溪 梅1671 嶺 煤1672 眉1673 湄1674 潭 蒙1675 孟1676 蒙1677 孟1678 家 莊 孟1679 津 孟1680 豬 孟1681 河 營 蒙1682 嵩 詔 蒙1683 化 猛1684 連 蒙1685 舍 詔

猛1686 丁 蒙1687 自 蒙1688 陰 毒1689 米1690 密1691 宓1692 苗1693 廟1694 列 廟1695 米1696 脂 綿1697 沔1698 綿1699 竹 冕1700 寧 緬1701 寧 緬1702 甸 綿1703 陽 沔1704 陽 宓1705 須 彌1706 勒 閩1707 岷1708 民1709 勤 閩1710 清 憫1711 忠 寺 明1712 明1713 光 宮 明1714 宮 名1715 明1716 堂 明1717

德 閩1718 侯 岷1719 閬1720 越 彌1721 渡 密1722 雲1723 貊 莫1724 墨1725 漠1726 靺1727 鞨 莫1728 賀 延 沒1729 來 鏌1730 鋣 麻1731 粟 坡 末1732 羅 磨1733 些 摩1734 地 那 懋1735 功 牟1736 婁 牟1737 牟1738 定 莫1739 邪 穆1740 木1741 瓜 木1742 蘭 木1743 壘 木1744 壘 穆1745 稜

木1746 鹿 木1747 葉 慕1748 容 納1749 溪 納1750 職 肭1751 脂 那1752 曉 那1753 馬 那1754 密 澳1755 漳1756 詔1757 召1758 溪1759 充1760 翔1761 雄1762 滙1763 猗1764 宮1765 盤1766 奔1767 毗1768 皮1769 部1770 誰1771 難1772 兜 兗1773 兗1774 營1775 豫1776 那1777 色 波 那1778 大 訥1779 內1780 內1781 邱 內1782 方 內1783

鄉 內1784 史 娘1785 娘 宮 鳥1786 鼠 碾1787 伯 泥1788 壤 甯1789 寧1790 寧1791 寧1792 津 甯1793 靜 甯1794 寧1795 洱 甯1796 夏 寧1797 陝 寧1798 鄉 寧1799 化 寧1800 岡 甯1801 國 寧1802 年 寧1803 波 寧1804 浦 寧1805 朔 寧1806 德 寧1807 定 寧1808 都 寧1809 武 寧1810 陽 寧1811

洋 寧1812 遠 寧1813 遠 甯1814 遠 惹1815 瑟 知 牛1816 莊 忸1817 密 嬈1818 水 街 怒1819 弩1820 支 奴1821 發 嫩1822 農1823 弩1824 失 畢 峩1825 眉 遏1826 根 陀 額1827 尒 勾 甌1828 雒 巴1829 霸1830 八1831 寨 霸1832 巴1833 齊 巴1834 吉 弄 拔1835 汗 那 排1836 持 拜1837

泉 白1838 白1839 蓮 白1840 馬 寺 白1841 衣 廟 白1842 蒲 延 百1843 色 白1844 沙 白1845 達 白1846 子 白1847 崖 巴1848 姥 酉 半1849 盤1850 潘1851 莊 邦1852 均 盤1853 盤 磐1854 石 保1855 寶1856 褒1857 寶1858 雞 保1859 德 寶1860 坻 寶1861 停 包1862 頭 寶1863 應 把1864 邊

拔1865 特 巴1866 彥 毗1867 沛1868 邳1869 貝1870 勒 廟 流1871 邛1872 北1873 平 府1874 栗1875 塘1876 大1877 通 地1878 庭1879 陪1880 尾 豫1881 運1882 彭1883 蓬1884 安 蓬1885 溪 彭1886 家 場 彭1887 懷 蓬1888 萊 彭1889 蠡 彭1890 澤 本1891 溪 奔1892 牛 奔1893 子 欄 庇1894 畢1895 皮1896 郫1897 驃1898

筆1899 架 畢1900 節 比1901 景 沂1902 沂1903 京 偏1904 片1905 馬 便1906 卑1907 陸 邠1908 豳1909 濱1910 濱1911 濱 并1912 平1913 平1914 舟 平1915 垻 賓1916 川 平1917 泉 平1918 番 平1919 和 萍1920 鄉 平1921 鄉 憑1922 祥 馮1923 翊 平1924 彝 平1925 壤 平1926 谷 平1927 利 平1928 涼 平1929

羅 平1930 樂 平1931 魯 平1932 陸 屏1933 平1934 潭 平1935 等 平1936 定 平1937 則 平1938 度 平1939 望 平1940 武 平1941 牙 平1942 遙 平1943 原 平1944 遠 平1945 越 賓1946 陽 溺1947 琶 囉 卑1948 品 皮1949 避1950 暑 山 莊 卑1951 闐 貔1952 子 寫 泌1953 陽 辟1954 雍

亳1955 博1956 婺1957 博1958 愛 博1959 愛 薄1960 知 波1961 知 孛1962 伽 夷 嶓1963 冢 渤1964 鉢1965 和 波1966 悉 播1967 仙 博1968 興 撥1969 換 勃1970 利 柏1971 梁 臺 博1972 羅 破1973 洛 那 婆1974 羅 娑 婆1975 露 薄1976 茅 播1977 密 滓1978 泥 博1979 白 博1980 平 波1981

斯 薄1982 提 鄱1983 陽 鄱1984 陽 白1985 雲 觀 蒲1986 濮1987 普1988 浦1989 蒲1990 圻 浦1991 蒲1992 知 布1993 不1994 忍 蒲1995 甘 薄1996 姑 僕1997 固 振 普1998 蘭 店 蒲1999 類 蒲2000 犂 蒲2001 里 嚕 普2002 樂 殿 勃2003 律 普2004 寧 濮2005 達 蒲2006 台 撲2007 挑 莆2008

田 普2009 定 普2010 陀 浦2011 普2012 文 濮2013 陽 蒲2014 陽 捕2015 魚 兒 塞2016 迦 審 撒2017 剌 薩2018 拉 納 三2019 場2020 三2021 橋 三2022 川 三2023 佛 齊 桑2024 植 三2025 合 三2026 姓 三2027 國 三2028 隴 三2029 苗 三2030 河 三2031 台 三2032 潭 印 月

三2033 都 澳 三2034 危 三2035 眼 橋 三2036 原 薩2037 毗 僧2038 加 剌 沙2039 沙2040 鍋 屯 沙2041 丘 沙2042 勒 沙2043 面 沙2044 漠 陝2045 鄯2046 單2047 善2048 丹 廟 商2049 上2050 上2051 金 商2052 郎 上2053 杭 上2054 饒 上2055 高 上2056 波 谷 上2057 林 上2058 洛 商2059 彌

上2060 思 上2061 黨 上2062 都 商2063 都 尚2064 都 上2065 猶 上2066 虞 山2067 戎 鄯2068 善 鄯2069 闌 丹2070 汕2071 頭 汕2072 尾 韶2073 紹2074 興 邵2075 沙2076 鉢 沙2077 市 沙2078 陀 沙2079 頭 角 沙2080 灣 涉2081 葉2082 支 葉2083 射2084 洪 賒2085 彌 賒2086 彌 申2087 祁2088 神2089

池 沈2090 邱 深2091 圳 勝2092 芳 澠2093 池 省2094 溪 昇2095 盛2096 樂 威2097 時 據 神2098 木 稔2099 深2100 澤 身2101 毒 瀋2102 陽 石2103 史2104 石2105 漆 石2106 家 莊 石2107 阡 尸2108 棄 尼 石2109 柱 石2110 莊 石2111 泉 什2112 加 施2113 咼 始2114 興 始2115 皇 石2116

會 石2117 鼓 施2118 浪 詔 室2119 利 佛 逝 石2120 樓 石2121 板 灘 石2122 屏 施2123 秉 恰2124 布 恰 攝2125 舍 提 水2126 師 營 石2127 首 石2128 石2129 亭 師2130 宗 石2131 彎 室2132 韋 石2133 玉 壽2134 朔2135 壽2136 張 壽2137 春 壽2138 光 壽2139 寧 首2140

都 壽2141 陽 舒2142 蜀2143 石2144 板 率2145 賓 雙2146 雙2147 橋 雙2148 流 雙2149 靡 雙2150 柏 雙2151 塔 寺 舒2152 殊2153 相 寺 稅2154 建 舒2155 蘭 順2156 舜2157 淳2158 順2159 承 順2160 慶 順2161 義 鼠2162 尼 施 順2163 寧 順2164 德 朔2165 朔2166 方 舒2167 都 沭2168 陽 莎2169

車 司2170 肆2171 泗2172 塞2173 斯2174 加 里 野 賜2175 支 思2176 恩 息2177 烽 四2178 會 思2179 惲 恩 惲 司2180 隸 思2181 林 思2182 樂 斯2183 羅 思2184 茅 四2185 明 思2186 斯2187 畢 莫 運 斯2188 賓 四2189 平 街 汜2190 蘇2191 宿2192 肅2193 清 肅2194 蘇2195 疏2196 附 宿2197

呵 多 蘇2198 蘿 隨2199 遂2200 隨2201 嵩2202 粟2203 弋 綏2204 綏2205 清 遂2206 溪 敘2207 遂2208 川 綏2209 中 綏2210 芬 綏2211 化 綏2212 來 綏2213 楞 綏2214 睢2215 甯 遂2216 寧 綏2217 甯 綏2218 濱 碎2219 卜 綏2220 德 綏2221 定 綏2222 綏2223 遠 蘇2224 閶 疏2225 勒 粟2226 摟

烽 蘇2227 碼 頭 宋2228 嵩2229 松2230 溪 松2231 雙2232 溝 松2233 岑 松2234 潘 崧2235 松2236 桃 松2237 滋 松2238 陽 宋2239 雲 循2240 鮮 蕭2241 寧 蘇2242 坡 橋 蕭2243 慎 粟2244 特 蘇2245 龕 汕2246 頭 達2247 大2248 塔2249 打2250 箭 爐 大2251 金 川 大2252 清 大2253 竹 大2254

大2255 和 達2256 曷 大2257 河 堤 大2258 夏 大2259 饗 大2260 興 代2261 泰2262 大2263 邑 台2264 台2265 莊 帶2266 方 太2267 行 泰2268 和 泰2269 台2270 拱 泰2271 來 太2272 白 太2273 平 塲2274 泰2275 順 太2276 倉 臺2277 灣 太2278 岳 太2279 原 大2280 沽 大2281 谷 大2282 孤 大2283

皖²⁹¹⁵ 雲²⁸⁹⁰ 永²⁸⁶³ 嶁²⁸³¹ 沇²⁸⁰⁵ 潁²⁷⁶⁸ 耆 明 武²⁶⁷⁹ 五²⁶⁵⁴ 進 護 顏 了 豫²⁵¹² 同²⁴⁸⁰ 鳳 多²⁴¹⁹ 天²³⁹³ 至 頭 懷 睿
善²⁹¹⁶ 內 和 兄 陵 瀛²⁷⁶⁹ 榿 陽²⁷⁰⁸ 威²⁶²⁹ 國 井 萬²⁵⁶⁶ 梓²⁵⁴¹ 敦²⁵¹³ 通 泰²⁴⁸¹ 嶺 彌²⁴⁵¹ 天²³⁹⁴ 鄧²³⁶⁷ 大²³³⁹ 單²³¹⁴ 大
見 右²⁸⁹¹ 兒²⁸⁶⁴ 餘²⁸³² 元²⁸⁰⁶ 應 杆 朔 清 烏²⁶⁵⁵ 溫²⁵⁹⁸ 煌 潼²⁵⁴⁰ 正 同 晉²⁴⁵² 跋²⁴²⁰ 回 川²³⁴⁰ 桓²³¹⁵ 理
師²⁹¹⁷ 北 新 干 謀²⁸³³ 營²⁷⁷¹ 列 揚²⁷⁰⁹ 為²⁶⁸⁰ 拉 武²⁶³¹ 文²⁶⁰⁰ 里²⁵⁸⁷ 于²⁵⁴² 化 潼 寧²⁴⁸³ 涪²⁴⁵³ 衝 登²³⁶⁹ 大²³⁴¹ 棱²³¹⁶ 荔
...

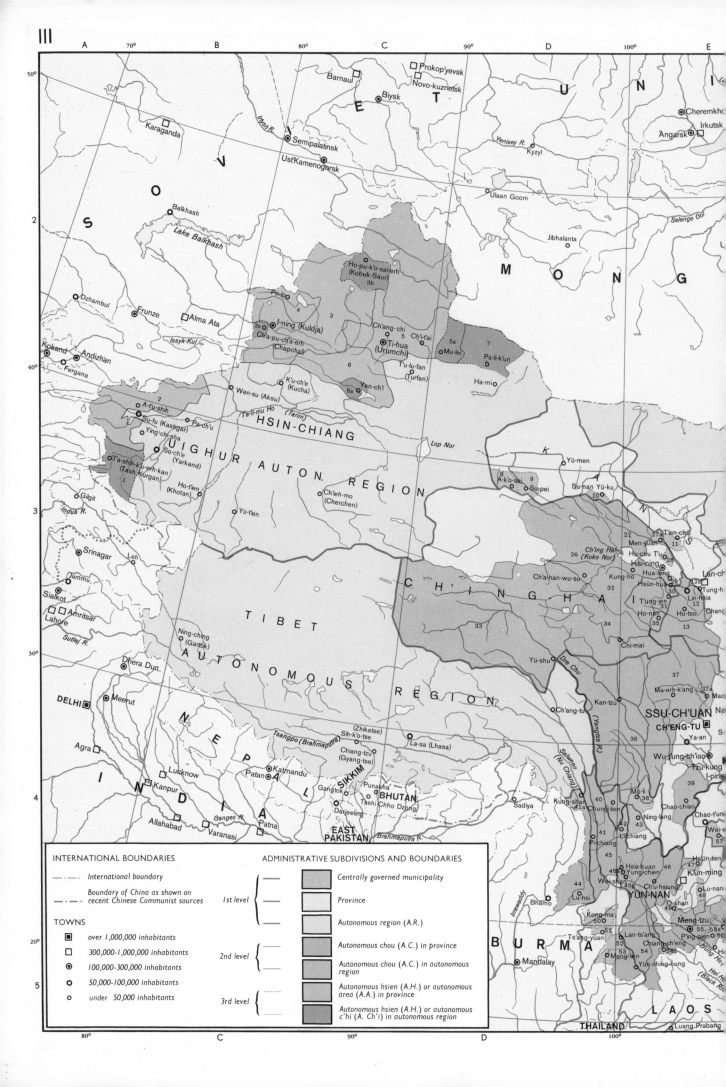